Ask Vance
Book Two

Memphis magazine's history and trivia expert solves even more local mysteries: who, what, when, where, why, and why not.

By Vance Lauderdale

Memphis, Tennessee

All Rights Reserved. © 2011

Special Thanks

Let me be perfectly candid with you: I deserve any and all credit, honors, accolades, and prizes for researching, writing, photographing, producing, designing, and publishing this fine book.

No, wait. That's not right. A surprisingly large number of people helped me over the years with various aspects of "Ask Vance" — the column and the book — and I'll try to name most of them here. Also, that way I can spread the blame around when you — dear reader — find something wrong on these pages. Keep in mind, though, that I like to sprinkle typos and mistakes throughout the book just to see if you are really paying attention.

My colleagues at *Memphis* magazine and the *Memphis Flyer* (where "Ask Vance" first appeared) have kept the column alive, and even lively, over the years. They've also helped launch my new blog, and in recent years have produced a series of eye-catching "Ask Vance" wall calendars. There are too many folks to mention here, but I'd like to give special thanks to Kenneth Neill, Bruce VanWyngarden, Jeffrey Goldberg, Molly Willmott, Penelope Huston Baer, Dennis Freeland, Frank Murtaugh, Mary Helen Randall, Richard Banks, Marilyn Sadler, Greg Akers, Susan Ellis, Leonard Gill, Matt Writt, Ashley Johnston, Hannah Sayle, Lindsay Jones, Britt Hall, and Kristin Mallory.

Many talented art directors and designers have given the column a fresh look since we first began publishing it in 1991, and have helped with related projects. Their names rarely appear on the final product, so special credit goes to Murry Keith, Hudd Byard, Hannah Johnson, Brian Groppe, Anthoney Carter, Kerri Mahoney, Serah DeLong, and Matt Wiseman.

My good friends at the local libraries have tolerated my persistent requests for information and photographs. I'm especially grateful to the patient assistance of Ed Frank, Sharon Banker, and Chris Ratliff at the University of Memphis Libraries Special Collections Department, and Wayne Dowdy (among others) at the Benjamin Hooks Central Library.

Other friends and associates have been helpful in more ways than they'll ever know. Among them: Bonnie and Nick Kourvelas, Kip Cole, Melissa and Caleb Sweazy, Andrew Northern, Gayle S. Rose, Amy LaVere, John Harkins, Lee Askew, Fran Catmur, Jorja Frazier, Joe Lowry, Gene and Betty Finger, and Sherri Weathers.

And most especially, thanks to Michael Finger at *Memphis* magazine. It would have been hard to do this without him.

For more from Vance Lauderdale, visit his blog: www.memphismagazine.com/Blogs/Ask-Vance

Copyright © 2011 by Contemporary Media, Inc.
All Rights Reserved.

No part of this book may be reproduced in any form or by any electronic or mechanical means without permission in writing from the publisher, except by a reviewer, who may quote brief passages in a review.

Library of Congress Control Number: 2011913143

All materials appearing herein were originally published in *Memphis* magazine.

ISBN 0964982153

Publisher of *Memphis* magazine, the *Memphis Flyer*, *Memphis Parent*, and *MBQ*
460 Tennessee Street, Suite 200
Memphis, Tennessee 38103
901-521-9000
www.memphismagazine.com

Preface

For many of you picking up this copy of *Ask Vance — Book Two*, this is one of those proverbial books which need no introduction. After all, over the past two decades, "Vance Lauderdale" has become a household name in Memphis, a man whose remarkable grasp of every aspect of this city's sometimes glorious, sometimes checkered past has made him something of a living legend in these parts. Our first *Ask Vance* book, published in 2003, has been a perennial local best-seller. So for those of you who have "been here before": Vance and I are delighted that you've been a regular reader of his columns over the years in *Memphis* magazine, and we hope you find this second volume of his collected works just as informative and entertaining as his first.

If you are new to the Lauderdale Legend, a little background is essential to your understanding of just what *Ask Vance* is all about. Exactly twenty years ago this fall, a new feature made its debut in the pages of our weekly newspaper, the *Memphis Flyer*, a column whose question-and-answer format addressed the who's, what's, when's, where's, why's, and how's of twentieth-century Memphis history.

Its author was a mysterious Memphis gentleman, little known, rarely photographed, but a bon vivant with a bon mot for every occasion, a man who goes by the peculiarly native name of Vance Lauderdale. Mr. Lauderdale's own background is shrouded in controversy; little if anything can be found in print about the man, except what can be found in his own unique writings. Peculiar, to say the least.

Since 1995, "Ask Vance" has appeared every month in the pages of *Memphis* magazine. Its author has won numerous national journalism awards by crafting one of the country's premier local-history columns. A man of a thousand answers, Mr. Lauderdale delivers them in whimsical, often downright comical, but always uncannily accurate fashion. You'll know volumes more about Memphis history if you simply take the time to read this one.

As *Memphis* magazine's most popular columnist, Mr. Lauderdale has made a smooth transition into the Internet era; indeed, you can now keep up with his ramblings daily, at www.memphismagazine.com/Blogs/Ask-Vance. These days, thanks to the wonders of modern technology, he rarely needs to come out of his basement. Probably just as well for all of us!

Whenever Vance does need fresh air, however, his long-time contact at our company, Senior Editor Michael Finger, is always on call, ready to serve as his intellectual companion, amanuensis, and purveyor of fine spirits. Indeed, this book would be impossible without Michael's dedication to duty, without his willingness to take on trying tasks despite their often deleterious effects upon both his physical and mental health. Thankfully, Michael is grounded in the key precepts of Buddhist philosophy, having imbibed them well, not to mention more than a few bottles of Vance's beloved Kentucky Nip.

So thank you again, Vance and Michael, for keeping Memphis thoroughly informed on how it got to be just what exactly it is today, whatever that is. Enjoy this book, and should you have any comments or questions, just "Ask Vance" himself: askvance@memphismagazine.com.

KENNETH NEILL
PUBLISHER/CEO
CONTEMPORARY MEDIA, INC.
MEMPHIS, TENNESSEE
1 AUGUST 2011

You are not a Lauderdale, and never will be.

So you have no idea what it's like to be the last descendant of one of the wealthiest and most powerful families in Memphis — if not all of America. Not that many years ago, the skies were filled with our gleaming dirigibles, our linotype factories cranked out hot-lead typesetting machinery, and our flax farms occupied most of Kansas, Nebraska, and Saskatchewan.

In those heady times, it was impossible to venture down into the Lauderdale vaults without stumbling over canvas bags of cash, and we used bundles of $100 bills for coasters, to keep Kentucky Nip stains off the Chippendale.

Nowadays, the only things in our underground vaults are mouse traps, the best furniture was hocked years ago, and most of the Mansion has been closed off to keep the utility bills down.

It wasn't always this way, you know — a Lauderdale reduced to writing local history columns to make ends meet. Why, back in the day, we hobnobbed with the Vanderbilts, the Carnegies, the Rockefellers, and the Hinkelstümpfelders of the world — grand names any schoolchild would recognize. They would travel to Memphis to attend the glittering balls on the fourth floor of the Mansion, or take part in the spirited games of Pictionary my family would hold in the east parlor. From my little cot in the basement, I remember those magical evenings — the raucous laughter, the clatter of roller skates on the mosaic tile floors, the breaking of liquor bottles against the marble fireplaces. And those were just the servants! The rich folks mainly just sat around in the den and polished their money and chatted about oil wells and gold bathtubs — the usual stuff.

But I look back on those days now with considerable bitterness, for I remember the scorn that Father had for the Vanderbilts, who — so he said — made their money from those old-timey steam-belching railroads, while the Lauderdales invested our considerable fortune in our fleet of airships that criss-crossed the skies.

It never dawned on us that the Commodore's locomotives could lug tons of precious cargo from coast to coast, along with thousands of passengers. Meanwhile, a Lauderdale dirigible could carry about 12 people and maybe, oh, 45 pounds of luggage, and that was on a good — meaning: non-windy — day.

So the dirigible business was "iffy," to use a technical term. And then came that god-awful incident with the *Hindenburg* — yes, a Lauderdale zeppelin crafted in our Düsseldorf factories — that spoiled the whole blimp industry. It hardly seemed fair. One epic catastrophe, broadcast live over the radio and filmed in all its blazing horror for the world to see, and all of a sudden the fickle public got the crazy notion that airships weren't entirely safe. Yes, perhaps it *was* unwise to ferry that cargo of roman candles and unstable phosphorous across the Atlantic, but that's the benefit of hindsight.

Everything tumbled down around us after that. The steam-driven linotype machines were replaced with newfangled "type-writers," and those replaced in their turn with the dastardly computing machines. The flax farms went belly-up, the crops withering and blowing away when people realized it was a lot easier to buy a linen shirt from Target instead of weaving their own. And when the nationwide chain of Lauderdale sno-cone parlors closed — oh, I just can't bear to think about it. It was the last straw.

Why am I even telling you this? Surely, the world knows my story by now — a sad tale described in tiresome detail on the Internet (easily found by searching for "great American bankruptcy trials" or "Lauderdale folly"), and covered relentlessly by Nancy Grace.

I'm just glad that I wasn't here to witness most of our family's decline, as I was shipped off to schools in Europe at the fragile age of 37. After earning degrees in Harvesting, with a minor in Oboe, I returned to my once-lovely home in Memphis, where I found the estate in ruins. Mother and Father had abandoned me, it seems, though years later I discovered they had simply moved to a mobile home park outside Millington. Left to my own devices in the lonely Mansion, I did little but wander the halls and dust the bowling trophies left behind on the mantels. Finally, as you know from Chapter 17 of my autobiography, *Bound for Glory*, the only way I knew to make a halfway decent living was this one — penning history columns about all sorts of odd and unusual matters, first for the *Memphis Flyer*, and nowadays for *Memphis* magazine and *MBQ*.

Old habits die hard, and I still carry the trappings of fortune. The cape and swordcane protect me from assassins and kidnappers, unwilling to believe that ransom demands would be met with hysterical laughter. The Mansion remains standing — most of it, anyway — though I'm somewhat leery of that odd tilt to the north tower, and we sold off the south lawn years ago for a miniature golf course (since closed).

I still have the rusty Daimler-Benz and Hispano-Suiza for those rare occasions when I venture out in search of answers to particularly difficult queries from readers. Plus, over the years, I've added to the rare collections of the Lauderdale library, whose holdings now include several hundred thousand photographs, scrapbooks, canned goods, and other historical ephemera of great value. To me, I mean. Not you.

In fact, even though readers have begged that I open the old home as a tourist attraction, I value my privacy and refuse to do so. Let the roof-mounted machine guns serve as a deterrent to anyone who wants to drop in for a visit.

Despite everything, my hopes are high. Among other "Ask Vance" ventures, I've started a new blog, as you may know, and I fully anticipate earning millions of dollars off that, as so many "bloggers" (as we are called) have done before me. And the first *Ask Vance* book was so successful (earning literally dozens of dollars), that I'm confident this one will do just as well.

But in case you can't figure it out for yourself — remember, you are not a Lauderdale — this handsome book contains 60 of the best columns published in *Memphis* magazine since the first volume came out in 2003. Or maybe these are just the ones we could find without going to any trouble digging through back issues.

As you read this book from cover to cover — as you must surely do — you'll notice that the design of the column evolved over the years. Even though my writing style today is as pure and award-worthy as always, various art directors have had their way with the look of "Ask Vance," so that explains why the earlier columns appear different from the later ones. I still think it's quite spiffy. I hope you do, too.

One day, the Lauderdale name will once again carry the dignity and grace that it deserves, and perhaps I can finally re-open those sno-cone parlors. Just you wait and see.

– *Vance Lauderdale*

Mail: Memphis Magazine
460 Tennessee Street #200, Memphis, TN 38103
Email: askvance@memphismagazine.com
Web: www.memphismagazine.com
Blog: www.memphismagazine.com/Blogs/Ask-Vance

ask vance

by Vance Lauderdale

Our Trivia Expert Solves Local Mysteries of Who, What, When, Where, Why, and Why Not.

An Interesting Undertaking

Dear Vance: What can you tell me about this vintage postcard (right), showing a grand mansion housing the Emma Wilburn Funeral Home? — J.M., Memphis.

Dear J.M.: I must tell you that's one of the most intriguing postcards I've ever seen from this area. For one thing, it's a great view of a fabulous home. And I don't imagine there were too many businesses of any kind owned by African-American women in the early 1900s, much less such an interesting, uh, undertaking as a funeral parlor.

Forgive me for sounding so sexist, but I all-too-quickly assumed that Mrs. Wilburn had inherited an establishment run by her husband, or perhaps another family member. Well, I was wrong. After checking through old newspaper files, I discovered that it was all hers, and Emma Wilburn & Company (as it was listed in the telephone books) opened at 913 Mississippi Boulevard in 1920. Not only did Wilburn work at this location, but she lived there, too. Now, no one has ever questioned the bravery of the Lauderdales, but I would certainly need nerves of steel to spend the night in a funeral home, considering all the other folks also "sleeping" there.

Your postcard mentions that Wilburn offered "special care for ladies and children" and I located an old advertisement that promoted her services as an "undertaker, embalmer, and most complete dresser." That same ad also noted that Wilburn provided "the very best ambulance service, day or night."

Did you know that during this time you would actually call a funeral home if you were in dire need of an ambulance? That just doesn't seem right to me. After all, is it really in their best interest to help you survive whatever accident has befallen you? I just don't think they would drive very fast — and probably wouldn't even turn their siren on. After all, what's in it for them?

At any rate, Wilburn ran her impressive funeral parlor until the 1930s. At one point, she married the funeral home manager, Fred Walton, and the fine print at the bottom of the postcard also shows her married name. But Emma Wilburn & Company apparently closed in the 1930s. The grand old home then housed a series of other undertaking establishments, including the Thomas Funeral Home and Southern Funeral Home, until the property was acquired by Walker Temple AME Church in the 1950s. I'm sorry to say that it is now a parking lot.

Remembering the Rose

Dear Vance: In the Cooper-Young neighborhood, there's a two-story brick building with an old sign at the top reading "Seraphim Rose Books." What can you tell me about this long-gone business? — P.T., Memphis.

Dear P.T.: The building at the corner of Walker and Tanglewood (opposite above) seems to be something of a mystery in that community. I've heard reports that it was once the old Mt. Arlington School, a county school that educated students in this area long before the board of education built the Fleece Station — now Peabody — School on Young. But Peggy Boyce Jemison, who compiled a marvelous history of Cooper-Young in 1977, claims Mt. Arlington School was actually located five blocks east, on Cox, and I think she's right. This building just doesn't look like a school.

The city directories don't list anything at 2072 Walker until 1923, when M.J. Lovett opened a grocery store in this building. He actually lived over on Tanglewood, and the second-floor was an apartment, occupied by a fellow named F.S. Roberts, who worked as a supervisor for a window and door manufacturing company here. In the 1930s, Lovett operated his grocery store out of one half of the ground floor, and J.A. Hicks ran a barber shop in the other half.

The building went through a variety of owners in later years, including Our Market Grocery, Haley Sundries, Floied Fire Extinguisher Company, and Walker Street Trading Company (an antiques store).

But the bookstore isn't as old as you think, P.T. A fellow named Leonard Ruck opened it in the early 1990s on Madison and then moved it to this location in 1996 or 1997. I first thought "Seraphim Rose" was a type of flower, but have learned that Eugene Rose was a prophet who lived in California from 1924 to 1982. He joined the Russian Orthodox Church, changed his name to Seraphim Rose, and published a number of influential books and a magazine, *The Orthodox Word*. That is his portrait, in fact, on the outside of the building, holding a scroll that reads "It is later than you think; hasten, therefore, to do the work of God."

The Seraphim Rose Bookstore closed just a couple of years ago. Some of the space is now occupied by Last Chance Records.

Remnants of Rawleigh

Dear Vance: I work in an old warehouse downtown (right) that has round stone plaques on the facade bearing the initial R. What used to be in this interesting building?
— N.H., Memphis.

Dear N.H.: You are lucky enough to work in what used to be the largest production facility in America of the W.T. Rawleigh Company.

W.T. (I never discovered his first name) Rawleigh was born in Wisconsin in 1889, and when he was a young man he borrowed a horse and buggy and started selling liniment and medicine to farmers. By 1895, he was so successful that he started making his own products. In the early 1900s the W.T. Rawleigh Company, with headquarters in Freeport, Illinois, was producing and selling more than 100 household products — medicines, salves, balms, spices, flavorings, seasonings, ointments, and cleaning products.

According to a company history that I scrounged up, W.T. Rawleigh was a forerunner of what they called the "direct-to-customers method," meaning you bought their products by mail order or from door-to-door salesmen. Then as now, you won't find Rawleigh products in any store. Their method certainly worked; by 1920 Rawleigh had more than 22 million customers.

The company built sprawling manufacturing plants in several cities across America. The 110,000-square-foot facility at 139 Illinois, which opened here in 1912, was the largest in the country, making patent medicines, cosmetics, insecticides, and spices. I presume they kept all those separate in some way; it would have been bad to mix them up. In 1958, however, the big manufacturing operation here shut down, and the buildings were converted to warehouses for the company.

Rawleigh closed its Memphis division in the late 1970s, and the complex — which is actually three adjoining buildings — was sold. In recent years, it has been used as production and distribution facilities for John Simmons' gift and art company, Carnevale.

The W.T. Rawleigh Company, however, is still around, and has changed with the times to the point where it even has a handy Web site. A "message board" allows customers to post questions about Rawleigh products. Just recently, somebody named "shinlee" pleaded, "Hope someone can help. Have spent a small fortune to resolve prickly heat rash." Within hours, "Trish" responded, "Rawleigh's Medicated Ointment is awesome for prickly heat."

No surprise there. Something tells me if "Trish" had suggested a non-Rawleigh product she would have been kicked off the site.

Got a question for Vance? Send it to "Ask Vance" at *Memphis* magazine, 460 Tennessee Street #200, Memphis, TN 38103, or e-mail him at askvance@memphismagazine.com.

[ask vance]

By Vance Lauderdale

Our Trivia Expert Solves Local Mysteries of Who, What, When, Where, Why, and Why Not.

The Life (and Death) of the Memphis Blues

Dear Vance: Help me settle a bet. Did a World War II plane called the *Memphis Blues* exist, and was it flown by a native Memphian? — J.V.M., Memphis.

Dear J.V.M.: It's interesting that you would bring up such a question at this time, since as we speak (or I write, while you read — oh, you know what I mean) the much better known *Memphis Belle* could be heading to the Air Force Museum in Dayton, Ohio. The *Belle*, as you surely know, is probably the most famous B-17 of World War II. It was the first to complete 25 missions over Europe, was featured in a popular wartime documentary, came back to America to "star" in a national war-bond drive, then was brought to Memphis, refurbished, and put on display at various places around town. Most of the other aircraft from that period were reduced to scrap when the war finally ended, but the *Memphis Belle* — and the famous love story of pilot Robert Morgan and his "Memphis Belle," Margaret Polk — remained a legend.

Not so well known — in fact, most people I spoke with had never even heard of it — is the story of our city's "other" Flying Fortress, the *Memphis Blues*, named after the famous W.C. Handy composition. I think that's mainly because the *Blues* had a short, albeit dramatic life. The plane, also a B-17F like the *Belle*, was based in England, where it was assigned to the 358th Bomb Squadron in April 1943. It completed six missions over the course of about four weeks. Then, on July 14, 1943, it took off on a raid to destroy the Nazi-held Villacoublay Airdrome outside Paris.

The *Memphis Blues* never made it. Heavily damaged by enemy anti-aircraft fire as it was flying over France, the plane turned around and tried to limp

back home. With three of its four engines out, the bomber was doomed, and its pilot, Lt. Calvin Swaffer, ditched the aircraft in the English Channel. "Swaffer decided against ordering his crew to bail out over German territory," according to a newspaper clipping. "Putting his faith in the Royal Air Force rescue service, he headed for the Channel and crash landed." All members of the crew were quickly plucked from the water by the RAF.

You are correct about the *Memphis Blues* pilot being a native Memphian. Records indicate that Swaffer worked as a cotton inspector here before joining the Army Air Corps. He served as a co-pilot on another bomber before being promoted to pilot on July 12, 1943. The crash into the Channel was his 25th mission, the maximum required of bomber crews in those days, so Swaffer was allowed to come home. After the war, he returned to Memphis, married a woman named Dorothy, and found a job as a pilot with American Airlines.

Most, if not all, of this information comes from an amazing Web site maintained by the 303rd Bomb Group Association (www.303rdbga.com). This organization has compiled a comprehensive account of just about every B-17 that operated in World War II, and it was here that I was able to locate a photo of the crew of the *Memphis Blues*, taken shortly after their rescue (left). That's Swaffer, the tall fellow fourth from the right.

Unfortunately, I was never able to find a photo of the plane itself, and even though there is a Web site devoted to the colorful "nose art" that adorned these bombers (again, the Petty girl on the nose of the *Memphis Belle* comes to mind), the artwork for the *Memphis Blues* is listed here, among that of many other planes, as "missing."

The future location of the *Memphis Belle* is still uncertain, but we do know where its "sister" ship, the *Memphis Blues*, is today — still lying at the bottom of the English Channel.

Circular Reasoning

Dear Vance: Is it true that Memphis once had (or still has) a circular school building? Many of these were built around the country in the 1950s and '60s. — B.H., Memphis.

Dear B.H.: The closest thing we have is Sheffield High School (opposite), constructed in 1966 and still in use today. It was not just one circle, but three linked circles designed by the Memphis firms of Adams and Albin Architects and Robert L. Hall. The designers called it "a compact and economical plan."

One domed building served as the gymnasium, another was the auditorium, and the main three-story structure housed the cafeteria on the ground floor and 60 classrooms on the upper floors. An unusual feature, according to a newspaper article, was the library, "suspended between the second and third floors." My pal Bonnie Perkins, a Sheffield graduate and producer of many of the popular *Memphis Memoirs* history programs aired on WKNO-TV, remembers, "It's actually a cool design because the library was very tall and spacious, and completely round. All the staircases had doors opening directly into the library, so naturally kids always cut through when they're in a hurry, but the librarians would get onto you if you did that."

The southeast Memphis school adopted the circular theme for the name of its mascot, initially calling its teams the Knights of the Round Table. That "Round Table" part got dropped pretty quickly — too long to fit on a scoreboard or football uniform — but Perkins tells me that developers of the neighborhood around the school apparently liked the notion, naming nearby streets Camelot and after vaguely English places, like Forest Glen and Forest View. You would think that the main street in that area, Knight Road, also came from Camelot, but it was actually named after a prominent landowner in the area. Just a coincidence. Or so I'm told.

Searching for Shelby Street

Dear Vance: My great grandmother wrote down her memories of living in Memphis from 1900 to 1906, when she lived on Shelby Street close to the river, in an apartment rented from her mother's cousin, Richard Lane. I found the address to be 437 Shelby Street, but I cannot find such a street on maps today. Does it still exist? Is the building still standing? — J.G., Memphis.

Dear J.G.: Yes, Shelby Street still exists. When your ancestor lived here, it ran along the river bluff, from Beale Street south to Georgia Avenue. (This was in the days before Riverside Drive, remember.) In 1907, it was renamed South Front Street, since it was basically just an extension of it, and it remains so today.

City directories show that a Richard C. Lane indeed lived at 437 Shelby Street and also worked out of his home as a cigar manufacturer. His wife, Alvira, was a dress maker. Then as now, this area was a mix of commercial and residential properties. Their home stood between a boarding house and Wm. C. Ellis & Sons, a machine-works firm that opened in 1862 and is still in business today.

Lane apparently died in 1912 (since the always-helpful city directories listed Alvira as a "widow" the following year). She continued to work after his death, and one of the telephone directories contained an ad for her business, announcing such services as "hemstitching at 10 cents per yard, all kinds of dress plaiting, briar stitching, smocking, pinking, and braiding. Work guaranteed." I believe she passed away in 1918.

I'm sorry to tell you that their residence, and your great grandmother's former home, has been demolished. It is now a parking lot at the corner of Beale and South Front. The photo above shows that block today. The home we've been talking about stood just past the Wm. C. Ellis & Sons building on the left, just about where that billboard is. **M**

Got a question for Vance? Send it to "Ask Vance" at Memphis *magazine, 460 Tennessee Street #200, Memphis, TN 38103, or e-mail him at askvance@memphismagazine.com.*

[ask vance]

By Vance Lauderdale

Our Trivia Expert Solves Local Mysteries of Who, What, When, Where, Why, and Why Not.

A Mighty Mouse

Dear Vance: Is there a story behind the big mouse (right) on the pest-control place on Elvis Presley Boulevard? It is so cute that I have to know more.
— K.D., Memphis.

Dear K.D.: Not only is there a story behind it, there's even a movie.

I drove out there myself one fine day in June and spoke with Carese Rice, president of the Atomic Pest Control Company at 2371 Elvis Presley Boulevard. Carese is the daughter of Les Tubbs, who founded Atomic back in 1958, and Les gets credit for this rather eye-catching addition to his company's headquarters.

The 10-foot-tall mouse began life as a promotion for the 1971 movie *Willard*, a charming little tale about a boy who befriends a pack of rats, which was then showing at the old Crosstown Theater on North Cleveland. Les saw the giant mouse, realized he could put it to good use after the movie (and its sequel, *Ben*) ran its course, and purchased it. He first loaded it on a trailer and hauled it all over town promoting his business — and as a press release rather cryptically says, "entertaining children" — but since 1978 it's been securely mounted on the roof of the business.

In case you're wondering, K.D, it's made of fiberglass and weighs more than 1,200 pounds. His thick wire whiskers are three feet long, and that big piece of cheese stands more than six feet tall. A few years ago, Carese had him (or her) restored and repainted, so now he really looks quite spiffy.

Needless to say, he's attracted quite a bit of attention over the years. Carese told me that people stop by all the time to snap his photo, and he's been featured in the syndicated comic strip *Zippy* and in an article by Pulitzer Prize-winning writer Andrei Codrescu. Carese even contacted the folks at the *Guinness Book of World Records*, who told her that though there is no official category for "world's largest mouse," they will definitely certify hers if she sends in the necessary paperwork.

Such fame deserves to be recognized, so as you read this, Atomic is having a contest to name the mouse. Some of the entries submitted seem a bit odd, such as "Cimota" (that's "Atomic" spelled backwards), "Elvin," "Adam Meeks" (huh?), and even "Mr. Ringles Ring Us To Control Your Bugs." Carese says, "I'd really like it to have some name that connects the mouse to Memphis," so if you have a suggestion, just call her at 774-0057 or e-mail her at atomicpest@aol.com. Hmmm. Mighty Mouse? No, I guess that name has already been taken.

Miracle Medicine?

Dear Vance: When I was a child, my mother treated all our aches and pains with a product called Penetro. I believe it was made in Memphis. What happened to this medicine?
— C.F., Memphis.

Dear C.F.: I confess that I received your query quite some time ago and carefully filed it away in my polished oaken crate labeled "Questions To Be Answered Later."

Actually, it's more like a battered cardboard box, but it accomplishes the same purpose — holding piles of letters that have stumped me. In this case, because I had never heard of Penetro, and neither had anyone else I contacted.

But then one day I happened to pick up a wrinkled brochure (below right) at the flea market and with a shout of "Eureka!" realized it contained all I needed to know to respond to you. Finally!

Your mother was right, apparently, for the makers of Penetro claimed it could cure an astonishing variety of ailments, including "sprains, bronchial irritation, cuts and scratches, tired and sore muscles, head cold discomfort, superficial burns and scalds, irritated feet, sunburn, bruises and abrasions," among others. Why, it could even treat frostbite!

What was in this miracle product, you ask? Mutton suet. Yes, mutton suet — in other words, lard from sheep.

The brochure describes Penetro as "Grandma's Discovery Perfected by Modern Medical Science." Mutton suet, you see, "is one of the earliest of all home remedies. Your grandmother, great-grandmother, and great-great-grandmother placed their faith in mutton suet." I'll bet you never knew that, did you? "Now, after generations of service, mutton suet has been taken by modern medical science and combined with menthol, camphor, methyl salicylate, turpentine, oil of pine, and thymol to create stainless, snow-white PENETRO."

First of all, I wonder how much mutton suet is left after they've mixed in all that other stuff (including turpentine!). And second, I wonder how much work Penetro actually does. After all, for headaches, the brochure recommends rubbing their product into your temples and then "lie down and remain quiet," which is a pretty good treatment for headaches, even without all that mutton suet.

I can't tell you how long Penetro stayed on the market. The brochure reveals it was manufactured here by Plough (now Schering Plough), but a call to the Memphis office, then more calls to their home office in Kenilworth, New Jersey, got me nowhere. It seems the company doesn't keep records of their old products, and no one had ever heard of this. So even though the brochure claims that Penetro "occupies an enviable position in the medicine cabinets of hundreds of homes," its once-grand reputation seems to have faded over the years. Even with the people who made it.

Harmon Baker with assistant Carla Reeves, in 1982.

The Magic Man

Dear Vance: What can you tell me about the elderly magician who billed himself as "The Baffling Mr. Baker"? — S.D., Germantown.

Dear S.D.: Space prevents me from telling the whole story of this extraordinary gentleman. Let's just say that the man who claimed he was "the world's oldest practicing magician" was probably correct; after all, he was still performing shortly before his death — at the age of 106!

Many things are still unknown about Harmon E. Baker, who was (perhaps) born in Memphis in 1887 and first began practicing magic at the age of 12. Baker liked to change his life story whenever it pleased him, and some accounts had him winning an Olympic gold medal for wrestling, piloting fighter planes during World War I, and studying judo in Japan. None of that really mattered, for he spent his entire life performing, and he was pretty good at it — good enough to be featured on *The Tonight Show with Johnny Carson*, *The Late Show with David Letterman*, and at the 1981 grand reopening of The Peabody.

Standing barely five feet tall, Baker cut a remarkable figure, and a profile published years ago in this magazine noted: "Baker is a study in perpetual motion. He darts back and forth, fluttering handkerchiefs and flapping ropes; his malleable face forms itself into expressive shapes. He bears a certain resemblance to Jimmy Durante, and sounds somewhat like him as well."

By all accounts, he was a nice man, who enjoyed performing for children. "I don't talk down to them," he told one writer. "I like to emphasize the fact that my work is educational, and show the children that all that I do is tricks to deceive the five senses."

Towards the end of his amazingly long life, Baker began writing books about magic, working out of the home on Carrington that he shared with his wife, Ruth. But I don't know if he ever finished them. He passed away in 1993 and is buried in Forest Hill Cemetery. **M**

Got a question for Vance? Send it to "Ask Vance" at *Memphis* magazine, 460 Tennessee Street #200, Memphis, TN 38103, or e-mail him at askvance@memphismagazine.com.

[ask vance]

By Vance Lauderdale

Our Trivia Expert Solves Local Mysteries of Who, What, When, Where, Why, and Why Not.

Home of the Horse Shoe

Dear Vance: I remember a rather large tourist court that stood on Summer Avenue in the 1960s called the Silver Horse Shoe. On my last visit to Memphis, I couldn't locate the place. Can you help me? — B.E., Nashville.

Dear B.E.: Certainly, for the Silver Horse Shoe stood as a landmark of sorts on that boulevard for almost half a century. In fact, when they — whoever "they" are — demolished the place in the early 1990s, I was there to capture the event with my trusty Nikon (above).

You have to remember that in the days before the interstate system gridded the nation, the main routes connecting cities and towns were the state highways, and Summer Avenue — otherwise known as State Highway 70, 79, and 64 — served as a main gateway to Memphis. In fact, its semi-official name was the Bristol Highway, because it linked our city on the western edge of Tennessee with the town of Bristol far to the east.

To take advantage of that tourist traffic, entrepreneurs set up quite a number of diners, gas stations, and motels along this busy road, among them the Alamo Plaza, the Chickasaw Tourist Court, the Palomino Motel, and — perhaps a bit better known — the world's first Holiday Inn.

The Silver Horse Shoe began life in the late 1940s as the Hester Motel, a row of one-story units that occupied the entire block on the north side of Summer between Berclair and Novarese. At first I puzzled over the name of the place, but then I noticed that the only residence in that entire block was occupied by a fellow named James R. Hester, and his house happened to be right next door to the motel. Though the telephone directories of the day list his occupation as farmer, I will go out on a limb here and presume that he built and operated the Hester Motel.

As I said, there was little else on that stretch of Summer at the time, but across the street stood an interesting collection of small businesses, including Bel-Air Cleaners, Saltz TV & Radio Repair, Dairy Dip Dairy Bar, East Pharmacy, Ollie Jones' Barber Shop, and Laster Hardware.

Sometime in the early 1950s (I don't have the exact date), the tourist court changed its name to the Silver Horse Shoe Motel. I don't really know why. I mean, that is certainly a swankier name than Hester, certainly, but there is nothing horse-shoe-shaped about the place — just a couple of rows of rather plain motel units clustered under the big trees, unadorned except for simple triangular pediments over each entrance, which were painted yellow to match the doors when I visited it last. In fact, the only thing "silver" about the place was the grey shingle roof. But at that same time Memphis also had a Silver Bell Liquor Store, a Silver Dollar Inn, a Silver Moon Cafe, and at least seven Silver Saver Super Markets, so apparently business owners thought "silver" was catchy.

Even if you never stayed there, many people remember the interesting Art Deco-looking diner that stood next door to the motel. That opened in the early 1960s as part of the citywide Gridiron chain, I believe, and eventually changed its name to the Horse Shoe Diner — without the "Silver."

But you won't find the Silver Horse Shoe or its matching diner no matter how hard you look, B.E. When the site was cleared in the early 1990s, it made way for a shopping center. The motel has been replaced by a Mega Market, and an auto-parts store now stands on the site of the old diner.

Matching Monuments?

Dear Vance: Why are two or three of the tombstones in the National Cemetery a completely different size and shape from the others, which are of a uniform style and color? Were those for officers or something? — P.G., Memphis.

Dear P.G.: It's only fitting you would ask such a question of the Lauderdales. After all, if it weren't for my family's bold military exploits as leaders of the local scrap-paper drive during the First World War, our country might not have emerged as victors. Of course, being of the humble sort, I have no intention of being laid to rest in the National Cemetery, since they rejected the plans for my impressive 500-foot quartz obelisk. The fact that I personally have no military experience whatsoever, except for being co-captain of my school's safety patrol, had nothing to do with their decision, I assure you.

National cemeteries were established by an act of Congress following the Civil War as hallowed places to bury our war dead. They were originally located in cities close to scenes of major battles, in fact, which explains why such cemeteries were opened in Memphis, Nashville, and Corinth, Mississippi. As you noticed, P.G., part of what makes these places so beautiful and impressive is the row upon row of nearly identical white marble markers — more than 41,000 of them in the National Cemetery in Memphis.

Certain cemeteries have their own rules, but in general, if you are a veteran, you are entitled to a burial plot and a carved headstone, furnished and maintained at government expense. If you (and they) so desire, your spouse and any unmarried son or daughter can also be buried with you, which explains why some of the markers have names carved on the front and the back.

Okay, but what about the headstones that don't follow this tradition? I actually drove through the National Cemetery and located six gravestones that literally stand out from the rest, and they do not mark the graves of famous soldiers or high-ranking officers. One of them, in fact, identifies the last resting place of a private, John Van Horn (1833-1903), who served with the Kansas Cavalry (below) and another, a small stone capped with a marble angel, stands over the grave, the 2-year-old daughter of Herman and Mollie Pass. Herman was a private during World War I.

According to cemetery director Margaret Dill, "A long time ago, families were apparently allowed to purchase and install a private monument at their own expense and their own maintenance. But very few people did so, for various reasons." One reason might be the cost. If the stone they purchased ever weathered or cracked, the family — not the government — would have to buy a new one.

At any rate, Dill explained that the regulations were changed, and later burials were required to use the standard headstones.

When the National Cemetery first opened in 1867, it was located way outside of town on what was then called the Raleigh Road. Now it lies in the shadow of the Jackson Avenue viaduct, and most people probably drive by it without noticing. Too bad. Those 41,000 veterans and their families deserve to be remembered.

Searching for Service

Dear Vance: Can you tell me anything about the old Baptist Service Center that operated in Memphis during World War II? — T.N., Memphis.

Dear T.N.: Actually, I can't, but at least I can show you a nice picture of the place. Will that do?

I managed to find an interesting old postcard (below) of this establishment in the Lauderdale Library, and presume it was a USO-type organization, offering a place of rest and recreation for our soldiers. It was located downtown at 78 Madison, on the north side of the block between Front and Main. The director was a fellow named Harry N. Hollis.

The front of the postcard notes that the place is "for the Armed Forces of our Nation." The back explains that it "represents an effort on the part of Shelby County Baptists to provide for the spiritual and physical needs of those in the armed forces." What's more, "featured is a homelike atmosphere."

A pretty impressive "home," huh? This grand building, with its massive Greek Revival portico and flanking Ionic columns, was originally constructed for the Liberty Savings Bank and Trust Company. After the war, it became the Unique Beauty Shop, Harry Hollis took a job as a salesman with the Carnation Milk Company. During the 1960s, the building was demolished to make way for a much more "modern" structure, which for years housed the Lerner Shop and is today home to the Six50 Sports Club. **M**

Got a question for Vance? Send it to "Ask Vance" at Memphis *magazine, 460 Tennessee Street #200, Memphis, TN 38103, or e-mail him at askvance@memphismagazine.com.*

[ask vance]

By Vance Lauderdale

Our Trivia Expert Solves Local Mysteries of Who, What, When, Where, Why, and Why Not.

Tropical Treasure

Dear Vance: I recently purchased a 1964 White Station High School yearbook. Inside is a double-page photograph of students parked around a fountain illuminated with colored lights and decorated with large seashells. Where was this unusual hangout? — B.R., Memphis.

Dear B.R.: When I first looked at this photo, I shouted "Eureka!" because: 1) I just like to shout "Eureka!" at random times throughout the day, and 2) after years of searching, I — or you, actually — had finally located a photograph of the elusive Tropical Freeze.

Opened in the early 1950s at the southwest corner of Poplar and White Station, the Tropical Freeze was a unique South Seas-themed drive-in restaurant. Even though it closed around 1967, it is remembered fondly by 97.5 percent of everyone who lived in East Memphis. That's just a rough calculation, of course. If memory serves correctly — and I'm getting some pretty bad service these days from those memory banks — the rather small building had three fake palm trees on the thatched roof illuminated by colored floodlights, and all sorts of other "tropical" embellishments, including fountains and sea shells. Needless to say, a bizarre establishment for East Memphis — heck, *any* part of Memphis, for that matter. And I have been searching for a photo of it for years.

So you can imagine my dismay when some friends declared this was NOT the Tropical Freeze, because (they said) the parking lot didn't have a fountain.

But what else could this be, I wondered? After all, Memphis couldn't have had that many tropical-themed joints in the mid-1960s. (Sure, I knew about the Luau, across from East High School, but this shot was not taken there.)

So I put my detective hat on, so to speak, and got to work. First of all, I reasoned that a WSHS hangout had to be close to the school itself, on Perkins north of Poplar. The kids wouldn't drive far across town to do their hanging out, even when they had spiffy cars like these.

Then I scrutinized the image itself for clues. Though it's hard to see here, the yearbook photo shows a red/yellow/green traffic signal in the right background. In

addition, dashed white lines — painted lane dividers — are dimly visibly in the street behind the fountain. In 1964, very few streets in the WSHS area were wide (or busy) enough to need lane dividers. In fact, Poplar was the only one that came to mind. And in the mid-1960s, the only traffic lights along Poplar were located at Perkins, Mendenhall, and White Station.

The final clue? What was *not* visible in the photo. Namely, there are no lights, signs, or businesses across the street.

Poplar at either Perkins or Mendenhall was more developed than this. But Poplar at White Station was different. In 1964, the Tropical Freeze was on the southwest corner of that intersection, but across the street, the north side of Poplar was still mainly residential.

This had to be the Tropical Freeze!

So I began to track down Memphians who went to White Station in the mid-1960s. One of them, attorney Tom Prewitt Jr., put me in touch with a priest at St. Mary's Episcopal Church. Father C.B. Baker graduated from WSHS in 1964 and he told me, "This is not speculation. The picture was taken at the Tropical Freeze, at the corner of Poplar and White Station. You can go to press with that!"

And so we will. Who am I to argue with a priest? Father Baker remembers the Tropical Freeze very well, and says that other students — oh, he wouldn't name names — "would drop those Salvo detergent tablets in the water, and suds would flow out into the intersection. And one time, somebody got some ducks from Audubon Park and put them in the fountain."

That probably explains why later owners of the site — Roy Rogers Roast Beef, Danver's, and now Starbucks — got rid of the strange fountain. But perhaps not entirely. The curved stone wall that wraps around the "lawn" at Starbucks today may be what's left of the wall behind the fountain in this photo.

So, after all these years — Eureka! — I finally located a photo of the Tropical Freeze parking lot. Perhaps someday I can find a photographer who bothered to turn around and took a picture of the actual building. Is that really too much to ask?

Business on Barksdale

Dear Vance: In your October issue, when you wrote about Dirmeyer's Drugstore at the corner of Barksdale and Nelson, you didn't mention the beautifully restored building (above) right next door. — T.S., Memphis.

Dear T.S.: No, I didn't mention it because nobody had asked about it. Until now. My column doesn't permit me to discuss in my typically longwinded way the complete history of every single building in Memphis. For that, you'll have to wait for my upcoming book, *Ask Vance: The Complete History of Every Single Building in Memphis*. I'm supposed to get to work on that any day now.

But the building you mentioned, T.S., opened in 1927 as Arrow Food Store #19, a grocery chain that, quite frankly, I am not familiar with. Perhaps because I wasn't even born then. Arrow apparently didn't remain in business very long. By 1930, this building was Piggly Wiggly #3. Then, just five years later, it became a Baker Brothers Grocery.

Over the years, many different owners moved in. In the early 1940s, it seems to have been a private residence for Mrs. Eva D. Jacobs, who worked as an inspector at Bry's Department Store. An inspector of *what*, I can't say. After that, 863 S. Barksdale became home to Wyatt Tomlinson's Upholstery Shop, then some business with the rather vague name of Home Specialty Service Company, then Wilson Manufacturing Company, and then Ajax Refrigeration Service.

Estes and Weeks Custom Metal Works moved in during the 1980s and 1990s. In recent years, though, all that hammering and banging and manufacturing has been replaced by a considerably quieter tenant — a psychologist's office. No one answered the phone when I called to make an appointment, even though I let it ring a long, long time, so it's possible the building may be waiting for yet another tenant.

When Walter Came to Walker

Dear Vance: Back in the 1950s, my father worked for International Harvester. He remembers national labor leader Walter Reuther coming here to open a very elaborate union headquarters somewhere in South Memphis. Do you know if that building still exists? — G.T., Memphis.

Dear G.T.: Indeed it does, and it looks as fine today — now home to Allied Electrical Contractors — as the day it opened.

Constructed in 1945, this two-story art deco building at 1190 Walker (below) originally housed Local 667 of the American Federation of Labor. In 1954, it changed hands, and you're right that Walter Reuther, all-powerful head of the United Auto Workers, came to Memphis to dedicate the building as the new headquarters of the UAW's Ford Local 903. This was back when Ford Motor Company had a manufacturing plant in Memphis, you see.

The June 19, 1954, *Memphis Press Scimitar* reported, "Reuther, whose red

hair matches his fiery temper, spoke on the lawn of the Ford Local Building this afternoon." The paper noted that Reuther was "head of the world's largest labor union, with 1,500,000 members." Pretty close to the same number who read *Memphis* magazine, I believe. **M**

Got a question for Vance? Send it to "Ask Vance" at Memphis *magazine, 460 Tennessee Street #200, Memphis, TN 38103, or e-mail him at askvance@memphismagazine.com.*

[askvance]

By Vance Lauderdale

Our Trivia Expert Solves Local Mysteries of Who, What, When, Where, Why, and Why Not.

Stunning Statues

Dear Vance: Please tell me more about the gorgeous statues outside the Shelby County Courthouse downtown. I'm especially in love with this stunning Roman fellow (right). — J.R., Memphis.

Dear J.R.: It's perfectly understandable that you are "in love" with this particular statue, since so many readers have noted that it bears a remarkable resemblance to *me*. And while I don't often wander the halls of the Lauderdale mansion dressed as a Roman soldier (well, not since the psychiatric treatments), this is often the magisterial pose I assume as I sit before the grand fireplace and ponder which questions from readers to answer each month.

Do you know that in all the years of writing this column, I believe this is the first one that concerns the Shelby County Courthouse. I find that remarkable, considering it is such an imposing structure — a massive, colonnaded building that takes up an entire city block, and exuding what the authors of *Memphis: An Architectural Guide* call "serene classical confidence."

Again, much as I do myself.

The courthouse opened in 1910 to replace a jumbled collection of courtrooms that had previously been jammed into rented space at the Overton Hotel at Main and Poplar. A plaque outside the building notes that this is the largest and most ornate courthouse in Tennessee, and who could argue with that? The city fathers wisely chose the sturdiest materials (blue limestone from a quarry in Bedford, Indiana) and best designers for this important civic project. A courthouse building commission selected the prestigious firm of Rogers and Hale, with offices in New York and Chicago. James Gamble Rogers would be the primary architect, and according to the official *Report of the Commission* published in 1910, he "was found to be specially qualified in designing buildings of a monumental character." What's more, Rogers . . . wait, you asked about the *sculptures*, didn't you?

Well, they didn't scrimp on those, either. The commission selected a prominent artist, J. William Rhyne, to carve six much-larger-than-life figures to guard the west and south entrances to the courthouse. Each figure is different, representing Wisdom, Justice, Liberty, Peace, Prosperity, and (that Roman fellow) Authority. Each was carved from a solid block of limestone, and each statue weighs — well, it's hard to say. But the other day, I leaned all my weight against one, and it didn't budge.

Born in Scotland in 1860, Rhyne moved to this country in the late 1800s. He rather quickly established a reputation as one of America's most gifted sculptors, and today the many monuments and memorials he carved grace public buildings, cemeteries, and parks from Washington, D.C., to Washington state. Perhaps his best-known works are the imposing figures of "Victory" and "Peace" that adorn the entrance to Grant's Tomb in New York City.

That *Report of the Commission* I mentioned earlier contains the budget for the original construction. This massive building, with all its marble and limestone and brass and hand-carved detail, cost the county just a bit over $1.5 million. Rhyne charged just $5,000 for each of the massive figures by the doors. He also carved other decorative elements for the building, including the elaborate pediments, bringing the total charge for all the sculptures to precisely $74,302.10.

That's probably what it would cost to carve just *one* of those figures today.

Home of the Future

Dear Vance: I picked up some old magazines at a garage sale, and a 1959 copy of *True Romance* contains an article on "Story-Book Homes." What surprised me is that a model home in the state-of-the-art "Futurama" design was constructed in Memphis. Is it still standing today? — B.N., Nashville.

Dear B.N.: I certainly didn't think so, because all too often my explorations in search of buildings from the past have taken me to parking lots or overgrown fields. Imagine my surprise, then, when I discovered that this particular "Story-Book Home" is not only still standing, it looks as good as new (opposite, above).

As your magazine article explains, "Story-Book Homes" were a series of mostly traditional home designs, among them the "New Orleans," the "Regency," and even a model called the "Abundant Villager." And these were special homes indeed. "Not even movie stars or millionaires can live a more luxurious or thrilling life than you can in your fabulous Story-Book Home," the article declared. What made these homes unique, or so their designers claimed, were the ultra-modern features and materials incorporated into each home. "For instance, the double insulation, the special roof decking, and the moisture-proofing are positively not combined in any other houses. And the beautiful and durable Flintkote Flexachrome vinyl-asbestos floors are easy to clean and require no waxing." What's more, the kitchens even featured Westinghouse appliances. Apparently, that was a big deal at the time.

Local builders could purchase these plans — for a whopping one dollar! — and in the Memphis area, developers W.D. Jemison and Sons erected several "Story-Book Homes" in the Forest Lakes subdivision they were developing around Beaver and Otter Lakes in Raleigh.

The "Futurama" home (below) was the most unusual of all the designs, described as a "home of the future with a magnificently simple exterior of great dignity and hospitality." Inside, "huge, exposed natural beams make this house look as strong and durable as it truly is." The deluxe model featured "a vast living room with handsome fireplace and shoji-screened entrance. A huge family and TV room surrounds a magnificent scientific kitchen with formal dining, which overlooks a beautiful 32-foot indoor swimming pool (heated and filtered)." The bathroom was tiled with "the revolutionary new Formica," which has a "smooth, gleaming surface that saves cleaning time and work for Mother."

Oh, there were plenty of other marvels. The master bedroom "offered all the elegance of your own private villa on the Riviera." And that indoor pool, just off the bedroom, was always available "for a relaxing, nighttime dip — in complete privacy, unhampered by bathing suits!"

This article ran in *True Romance* magazine, remember.

As far as I can tell, only one of these was constructed in Memphis, at 3991 Lakemont Drive.

"When it was first built, the home was featured in the Sunday newspaper, and my mother took us to see it," says "Futurama" homeowner Jan Beaty. "I was only 14 years old at the time, and never knew that would one day it would be my home."

Beaty and her husband purchased the house in 1970. This was quite a change from their previous residence, a small home in Frayser. The "Futurama" still had most of its original features, including the indoor swimming pool, sunken bathtub, separate "his and hers" bathrooms, and brick fireplace.

Over the years, Beaty has made quite a few updates. She lightened many of the darker paint colors that originally covered the walls, added a cedar-lined attic in the home's distinctive rooftop "turret," and completely modernized the kitchen. Moisture from the pool weakened the overhead beams in that room, so when she had those rebuilt she also replaced the original styrofoam-panel ceiling with a more environmentally friendly material, which absorbs moisture.

"One of the features mentioned in the magazine article was that you could just open the door leading to the swimming pool room and that would draw moisture into your house, like a humidifier," says Beaty. "Well, they omitted the fact that if you have chlorine in the water, that's not a good idea. Your whole house smells like chlorine."

Beaty also added more windows at the rear of the house to give a better view of the lake. "It's so beautiful, looking out there. That's what's kept me here all these years; you just have such a sense of spaciousness."

"I don't know why these homes were featured in a *True Romance* magazine," she says, "but it really was a 'true romance' story. My husband and I just adored each other, and we really had fun here. It's really been a wonderful home." **M**

Got a question for Vance? Send it to "Ask Vance" at Memphis *magazine, 460 Tennessee Street #200, Memphis, TN 38103. Or e-mail him at askvance@ memphismagazine.com.*

[ask vance]

By Vance Lauderdale

Our Trivia Expert Solves Local Mysteries of Who, What, When, Where, Why, and Why Not.

The Rambling Rex

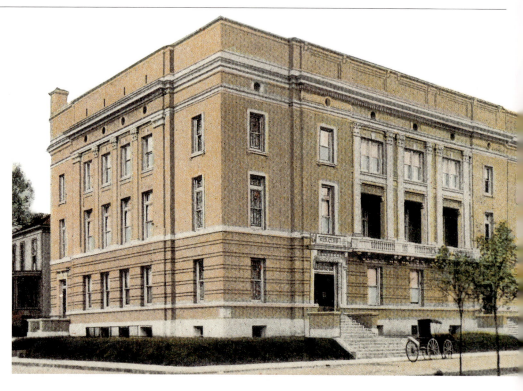

Dear Vance: What happened to the old Rex Club? I've seen references to it in various articles about Memphis history. — H.H., Memphis.

Dear H.H.: I'm afraid you're going to have to be just a bit more specific. After all, the Rex Club had a long history — longer, even, than the famed Lauderdale Literary Society — and it moved all over town, occupying various buildings here and there. I just can't spare the time to talk about all of them — well, come to think of it, I really don't have much else to do today, so I might as well tell you what I know.

From what I understand, this club was originally formed as a social association for young Jewish men way back in 1861. At the time, it was called the Southern Club. Not a very original name, I know, and when the Union forces captured our city the following year, they didn't like that "Southern" part and made the members change it to something even less original — the Memphis Club. I found an old newspaper article that said this club "was upstairs in a building at the southwest corner of Second and Union" — in other words, right above where Huey's is today.

This same helpful newspaper article noted that around 1908, a "group of rebels" (and by that, I don't think they meant Confederates, since the war was long over) broke away from the Southern/Memphis members and formed their own little club, which they called the Rex Club, for reasons that no one has bothered to explain to me. Apparently the new club was more fun than the old one, so the members of the *other* club disbanded and everybody became part of the Rex Club. At this time, they were having meetings and all sorts of activities on the second floor of the Lyric Theater, which once stood on Madison.

Are you still with me, H.H.? After all, you *did* ask. In 1910, the Rex Club erected its own building at Madison and Dunlap, and I located an old postcard (above) which shows this structure. Even with such an impressive headquarters, the club didn't stay there very long. In 1933, they sold the property to the University of Tennessee, which converted it into a student/alumni center. It served that purpose until 1973, when it was demolished to make way for more modern medical buildings. When the building came a-tumbling down, they discovered a time capsule in the old cornerstone, which contained some campaign material for Tennessee Governor Malcolm Patterson and a 1910 copy of *The Commercial Appeal*, among other things.

Okay, but what about the Rex Club? Well, in 1919, the members — who apparently never liked to stay in one location for long — purchased "the old George Bennett place" on Poplar about a mile east of White Station, where they built a very fine complex known as the Rex-Ridgeway Club. William Langford, identified as "the famous golf architect," came to Memphis and declared, "It's the most natural course I've ever seen." He laid out a very challenging nine-hole course — supposedly the toughest in the county — and left plans for the remaining nine. At the time, some club members thought the site was a mistake, believing "it was too far from town to ever be used." Over the years, they also erected a fine two-story clubhouse, swimming pool, and tennis courts. Eventually, the name became the Ridgeway Country Club.

Well, are you seeing a pattern emerge here? In 1969, a joint venture of Cook Industries and Boyle Investment Company bought the Ridgeway Country Club site for some $2.5 million, and transformed it into an office park. Ridgeway moved even further east, to property outside Collierville, where they remain today. For now, anyway.

18 • ASK VANCE II

Mystery on Milton

Dear Vance: We own a building at 2641/2643 Milton Avenue that we think was originally the Frulla Grocery Store. We were wondering about the history of the place. — J.T.B., Memphis.

Dear J.T.B.: It's easy to see why you think this little building, which has obviously seen better days, once housed the Frulla Grocery. After all, the old sign is still painted on one wall (below). But the building, which was constructed in 1931, was originally home to a grocery owned by a gentleman named Rufus C. Myers, who owned the property until 1943.

The following year, Claude Frulla, who had previously worked as a checker at Liberty Cash Grocers #2 at 1329 Union, moved into the little building on Milton and opened his own store there. It's interesting — to me, at least — that the city directories show that Claude lived at 893 East Trigg with two brothers, Eugene and Pacifico, who also worked with him at the Liberty Cash store, but for some reason they didn't join him at his own store.

I might add that even though the little building has two addresses (2641 and 2643) nothing indicates it ever housed separate businesses. Both sides seem to have held the same company, in this case, Frulla Grocery, which stayed there until 1976, when Claude retired. The building has been vacant for years. But you probably already knew that.

Death in the Afternoon

Dear Vance: I am writing in the hope you may be able to find information about a distant relative, Aileen Embury, a child who died in the Memphis area in 1913. It is possible the family was living in Boston at the time and the child was only visiting here. — M.W., York, England.

Dear M.W.: This is a sad

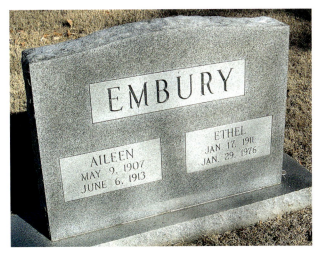

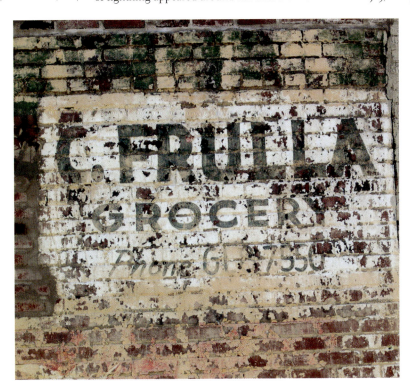

story indeed. I managed to turn up an old *Commercial Article* dated June 7, 1913, with the headline, "Child Was Killed by Thunderstorm." How could this possibly happen, I wondered? "A short but terrific thunderstorm flashed over Memphis yesterday afternoon," the article read, "killed a six-year-old girl, and did damage to buildings in several sections of town."

Little Aileen "was at play with children of the neighborhood," across the street from her parents' house at 1677 Lawrence Place. A black storm came up quickly, and the kids ran for cover, but as she ran across the street, "a blinding flash of lightning appeared around her and the girl sank to the ground."

Funeral services were held at the family's home, which was common practice at the time. In fact, the term "funeral parlor" is derived from the parlor of a home, the large downstairs room where such somber occasions were usually held. After funeral parlors became more established, a leading woman's magazine — I believe it was *Ladies Home Journal* — began a campaign to give that room a happier name. The result: the "living room." (I am *not* making this up.)

Aileen Embury was laid to rest in Forest Hill Cemetery, which maintains extremely complete records about each grave site, and even attaches the original obituary notice to cards that identify each burial. With that helpful information, I can tell you, M.W., that the family was indeed living in Memphis at the time. Aileen's father, John Embury, was born in Birkenhead, England, and came here in 1898 to work as a cotton buyer for a Liverpool firm. In 1925, he opened his own nursery in Germantown, which he maintained until he retired in 1950. Aileen's mother, Alice, died in 1953. John passed away in 1964. The Embury family, which included another daughter, Ethel, shares a tombstone (above) in the northwest section of Forest Hill. **M**

Got a question for Vance? Send it to "Ask Vance" at Memphis *magazine, 460 Tennessee Street #200, Memphis, TN 38103, or e-mail him at askvance@memphismagazine.com*

[ask vance]

By Vance Lauderdale

Our Trivia Expert Solves Local Mysteries of Who, What, When, Where, Why, and Why Not.

The Story of Stewart's

Dear Vance: What can you tell me about this interesting old photograph? What was Stewart's, Inc., and where was the picture (below) taken? — B.K., Memphis.

Dear B.K.: At first glance, I thought you had stumbled upon a snapshot from one of the Lauderdale family's surprise birthday parties. A surprise for the *servants*, that is, who were hustled down into the basement and forced to sing "Happy Birthday" and hand out gifts to the Lauderdale children. All that merriment came to an end, of course, when the family filed for bankruptcy and some of the more pesky servants claimed we had violated several dozen labor laws.

But with my keen eyes, I first noticed that these folks, though nattily dressed, as required of anyone who worked in the Lauderdale household, didn't seem to resemble any of the servants that I remembered from my childhood. And also, I noticed a jukebox off to the left (strictly forbidden in the Lauderdale mansion, ever since Mother's ill-advised affair with that jazz musician) and just behind it, two soft-drink machines — one for Grapette and another for Coca-Cola. Another no-no. The only beverage served at home was Kentucky Nip.

Then, of course, there is that inscription for Stewart's, Inc., at the bottom of the photo, with the date of June 7, 1951.

A moment captured in time by an unknown photographer, though just *what* moment is hard to say. After all, June 7th is no holiday that I am aware of. The photo seems to show an area of a warehouse, set up for some kind of special event, with rows of tables covered with white paper, and several large sprays of flowers to brighten up the otherwise bleak surroundings. Forty-seven women and just three men are facing the camera, apparently finishing a meal, since there are plates on the table, coffee cups, and glasses of tea.

At least I *can* tell you that Stewart's, Inc., was a Memphis food-products company, founded by William C. Stewart in 1932. A 1945 *Press-Scimitar* article proclaimed, "He's the coffee man. Everybody knows him by his coffee. He's really stepped out. Today, Stewart has a fleet of trucks. He has a nationwide business. He advertises on a nationwide scale."

In fact, this same newspaper article showed a photo of William and his wife, Natalie, and I believe they are the man and woman in the middle foreground of the photo you sent in, B.K.

The Stewart company started out selling Rosebud brand coffee, and then quickly expanded to include mayonnaise, potato chips, vanilla wafers, almonds, and other tasty snacks. By the time this photo was taken, the firm had 450 employees. Apparently, 400 of them weren't invited to the party shown here.

In the mid-1950s, the company was sold to Continental Baking Company, one of the largest bakers in the U.S. and perhaps best known as the makers of Wonder Bread.

You asked where the picture was taken, but that's hard to say. In 1951, Stewart's had a main office at 85 W. Virginia and a half dozen manufacturing operations all over town, as well as branch factories in Little Rock and Chattanooga. I suppose I could travel to all those places with this picture and see if I could match the location up with any of them, but most of those places have changed in the past half-century. And besides, that seems an awful lot of work, by my standards of "work." Surely, I've told you enough by now?

Remembering Ronnie

Dear Vance: What is the story behind the very curious "Memorial to a Little Boy" that graces the Gaisman Park Swimming Pool? — M.A., Memphis.

Dear M.A.: You have indeed uncovered a curious — and controversial — story. Massive cast-concrete letters on the southeast corner of the pool building spell out the inscription you noticed, while a bronze tablet below reads, "Dedicated to the Memory of Ronnie Jones. Age 9. Drowned in Wolf River, July 23, 1954."

At first I was befuddled (more than usual, I mean) by this. It seemed very strange to dedicate a swimming pool to a *drowning* victim — that just seemed to put a damper on the fun you might have there. But then it struck me that this pool was constructed precisely because of what happened to this boy.

And that's the story behind the plaque. Ronnie Jones lived with his triplet brothers, Richard and Robert, at 4076 Westover, in the Highland Heights part of town. On a hot afternoon in July, the boys walked about a mile north to a popular swimming hole in the Wolf River, near the Jackson Avenue overpass. One of the brothers later told reporters, "Ronnie could swim a little and he got out over his head. I tried to hold a branch to him but he kept going under." The little boy's body wasn't recovered from the murky river by rescue workers until the next morning.

So many children had recently drowned in that same stretch of the Wolf that newspapers back then called it the "Ghost River." Nowadays, that name is given to the river many miles to the east — only because the headwaters seem lost and mysterious, not because it is haunted by the spirits of so many of its victims.

City leaders decided Ronnie's death was the last straw. At the time, there were very few public pools in the city, and none at all in East Memphis, so they began raising funds to build the "Ronnie Jones Pool" in Gaisman Park on Macon Road. Inspired by the tragic death of the little boy, money poured in, and companies and individuals — painters, contractors, concrete workers, you name it — donated their services. The newspapers kept a running total of the contributions, and then reported that construction had begun.

And here's the controversy. Imagine everyone's surprise and dismay when the Memphis Park Commission announced the new facility would not be named after Ronnie Jones after all. It would be called "Gaisman Park Pool." When contacted by reporters, park commissioner John Vesey said, "That little boy business is news to me." Well, donors weren't happy about *that*. And they weren't made any happier when the huge "Memorial to a Little Boy" carving was unveiled, but without even mentioning just who that boy was and why he should be remembered. The *Press-Scimitar* even ran a photo (above) of Ronnie's brothers and a friend posed somberly around the empty marker, trying to drum up support for a more fitting monument.

To no avail, though. Eventually, a simple bronze tablet was mounted in the niche shown in the photo, and an identical tablet was mounted on the outside of the building. But the name of the pool, then as now, remains Gaisman Park Pool.

Looking for Lowry

Dear Vance: In 1952, my parents enrolled me in the Lowry Private School. I have no idea where it was located, but a friend attended high school there in the 1960s. Can you help me find it? — A.S., Memphis.

Dear A.S.: I can help you find the former school, but I wasn't able to locate much — if anything — about the woman who owned it. I can only do so much, you see.

City directories show that Mary Frances Lowry ran a private school out of her home at 1087 North McLean from around 1950 to the late 1960s. But nothing indicates it was ever a high school. In fact, the directory mentions only "piano studio, kindergarten, grades 1-6, and summer school June and July." I believe you, or your friend, may be mistaken about attending high school there.

The building is now a private residence and, to me, doesn't look like it was ever a school, but when I sent A.S. this photo (above), she replied, "My mother is sure this is the house where I attended first grade. There were only about 10 students in the class. I remember saying the Pledge of Allegiance, singing 'America the Beautiful,' and having a happy time."

Unfortunately, I was unable to learn anything about Mary Frances Lowry. Perhaps some of her students can tell me more about this woman. Besides, it's time to relax with a cold bottle or two of Kentucky Nip. That first question this month made me thirsty. **M**

Got a question for Vance? Send it to "Ask Vance" at Memphis *magazine, 460 Tennessee Street #200, Memphis, TN 38103, or e-mail him at askvance@memphismagazine.com.*

[ask vance]

By Vance Lauderdale

Our Trivia Expert Solves Local Mysteries of Who, What, When, Where, Why, and Why Not.

Memories of Mulford's

Dear Vance: I found an old milk-glass jewelry box while cleaning out a house, and underneath was a sticker for Mulford Jewelers, Memphis. Can you tell me the dates they were in business and where they were located? — B.W., Nashville.

Dear B.W.: I certainly remember Mulford Jewelers. It was where the Lauderdales purchased all the gold, silver, and platinum baubles and beads that made our house glitter like a comet flashing through the night. Of course, that sparkle lost most of its luster when the Lauderdale bankruptcy proceedings — which made front-page news in every newspaper in the northern hemisphere — took away just about everything except the grimy clothes on our backs. How were we to know the linotype boom, where we sank all our fortune, wasn't to last?

But that wasn't the fault of John N. Mulford, who owned and operated one of this city's oldest and finest jewelry stores. Mulford, born in London, came to this country in the 1870s. He loved to hunt and fish and roamed America in search of a place where he could pursue those interests, eventually settling in Memphis. In 1880, he opened Mulford Jewelers at 6 South Main Street in a building known as the Marble Block — presumably because it was made of marble. The store remained at that location until 1942, when it moved a few doors down, to 26 South Main.

Mulford was a hard-working fellow, and was still going strong in 1929, when *The Commercial Appeal* ran a story that commented on his half-century in business up to that point. "Lots of people think the company is run by a successor under another name," he told the reporter. "People come by and say, 'I didn't know you were still living.' But I'm very much alive."

Mulford explained why, in his 70s, he remained hard at work behind the jewelry counter. "It's not like labor, because I enjoy working so," he said. "It's as much

John N. Mulford

play to me as it is to frolic in the South Sea Islands or Alaska, where I go frequently."

Why, that's exactly how I feel about *this* job! In fact, replace "South Sea Island" with "Sardis Lake" and "Alaska" with "Alabama" and we are like twins. It's uncanny, really.

Mulford changed with the times, and I understand he began the first mail-order jewelry business in the South. He and his wife were well-known in Memphis, and according to a faded press clipping, "They were a familiar sight to residents, riding to and from work in their electric auto." And Mulford's enthusiasm for hunting "was even indicated in the store, where he had a beautiful hunting scene painted on his largest safe."

Mulford's stayed in business on Main Street through the turbulent Sixties, when other firms along the street struggled and failed. All good things must come to an end, though, and the store finally closed in 1973.

Hmmm. Wonder where that nice safe is today?

Plaster Puzzle

Dear Vance: There's an unusual Mediterranean-style house at 694 Landis in Midtown. We heard that it was built by an Italian plasterer who was brought here to work on the Pink Palace. Is that true? — D.M., Memphis.

Dear D.M.: Ah, a real "history mystery." And it turns out some of this story is indeed true.

The Shelby County Tax Assessor Web site claims this property was constructed in 1927, but I've discovered those dates rarely jibe with telephone directory listings. And if somebody has a telephone, I assume they also have a house, unless they are living out of a phone booth, as my Uncle Lance did during the summer of '34. But normal people aren't like that. The telephone books show that in 1922, only four houses were standing on that short street:

660, 663, 687, and 700 Landis. The next year, though, the developers had apparently done their work, for now there are 17 houses listed, including 694 Landis.

Telephone books are usually a year off, since it takes time to compile all those names and numbers. In other words, since the home in question was listed in 1923, it was almost certainly built in late 1922.

The first owner was a fellow named Thomas G. Johnson, and by checking the business section of the old telephone directories, I discovered that Johnson was indeed a plasterer. In fact, he ran his own plaster company on South Third.

But I have to tell you that I don't think Johnson is an Italian name. What's more, he seems to have been living and working in Memphis for several years before the Pink Palace was built. The first time he shows up in the local phone books is 1914, living at 958 Elizabeth Place and identified as a plasterer with Alexander Plastering Company.

Grocery store magnate Clarence Saunders, who founded the Piggly Wiggly chain that manages to get mentioned in this column about, oh, every month, began construction on his Central Avenue mansion in 1921. Ron Brister, curator of the Memphis Pink Palace Museum, tells me that the interior was not finished when Saunders lost his fortune — and his house — in a stock market mishap. The mansion remained empty for years, until the city of Memphis acquired it in 1926, completed the exterior and interior, and opened it to the public as a museum in 1930.

So even though Johnson was apparently not an Italian immigrant "brought over" to Memphis to work on the Pink Palace, did he do any labor on it at all? Well, I just don't know. Most homes at this time (in the days before sheet rock) had walls, ceilings, and moldings of plaster, so there were lots of plaster workers in Memphis in the 1920s — more than 50 listed in the city directories, in fact, including Johnson. But any records that may have shown exactly who worked on this building — either when Saunders owned it, or later after the city took it over — have long disappeared.

The plaster master's home at 694 Landis

What's evident, however, is that Johnson was indeed a plasterer of remarkable skill. The house at 694 Landis features incredibly detailed moldings, ornate columns across the front porch, and such unusual details as a fountain mounted on a wall in the dining room. Even the telephone nook in the hallway (above), which in most homes is just a recessed shelf, is almost a "temple to the telephone" in this house. The current owners, who are restoring the interior, tell me that plaster workers have commented on the unusual consistency of the plaster. Among other things, it contains no horsehair, which was often used as reinforcement, and the plaster itself is as hard as concrete. Corners and other elements are very sharply defined, which is usually not the case with soft plaster.

At the same time, some areas are not completed. Half of an elaborate frieze over the front entrance is finished, while portions of the other side are just roughed in.

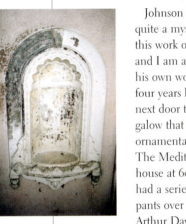

Johnson himself remains quite a mystery. After all this work on his house — and I am assuming he did his own work here — just four years later he moved next door to a smaller bungalow that features no ornamental plaster at all. The Mediterranean-style house at 694 Landis then had a series of other occupants over the years — Arthur Davant, Warner Partin, Luella P. Wall, and others. None of them were plasterers.

But why did Johnson move out of such a place? The current owners joke that maybe he was just sick of looking at so much plaster! But four years later, he moved again, down the street to yet *another* small bungalow. He is no longer listed in Memphis city directories after 1942, so I assume he either passed away or moved to another city — no doubt worn out by all the hard work he did at 694 Landis. It really is a unique house, and a testament to one man's remarkable skill. **M**

Got a question for Vance? Send it to "Ask Vance" at Memphis magazine, 460 Tennessee Street #200, Memphis, TN 38103, or e-mail him at askvance@memphismagazine.com

[ask vance]

By Vance Lauderdale

Our Trivia Expert Solves Local Mysteries of Who, What, When, Where, Why, and Why Not.

Mystery Motel

Dear Vance: How did the old motel shown on this postcard (below) get such an unusual name, and where was it located in Memphis?
— D.O., Jackson.

Dear D.O.: The Ditty Wah Ditty Motel is considered one of the oddest names ever attached to a business. It's mentioned in quite a few books about pop culture and "roadside" America. And in the tomes I've consulted, no one seems to have a clue what the name means.

John Margolies, an authority on such things, includes this exact same postcard in his fine book, *Home Away From Home: Motels in America*. He calls the Ditty Wah Ditty "among the all-time greatest names in all of moteldom," but then claims it "made some sense because it was located in one of the great jazz centers in the U.S.A." Huh? Jazz? I think he has us confused with New Orleans.

Another history buff, John Baeder, also features this postcard in *Gas, Food and Lodging: A Postcard Odyssey Through the Great American Roadside*. Baeder notes that the name "would arouse your curiosity chords" but he can't seem to explain it, either. He mentions that other writers have told him, "In folklore, Didy Waw Didy (sometimes spelled Ditty Wah Ditty) was the last stop on a mythical railroad bound for hell." My, what a pleasant name for a place to spend the night! Then he rather obliquely refers to an old blues song written and performed by a long-deceased musician named Blind Arthur Blake, who has been called "the king of ragtime blues."

I finally scrounged around in my usual haphazard way and found the lyrics to Blake's tune — only to discover that the song itself also wonders about the name! It begins:

*There's a great big mystery
And it sure is worrying me
It's a ditty wah ditty
Mister ditty wah ditty
I wished somebody would tell me what ditty wah ditty means.*

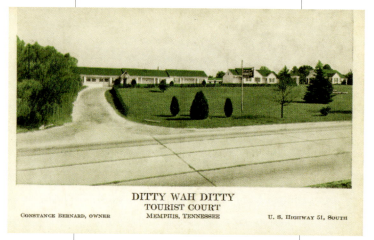

DITTY WAH DITTY TOURIST COURT
CONSTANCE BERNARD, OWNER   MEMPHIS, TENNESSEE   U.S. HIGHWAY 51, SOUTH

It became clear to me, though, as I read over the lyrics and began to hum the song, playing along with my kazoo (the Lauderdales have always been musically inclined) that "ditty wah ditty" just might refer to something a bit, uh, improper. Especially when I encountered these lyrics a bit farther along:

*Then I got put outta the church
'Cause I talked about ditty wah ditty too much
Mister ditty wah ditty
Mister ditty wah ditty
I wished somebody would tell me what ditty wah ditty means.*

Yes, and then I wish they would tell *me*. It's all very confusing. Perhaps that's why more recent owners changed the name to the Iris Motel. That's right; the place is still standing today on South Bellevue, though it's been considerably altered over the years and looks as if it might close any day now. As you can see from the recent photo (below), the trees and bushes that once lined the driveway have been reduced to a double row of stumps, and a mysterious green tarp blocks all view of the motel from the traffic rushing by.

Determined to solve the mystery of this place, I gathered some friends, cranked up the Daimler-Benz, and headed for Bellevue. I turned up the motel's long gravel driveway, where I confronted an elderly woman who seemed to run the place. Imagine my consternation when she sauntered up to the car, winked at me, and said, "Why, if it's not Mr. Lauderdale! Would you like your regular room?"

My, *that* was embarrassing. I turned the car around and roared out of there in a cloud of dust. She must have me confused with some other distinguished gentleman, who drives a Daimler-Benz and journeys about town with a cape and sword-cane. Really, it could be just about anybody.

Corner Questions

Dear Vance: I purchased 2129 Central several years ago and would love to know the history of the building (right). It was actually two separate businesses for many years, but is now one address. I understand it once housed one of the first Piggly Wiggly stores in Memphis. Currently it is Toad Hall Antiques.
— D.W., Memphis.

Dear D.W. — Your building, and in fact that entire corner of Central and Cooper, has a long and rather complicated history. And any story about your particular location must begin with an enterprising fellow named Caleb Andrews, whose name just happens to be carved in stone at the top of 2129 Central.

At the turn of the century, Andrews was a clerk with a grocery store at 2128 Central, which would have been on the *northwest* corner of Central and Cooper (where Love's Feeds stands today). By 1908, he had become the manager/owner of this establishment which, according to telephone directory listings, specialized in "staple and fancy groceries, wines, liquors, cigars, and billiards." Quite an eclectic mix of merchandise, I must say. Not many people go shopping for eggs and milk and come home with a new pool table. Other than the Lauderdales, I mean.

Andrews must have been an ambitious fellow, because he very quickly decided he needed a bigger, better building, so he had one constructed across the street, on the southwest corner of that same intersection. That's *your* building, of course. And from 1909 to 1919, C.L. Andrews Grocery occupied 2129 Central. Advertisements for his establishment announced he was still carrying those "staple and fancy" groceries, along with "general merchandise, hardware, notions, flour, and soft drinks." What? No billiards? I guess it was too much trouble to haul the heavy pool tables across Central.

About this time, other buildings went up next door, and since your building has merged with them, I suppose I have to touch on them here. Remind me to charge double my usual fee for this query.

Next door, 2127 Central first opened in 1914 as Mizell Plumbing. A few years later, it became Central Avenue Pharmacy, and then housed a series of barber shops.

Meanwhile, back at the corner, in 1919 Andrews sold his grocery store to Ernest and Joseph Dardano, who lived upstairs above the store with their wives, Rose and Louise. The Dardano brothers operated their grocery business at 2129 Central for about six years, when they inexplicably moved two doors west, to a considerably smaller location at 2125 Central.

This is getting confusing, isn't it? Well, it's not my fault all these folks kept moving around. A chart would help, but I can't draw charts without a ruler, and we certainly don't have a budget for *that*. I'll try to wrap this up.

In 1925, Piggly Wiggly #21 opened in the corner building formerly occupied by Andrews and the Dardanos. The Piggly Wiggly chain already had 54 stores in Memphis at this time, including three others on Cooper alone, so I'm sorry to say yours wasn't one of the first. And I know what you're thinking: If Piggly Wiggly already had 54 stores, why was yours numbered 21 when it opened? Why not #55? I don't know. I can't explain it. I can only do so much.

Meanwhile, next door, Gilbert and Maude Edwards opened a little drugstore that would eventually become a Memphis institution. Edwards Pharmacy, located at 2127 Central, stayed in business for more than 40 years, and before it closed in the mid-1980s was one of the last places in Memphis to have a working soda fountain. In fact, I had a mighty tasty milkshake there a few weeks before they shut their doors.

But back to your building. Piggly Wiggly moved out in 1945. In the late 1940s, it housed American Appliance Company, in the 1950s Railroad Salvage Company, and in the 1960s Honeycutt Furniture and Appliances. An antiques store called Second Hand Rose moved there in the late 1970s, took over the Edwards Pharmacy space when that establishment closed, and for the past several years, the combined building has been home to Toad Hall Antiques. The owners have put considerable work into the old place, such as rebuilding the roof and replacing the wooden floors with boards pulled from an old high-school gymnasium someone was tearing down in Mississippi. Some of those planks still have grafitti scribbled on them by the former students (above).

Does all that make *any* sense? Whew! Too bad Edwards Pharmacy is closed. After all this work, I could certainly use a cold soda. **M**

Got a question for Vance? Send it to "Ask Vance" at Memphis *magazine, 460 Tennessee Street, Suite 200, Memphis, TN 38103, or e-mail him at askvance@memphismagazine.com*

[askvance]

By Vance Lauderdale

Our Trivia Expert Solves Local Mysteries of Who, What, When, Where, Why, and Why Not.

The Last Days of the Lyric

Dear Vance: In your magazine's recent story about the 1921 Ford Motor Company robbery (July/August 2005), the author mentioned a town-hall meeting at the old Lyric Theatre. Where was that theatre, and what happened to it? — F.E., Memphis.

Dear F.E.: The Lyric, located at 291 Madison, was one of the favorite gathering spots for the Lauderdales. Many a night we would drive to the stunning theatre, climb the red-carpeted steps to our reserved box so we wouldn't have to mingle with the commoners, and laugh ourselves silly at the wondrous acts presented by the best vaudeville performers of the day.

Inspired by their creativity, I must confess that one evening, when I was 14 or so, during one of our family's talent shows, I myself ventured onto the broad stage and — clad in what I considered a fetching outfit of lederhosen, jaunty cap, and buckle shoes, sang my little heart out — a song of my own composition that lamented the death of my dearest pet, Spikey, the horned toad. Critics who had been paid by my parents to attend the performance were clearly in awe of my abilities. "I've never seen, or heard, anything like it," wrote one. "The sounds that came out of young Vance Lauderdale's throat cannot be replicated by any known species of animal," wrote another. Yet another resigned on the spot, no doubt thinking that, once he had witnessed perfection, anything else would be a bitter disappointment.

Oh, how I basked in their praise. Unfortunately, my classmates, oafs one and all, mocked me when I wore the lederhosen to school the next day, and being the sensitive child that I was, I decided to draw my theatrical career to a close. And also begin home schooling. Clearly, I was ahead of my time.

The Lyric met a similarly tragic

fate — a double loss to Memphians, if you don't mind my saying so.

Constructed in 1908, the theatre was originally called the Jefferson (even though it was, as I said earlier, on Madison), and two years later changed its name to the Lyric. An old newspaper clipping described its elaborate facade, which included "two scantily clad Greek maidens lounged prettily over the building's high arched entrance. They supported with their arms a huge shield and scroll." I believe they were based, loosely, on the Lauderdale coat-of-arms.

The Lyric remained a vaudeville house until about 1924. Thereafter it was used for YMCA meetings, dramatic clubs, and other gatherings — such as the talent shows produced by the Lauderdales.

All good things come to an end, it seems, and in 1941 the Lyric burned in one of this city's most spectacular blazes. I managed to find a photo of the building shortly after the fire (left). Salvage crews later attempted to remove the statues of the Greek maidens, but their chains slipped, and the sculptures came crashing to the ground and shattered.

Still, portions of the old theatre survive here and there around town. One woman bought 60,000 of the old fire-scorched bricks for a "rambling, English style home"

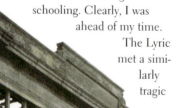

she was building on South Parkway, but the paper wasn't very specific about just where this home was to be, so I didn't go searching for it. One fellow obtained the massive chains that once held up the theatre marquee and used them for a footbridge at his home on Princeton. I drove up and down Princeton several times but failed to locate such a bridge. I had better luck with George Watson's project. He bought 10,000 of the old building's bricks and used them to build a nice wall around his home at Highland and Watauga. This part of the Lyric, at least, is still standing today (left).

And the building itself? Like so many former landmarks in Memphis, it was torn down. The site is now a parking lot.

Decades of Dirmeyer's

Dear Vance: What can you tell me about the very handsome stone building (above) that stands in Midtown at the corner of Nelson and Barksdale? — V.T., Memphis.

Dear V.T.: This is what I can tell you: In 1916, a fellow by the name of William C. Dirmeyer opened this establishment at 1904 Nelson. He advertised himself as a "prescription druggist" — apparently to distinguish himself from those rough-and-tumble druggists who prowled Cooper-Young handing out drugs *without* a prescription.

Dirmeyer stayed in business there for ages, it seems. In fact, according to the city directories I consulted, the drugstore remained in operation until 1970, but it's not clear if William C. was still running the place. I do know that in the mid-1950s, a woman named Ruth Ditto began to lease the western portion of the building, at 1902 Nelson, for Ditto's Beauty and Barber Salon, but the records are a bit unclear how long she remained in business. I was not a customer there myself, you understand.

In 1970, Litton Photographic Services moved into the old building, which explains the faded Kodak sign that still hangs over the front door. Five years later, Bluff City Photo Service took over. In the 1980s, the city directories show that someone named Steve Grubbs occupied the building, but they don't explain just what he was using it for. And in fact, I'm not sure if it is still occupied today. I do know that Sounds Unreel recording studio moved into the former beauty parlor space at 1902 Nelson, and perhaps they also took over some of the old drugstore space as well.

I guess I could call them and find out, but after that traumatic experience on stage at the Lyric, I don't like dealing with musicians. Who could blame me?

More About Miss Lowry

In our May issue I discussed, in my typically vague and rambling way, the history of Miss Lowry's private school at 1089 North McLean. I didn't have much to go on, just some small ads about the school that I had encountered, so wasn't able to tell anyone much about Miss Lowry herself.

Well, as always happens, after the story came out, one of her relatives gave me a call, and it turned out to be my old pal Joe Lowry, who knows as much about the history of Memphis as just about anyone. Mary Frances Lowry (right), it seems, was his aunt! Among other things, Joe told me that Miss Lowry lived in one half of the building and ran a school — basically a large classroom and library — in the other half.

"Back then we didn't use the word dyslexia," says Joe, "but that's the kind of students she concentrated on, and I have to say that quite a few well-known Memphians wouldn't be where they are today if it weren't for my aunt."

Born in Helena, Arkansas, Miss Lowry attended Columbia University and the Washington University School of Music in St. Louis. She employed a half dozen other teachers, and was especially interested in teaching piano and swimming. According to nephew Joe, as a certified Red Cross swimming instructor "she taught thousands of Memphis kids how to swim at various pools around town."

An avid traveler, Miss Lowry journeyed through most of the U.S., Europe, and Cuba, and even attended the Olympics in Moscow. She passed away on September 17, 1973, leaving a legacy of hundreds of students who benefited from her kindness and guidance. **M**

Got a question for Vance? Send it to "Ask Vance" at Memphis *magazine, 460 Tennessee Street #200, Memphis, Tennessee 38103, or e-mail him at askvance@memphismagazine.com.*

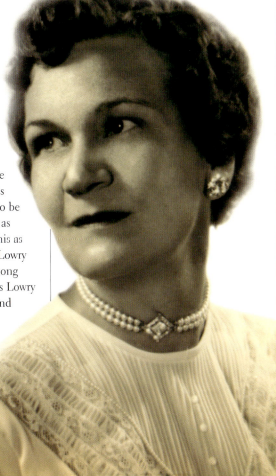

[ask vance]

By Vance Lauderdale

Our Trivia Expert Solves Local Mysteries of Who, What, When, Where, Why, and Why Not.

A Modest Memorial

Dear Vance: Why is the grave of Mary Hutchison, founder of the prestigious Hutchison School, marked by such a nondescript little gravestone at Forest Hill Cemetery? She shares space with the Halliburton family. Surely she deserves better than that. — J.T., Memphis

Dear J.T.: I drove to Forest Hill one day and, after wandering over hill and dale for what seemed like hours (okay, 15 minutes, tops), I discovered the marker you mentioned (below right). You're correct. It's just a plain granite block with no mention of the fact that this remarkable woman, a leader of the Memphis educational community for decades, founded one of the better private schools in this region. What's more, it looks like a lawn mower had crashed into the gravestone, knocking it askew.

So dismayed was I by this that tears ran down my handsome face, and I immediately considered building Miss Hutchison (as she was known to generations of students) a more fitting marker. I could easily recruit some of the Scottish stonemasons who have been employed for some 30 years now at Elmwood Cemetery, hard at work on the Lauderdale Mausoleum. Dubbed by many as the "Taj Mahal of Memphis," this soaring edifice is being constructed of the finest onyx, quartz, formica, and aluminum siding that money could buy.

Oh, I can't wait to get there!

But then it

This painting of Mary Hutchison, by Edith Bailey Wilkinson, is on display at The Hutchison School.

occurred to me, why squander my own resources on this project? I would ask — no, *demand* — that the editor of this very publication launch a fund-raising drive for a better memorial. After all, she has always bragged that she is a "Hutchison girl," though there is really no indication that the poor creature ever finished the fourth grade — at Hutchison or anywhere else for that matter. How could she, after spending so much time in reform schools?

Before we embarked on such a project, however, I thought I would notify the school of our noble plans and discovered, to my surprise, that this is just how Miss Hutchison wanted it.

According to Kathie Alexander, public relations coordinator for The Hutchison School, "Miss Hutchison always maintained that she wanted no special marker or monument. The school was to be her memorial."

She's buried in the Halliburton family plot at Forest Hill because she was always considered a part of that family, best known for their son Richard, adventurer and author, who was lost at sea in 1939. When she first came to Memphis from Brownsville, Tennessee, in 1902, she lodged with Nelle Nance Halliburton, whom she met when the two women taught school in Athens, Tennessee. Miss Hutchison first opened her little school in the Halliburton home here. In the 1920s, she squeezed it into a pair of bungalows on Union Avenue (since demolished), and the school now has a fine campus in East Memphis.

After Miss Hutchison's death in 1962, Alexander says that Richard's father, Wesley, "arranged for Mary Grimes Hutchison to be buried in the Halliburton family plot in Forest Hill with a trust company to give continual care to the family plot."

Well, that explains it. And I must say I'm relieved. I was worried that if I used some of my own workers for this project, they would never finish my own tomb, and my health is so frail lately, I may need it any day now.

Main Street Survivor

Dear Vance: Is the impressive Tennessee Block building, shown on this old invoice for Lemmon & Gale

Dry Goods Company (below), still standing somewhere on Main Street? — G.H., Memphis.

Dear G.H.: After days of exhaustive research, I can finally give you a definitive answer: It is . . . and it isn't.

Your apparently simply query turned into quite a conundrum. After all, the invoice showed a detailed illustration of the building, and it gave its address — 326 and 328 Main Street, so I would just stroll over there and tell you if the building was still standing.

But then I noticed the 1886 date on the invoice, and realized I had a problem.

Memphis revised all its street numbering around 1904. Before then, whoever erected a building or house here apparently guessed at what the address should be. This caused problems, because all too often, they didn't leave enough "space" between the numbers for other buildings to squeeze in, and in some cases, the numbering wasn't even consecutive — creating a nightmare for the poor postman. So sometime around 1904, city officials assigned new numbers to just about every place in town.

What all this means is that 326-328 Main Street is no longer a valid address. For one thing, it doesn't even specify North or South Main.

So I began rooting through old city directories. In 1903, just before the street numbers changed, Lemmon & Gale Dry Goods is indeed listed at 326-328 Main Street. In 1905, the address is now 56-58 South Main — the new address for the same building.

I scampered over to 56-58 South Main, where I found this impressive brick and stone building (below). It's a grand structure, all right, described by the authors of *Memphis: An Architectural Guide* as "one of the several good commercial Romanesque buildings in town." More to the point, they clearly identify it as the Lemmon & Gale Building, and if you look very carefully, you can see the word "Lemmon" carved in stone in a panel close to the roof line. For some reason, the panel on the other side, where you might expect to read "Gale," is blank. And speaking of that roof line, the *Architectural Guide* authors note, "The machiolated attic, a bit of fortress architecture unexpectedly erupting on Main Street, gives the building a certain romantic air." According to the dictionary, "machiolated" is a series of openings along the top of a building "for discharging missiles upon assailants below." I should mention that the Lauderdale mansion has this same feature, and it has proven quite effective at keeping creditors at bay.

The *Architectural Guide* folks claim the building was constructed in 1881. This, then, must be the building shown on the 1886 invoice.

But here is the mystery — why don't they look the same? The invoice illustration shows different arches, a central column topped with a statue, and — more significantly — a huge arched pediment with the words "Tennessee Block." The present building lacks all these features.

The building went through many owners over the years. Lemmon & Gale changed its name to Buckingham Dry Goods in the 1920s and moved to a smaller building down the street, and Memphis Photo Supply and The Art Shop moved in. In the 1940s and 1950s, it housed Lawrence Furniture and Dreifuss Jewelers. Cook and Love Shoes occupied the ground floor in the 1960s through the early 1990s. Certainly the various owners added signs and new designs at the street level, but that doesn't explain the significant changes to the entire five-story facade.

Something kept nagging me about this — something that might explain it — and I finally remembered what it was. Historian Paul Coppock, in one of his many history books, noted that Main Street had a terrific fire back on February 8, 1892, and he wrote, "Every building on the east side of Main, between Monroe and Union, was destroyed or heavily damaged." Lemmon & Gale would have been included in that area. My theory is that the building was damaged, or even partly destroyed, by this fire. The 1886 invoice shows the original building as it looked before the blaze, and the structure that is standing today is the one that was rebuilt following the fire.

That's my story, and I'm sticking with it. But if someone has a better explanation, I'm willing to hear it. **M**

Got a question for Vance? Send it to "Ask Vance" at Memphis *magazine, 460 Tennessee Street #200, Memphis, TN 38103, or e-mail him at askvance@memphismagazine.com.*

[ask vance]

By Vance Lauderdale

Our Trivia Expert Solves Local Mysteries of Who, What, When, Where, Why, and Why Not.

Vanished Village

Dear Vance: Whatever happened to that very popular Italian restaurant that was on Highway 51, between Memphis and Millington? — P.G., Memphis.

Dear P.G.: As a result of our many accomplishments, I'm proud to say that the Lauderdale name has been attached to counties, schools, streets, and our fleet of sleek dirigibles. Not to mention hundreds of bowling and roller-skating trophies. But, modest and unassuming creatures that we are, not a single member of my illustrious family ever had the audacity to name an entire town after ourselves.

But then, perhaps we didn't have the gumption of Joseph Forgione, an Italian who came to this country in 1911 and settled in Memphis in 1916. He worked here for years as a building contractor, and in 1948 boldly announced he was going to build his own town.

"I drove through Arkansas and I saw Jonesboro," he told a *Press-Scimitar* reporter one day. "And I've heard of a Youngstown in Ohio. So I wanted a Forgione Town."

Forgione (the newspaper helped readers understand the name was pronounced "for-jo-ny") picked a rather unusual location for his new village — the intersection of Highway 51 North and Lucy Road. On June 18, 1948, he broke ground for what he hoped would include a "motion picture theater that could double as a community center, a Baptist church, a water system, and two comfortable homes for his family." He also planned to build some 30 stores and a restaurant.

Forgione explained his common-sense approach: "You build four stores and sell 'em, then you build four more and sell 'em, and build four more. That way we build a town — if the Lord doesn't fool me and the people help."

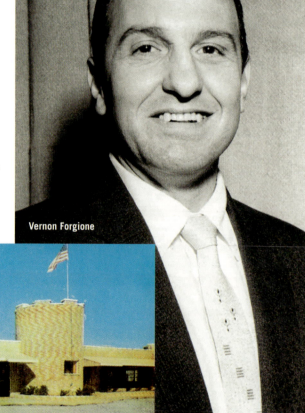

Vernon Forgione

As far as I can tell, Forgione never built 30 stores, but he did open a fine Italian restaurant, a gas station, and a couple of other businesses at that intersection. The restaurant, called Forgione's, seated 475, and ads proclaimed it "the South's largest and finest Italian restaurant." I haven't been able to confirm that; my dog-eared copy of *The Guinness Book of World Records* seems to be lacking a category for "South's Largest Italian Restaurants."

In 1957, however, a fire broke out, and the six buildings in Forgione's little "town" were destroyed. The problem was its remote location. Vernon Forgione, who had taken over the restaurant from his father, complained that it took more than an hour for fire trucks to arrive from Millington, and even then there wasn't enough water to use on the fire. Apparently the water system Joseph had talked about never got installed.

Vernon (above) told reporters, "Please tell my customers that everything is gone so they won't make a trip out here in vain. We didn't even save a cigar." Even so, he declared, "We will rebuild. I just don't know when."

But rebuild he did, constructing an odd orange-brick building with a pair of round turrets topped with a flagpole (above). The restaurant stayed in business for several years, as I recall, before changing hands. In the early 1990s, the eatery — whose name now escapes me — was no longer serving Italian fare, but proclaimed that it was "Home of the Mooseburger." Sadly, I never got the chance to taste such a unique concoction before the restaurant closed. It is now home to a daycare center — the only building remaining from "Forgione Town."

East Vs. West

Dear Vance: I'm familiar with Anderton's East, the popular restaurant in Midtown. But was there ever an Anderton's West, North, or South? — A.J., Memphis.

Dear A.J.: Well, there were indeed two other eateries in the Memphis chain, but compass directions weren't part of their name. They were just called Anderton's, named after their founder, a former professional boxer named Herb Anderton (below right).

I found quite a few old newspaper articles about Anderton, as you might expect, and one of them casually mentioned that he was "one of the 11 well-known Memphis Anderton brothers." So well-known, I gather, that the newspaper didn't feel compelled to mention their names or tell why they were so famous.

It doesn't matter, really. I'm just going to tell you about Herb. Born in 1913, he worked in the printing business most of his life, and first learned to cook while he was stationed at an Army base in Texas during World War II. When he left the service, he began to manage some restaurants around town that were owned by other folks. I would be glad to list them all here, but that would just make my story confusing. Please, pay attention.

In 1945, he opened his own place, Anderton's Oyster Bar, downtown at 151 Madison (bottom right). It was hugely successful. In fact, when the company celebrated its tenth anniversary, Anderton had his employees prepare a 400-pound birthday cake designed to serve 2,500 people, and every visitor to the restaurant that day got a free slice. In that first decade, Anderton claimed he had served more than two million customers, who gulped down more than six million oysters. He also began something that became an Anderton's tradition: In addition to menus, he placed "prayer cards" on tables that urged diners, "Go to Church on Sunday."

In 1956, Anderton purchased the old Gilmore Seafood Restaurant at 1901 Madison and renamed it Anderton's East. What I found amusing was a newspaper story about the renovation of that establishment and described the new design as having "an air of quiet elegance." Let's see — it had (and still has) a bar designed like a pirate ship, organic "blobs" that float like clouds over diners, a blue glass panel etched with sea creatures, and — at one time — an outside waterfall. Unique? Yes. Even a bit bizarre? Certainly. Quietly elegant? No.

In 1960, Anderton's Oyster Bar doubled in size, expanding to the east and south, and could now seat 250. Even that couldn't apparently meet the demand, because two years later, Anderton opened a third restaurant, on Highway 51 South directly across the street from Graceland. Managed by his son, Robert, this one was called Anderton's Oak Acres.

All of the Anderton's remained three of this city's most popular restaurants for years, and Anderton himself became wealthy enough to build a nice house on East Parkway that had an oyster-shaped swimming pool. It was designed by the same fellow who built his restaurants, so you can just imagine how the interior must have looked. More of that "quiet elegance," I presume.

But downtown, as anyone who lived here during the late 1960s and '70s knows, went through a rough period. Anderton closed the original restaurant at 151 Madison in 1975. "People can still come downtown if they want to," he told a reporter. "But they just don't want to." He said he might re-open again after a few years, but that never happened. The building later became a Burger King, and today stands empty.

The Anderton's by Graceland also closed, and the site is now occupied by rows of gift shops operated by Elvis Presley Enterprises.

And here's some really sad news. As we went to press, I learned that Anderton's East was also closing. That's too bad. If you never ate there, you missed a unique Memphis dining experience. The pirate-ship bar alone was worth the trip. In fact, if nobody else buys the place, I may see about purchasing that. It would look very fine indeed in the Lauderdale lobby. **M**

Got a question for Vance? Send it to "Ask Vance" at Memphis *magazine, 460 Tennessee Street #200, Memphis, TN 38103, or e-mail him at askvance@memphismagazine.com*

[ask vance]

By Vance Lauderdale

Our Trivia Expert Solves Local Mysteries of Who, What, When, Where, Why, and Why Not.

Searching for Sherron

Dear Vance: What can you tell me about this nice old postcard (below) for the Sherron Shoe Company? — D.N., Memphis.

Dear D.N.: After taking this vintage card down to the Lauderdale Laboratories and subjecting it to spectrographic analysis and microscopic examination, I can tell you with 99.5 percent certainty that it is: 1) a postcard, 2) for a Memphis company, 3) that sells shoes. We can also presume that the name of the store was Sherron.

Whew! Done for the day! Next question?

Okay, I have to admit I found the card rather fascinating. Just look at all those hundreds and hundreds of perfectly organized boxes of shoes, the ornate carpeting, and the rows of dapper clerks helping customers try on the latest fashions. Why, there are even ladders stretching to the ceiling, apparently mounted on some kind of track, so the hired help could roll the ladders back and forth to reach the topmost boxes. Just like they do in Rack Room today!

The back of the card offered this friendly entreaty: "We want you to make this your Shoe Store, and feel that you are perfectly safe when you buy Shoes here." I liked the capitalization of the word "Shoes" as if they were something precious and special, but I have to wonder why they made it a point to mention that their customers were safe here. Were the shoes at other stores dangerous in some way? If anything, I might feel nervous shopping at Sherron's, since a clerk high atop one of those ladders might drop a box of size 13 wingtips on my head, but that's just my cautious nature.

I don't know exactly when the Sherron Shoe Company opened. It is listed in 1903 city directories, the earliest I have at my disposal. Located at 78 South Main, the company president was Thomas Sherron, the vice president was Frank Sherron, and the secretary-treasurer was William — no, not Sherron, as you were expecting, but Schwalmeyer. I guess they couldn't find another Sherron to take that job.

In 1934, the company moved around the corner to 122 Madison. The former location became the office of George W. Walker, and it irritates me that the city directories don't bother to tell what Walker did for a living, or why he needed such a large office. I wonder if he kept all those ladders? I certainly would've.

I'm sorry to tell you that the Sherron Shoe Company closed in 1941. The building became home to the Harrell Insulation Company, selling siding, rock wool, and insulating materials. The place makes me itch just to think of it.

Today, 78 South Main stands empty, and 122 Madison houses a loan company. Don't bother looking for shoes, or insulation, or George Walker in either of those places.

Memories of Britling

Dear Vance: When I was younger, my parents took me to the Britling Cafeteria downtown. This would have been in the early 1960s, but now I can't remember where this restaurant was. Can you help me locate it? — S.L., Memphis.

Dear S.L.: If I couldn't, I certainly wouldn't be including your question here, would I? And then I could just sit back and leave the rest of the column blank. But since I am paid by the word (and not paid one-tenth of what I'm worth, if you ask me), I'll go ahead and ramble on in my charming fashion and tell you a bit about Britling.

First of all, there were two Britlings downtown. The first one opened way back in 1921 at 155 Madison. Then a second location opened in 1938 at 75 Union Avenue, right next to the Loew's Palace theater. The founder's name was not Britling, as you might expect. It was A.W.B. Johnson, who decided that "Johnson's Cafeteria" didn't have much of a ring to it, and I have to agree. The story goes that he was reading a collection of short stories

32 • ASK VANCE II

by science fiction writer H.G. Wells and encountered one called "Mr. Britling Sees It Through" and decided that was a fine name for his new restaurant. He eventually opened others in Nashville, Louisville, Lexington, and Frankfort, Kentucky. The company's slogan, as promoted on matchbooks and menus, was a simple one: "Good Food Is Good Health."

Still, eating there could, at times, be a bit risky. Customers at the Madison Avenue Britling had a narrow escape on the afternoon of November 4, 1929, when rags stored in the basement burst into flames. In a matter of minutes, the whole restaurant was ablaze. Firemen rushing to the scene discovered a tragedy in the making, as more than 300 people jammed the exits trying to escape. But an odd thing happened, as reported by the *Memphis Press-Scimitar*: "A phonograph that changes records automatically kept playing as the patrons filed out of the burning building. Officials believe this helped to prevent a panic." Thankfully, except for a few cases of smoke inhalation, nobody was seriously injured.

The owners rebuilt the cafeteria, and the photograph from the mid-1950s (right) shows a stunning building with a truly fantastic ground-floor facade — all sweeping curves and polished marble and gleaming stainless steel. But that location closed in 1956, and the fine building was demolished just a few years later to make way for First Tennessee Bank's headquarters.

So if you ate at a downtown Britling in the early 1960s, S.L., that means

you and your family no doubt dined at 75 Union (left), which was greatly remodeled in the late 1950s. Among other features, this Britling had murals by noted Memphis artist Burton Callicott, and "one wall will be a precast terrazzo panel in three dimensions in an off-white shade," which the designers bragged was "the first of its kind in Memphis."

Britling built another cafeteria in Poplar Plaza in the late 1950s, and by 1970 also had branches in the Laurelwood and Northgate shopping centers. But as I've pointed out more than once in this column, downtown Memphis was rather dormant in the late 1960s and early 1970s, and the company decided to close the Union Avenue store in 1971. I can't recall if the new owners kept that striking Greek Revival entrance when they converted the building to a computer-service company, but it doesn't matter, because the whole thing came tumbling down, along with the Loew's Palace, to make room for Parking Can Be Fun. There are other cafeterias in Memphis today, but not a single Britling. And the next time I venture to Nashville, Louisville, Lexington, and Frankfort, I'll let you know if any of those Britlings survived, either. **M**

Got a question for Vance? Send it to "Ask Vance" at *Memphis* magazine, 460 Tennessee Street #200, Memphis, TN 38103, or email him at askvance@memphismagazine.com

▶ ## ASK VANCE
Our trivia expert solves local mysteries of who, what, when, where, why, and why not.

THE REPLICA RESTAURANT

by VANCE LAUDERDALE

DEAR VANCE: What is the story of that World War II–themed restaurant that used to be out by the airport? It didn't last very long, for some reason. — G.B., MEMPHIS.

DEAR G.B.: Oh, the dark days of World War II were dark days indeed for the Lauderdales. Not because we lost any members of our family on the field of battle. Quite the opposite. Nobody was even wounded. You see, as soon as the war began, Father began proclaiming that the Lauderdales were actually Swiss, and since we were natives of a neutral country, we really weren't allowed to participate in any part of that pesky war. So my family never joined the armed forces, never fought overseas, never helped with paper drives, never planted a victory garden — never did anything, really, but talk longingly about Lucerne and the Alps whenever the topic of war came up.

So you can imagine our mortification when, just as the war was coming to an end, that nosey-parker newspaper reporter revealed that our particular branch of the Lauderdales didn't hail from Switzerland at all, but was, in fact, from Itta Bena, Mississippi. Mother had to resign her presidency of the East Parkway Petunia Club in disgrace, and Father drowned his sorrows in drink. It was a low point for my family, one of many that I had to overcome as a child. And let's not even bring up those awful days in school, when the bullies would grab me by the collar and say, "Let's hear you yodel, you Swiss sissy!"

Why do I bring this up now? Because World War II was a horrific period for our country, but years later, certain people must have thought it was actually a pretty fun time, because they came out with all sorts of war-related entertainment — television shows (I mean, what lunatic conceived of *Hogan's Heroes*, a comedy set in a German P.O.W. camp?), movies, games, and even restaurants.

And the somewhat awkwardly named 91st Bomb Group (H) Restaurant was part of that

fad, a cozy establishment designed to resemble a bombed-out French farmhouse. Of course, it was a very sanitized version of the war. The developers cleverly omitted such depressing details as dead civilians, wounded soldiers, and any mention whatsoever of Nazis. Instead, they constructed a rambling building that was surrounded and filled by all sorts of World War II memorabilia — guns, jeeps, photos, posters, and more. At one time, even the famous *Memphis Belle* was parked outside.

The restaurant, located at Democrat and Airways, was originally going to be based on the *first* World War. It was the brainchild of a national chain called Specialty Restaurants, headquartered in Long Beach, California. An early press release announced that the place would be called the "94th Aerosquadron Restaurant." Featuring a nice lounge and dance floor, "the plan is to use a central theme of an old World War I vintage farmhouse, decorated with artifacts from the period."

Well, the owners must have realized it would be a heck of a lot easier to incorporate a World War TWO theme, so they made the place an English farmhouse instead and changed the name to the 91st Bomb Group, the group that included the *Memphis Belle*.

Over the years, I've searched for a decent photograph of this unusual eatery, but found nothing. I did, however, locate a couple of old menus (left), and one of them includes a rather crude drawing of the "farmhouse." As you might expect, the fare was also WWII-themed, with such offerings as "Officer's Club Specialties," a "Commander's Dinner," and even "Farmhouse Favorites" that included a "Captain Morgan Steak" and "Veal Memphis Belle." Robert Morgan was captain of the *Belle*, remember.

The restaurant opened in early 1980 and was a tremendous success, serving some 170,000 patrons that first year, according to one newspaper story. But on June 12, 1981, it suffered a disaster. An outbreak of salmonella sent more than 20 diners to the hospital and forced the health department to close the place.

The Commercial Appeal reported that it finally reopened on July 3rd with "a sparse crowd."

"This was a one-in-a-million occurrence, just one of those things that can happen," the manager told reporters. "It's going to take some time to overcome this. The damage done to a restaurant that closes for 10 days is immense, especially when it's because of food poisoning."

The damage, in fact, was irreversible. The restaurant locked its doors a few months later and never reopened. It was eventually demolished, and if you drive by that corner today, no trace remains of the quaint old "English farmhouse" that once attracted thousands of diners.

HIGH SCHOOL HOT SPOT

DEAR VANCE: I always heard about a popular eatery in town called Chenault's. Where was it, and what happened to it?
— J.W., GERMANTOWN.

DEAR J.W.: Chenault's was indeed a hot spot for more than 20 years, if not longer, and served as a big hangout for the Whitehaven High School crowd.

I'm glad you didn't ask me when, exactly, the establishment was built, because I just don't remember. There were actually two different Chenault's, you see — an old one and a new one. Most people remember the new one.

I know this because I turned up a 1955 *Press-Scimitar* clipping announcing that Reginald "Rex" Chenault was planning to build a brand-new restaurant at 1400 South Bellevue, to replace his older and smaller establishment right next door. Calling it "an interesting modern building," the newspaper observed that the new Chenault's Drive-In "would include a public dining room of exposed brick and wood paneling, a private dining room, a tap room, and an upper level to be rented for private parties."

As you can see from the postcard (left) I discovered in the Lauderdale Library, the interior was indeed pretty snazzy, with gleaming white countertops and tables, and rows of pink booths and seats. In the back, the massive kitchen included "an enormous barbecue pit of unique design worked out by Mr. Chenault and the architects."

The place was dishing out hamburgers and milkshakes as late as the 1980s. It closed, though the old building is still standing today.

A SNIP IN TIME

DEAR VANCE: When I was growing up in Memphis in the 1950s, I was sent with my brother to get our Buster Brown haircuts at a barber shop that stood next door to present-day Cafe Olé. What was the name of that barber shop?
— L.H., MEMPHIS.

DEAR L.H.: It didn't actually stand next door to Cafe Olé, in the vacant area now taken up by the nice patio; it occupied the western half of that restaurant. If you stand on Young and look at Cafe Olé, you can see it is composed of two separate structures standing side by side. See that mortar seam between them? In the 1950s, the building closest to Cooper, back then 2129 Young Avenue, was Weona Food Store #11. And the building next to it, 2127 Young (above), was your childhood barber shop, a place called Troutt Brothers. It was owned by Virgil and Buck Troutt, who also lived in the neighborhood. Virgil and his wife, Nona, owned a house just down the street at 2001 Young, and Buck and his wife, Dorothy, lived a few blocks away at 2266 Evelyn.

The old city directories tell me that in the 1950s, a place called Sue's Beauty Shop operated out of the back of that barber shop. I wonder if you went there, L.H., when you grew out of your Buster Brown hair styles?

Someday, I will find out what business stood in the gap between Cafe Olé and the Young Avenue Deli. But that's for another column. Right now, I have to get a haircut, and I'm thinking Vance would look quite dashing in a Buster Brown. **M**

GOT A QUESTION FOR VANCE? *Send it to "Ask Vance" at* MEMPHIS *magazine, 460 Tennessee Street #200, Memphis, TN 38103 or email him at askvance@memphismagazine.com*

▶ # ASK VANCE
Our trivia expert solves local mysteries of who, what, when, where, why, and why not.

CRYSTAL QUESTION

by VANCE LAUDERDALE

DEAR VANCE: *What is the story behind the bizarre "grotto" in the middle of Memorial Park? It seems like a strange thing to have there.*
— J.L., MEMPHIS.

DEAR J.L.: I'm halfway sorry you asked me about this place. As you may know, for the past 12 years or so, workers have been constructing a magnificent mausoleum that will serve as a final resting place for my weary bones. Oh, it's a marvel, and I'm told that when it is finished it will be the only manmade object in all of Shelby County that will visible to crews of the space shuttle. That's probably due to the giant neon letters at the top spelling out V-A-N-C-E.

But after paying a recent visit to the Crystal Shrine Grotto, an interesting place indeed, I began to wonder if something like that would be more to my liking, and more suitable to my true character. It's lovely, charming, rustic — all words used to describe me in various published biographies. Oh, I can't decide what to do. I'll just let the Nobel Prize committee have the last say in where I shall be entombed — and how much they will charge for admission.

Besides, even if I wanted to build a monument like the Grotto, I couldn't, because its creator passed away in 1955 and is buried in San Antonio. Born outside Mexico City in 1890, Dionicio Rodriguez came to this country in the early 1920s. Since he spoke little or no English, and always traveled from place to place, much of his life is shrouded in mystery. But somehow, he perfected a technique for chemically tinting concrete and then carving or molding it into naturalistic forms that closely resembled stones, branches, trees — whatever he wished — even down to artificial worm holes, cracked branches, and peeling bark.

It's hard to say how well he was received in his own lifetime, but in recent years remaining examples of his amazing work have been documented and preserved, wherever possible, and good examples of it can be found in seven states. In Little Rock, there's a beautiful park with bridges and an old wooden mill — all formed of concrete — that was used in the opening scenes of *Gone With the Wind*.

In the 1930s, Rodriguez met up with another remarkable fellow, E. Clovis Hinds, who in 1924 had purchased some 160 acres of land on the outskirts of Memphis and began to transform it into a tranquil graveyard he would call Memorial Park. A cemetery brochure describes his dream: "He sought not simply a pleasant peaceful place of repose but an atmosphere steeped in tradition, linking the ancient past with the eternal future."

Rodriguez came here in 1935 and, under Clovis' guidance, began construction of what I would consider his masterpiece — the Crystal Shrine Grotto. If you haven't been there, my photographs and words really can't do it justice. Using tons of tinted concrete, Rodriguez recreated scenes from the Bible and literature. The Cave of Machpelah overlooks the scenic Pool of Hebron (above). Nearby is Abraham's Oak, the Ferdinand IV Sunken Garden, Annie Laurie's Wishing Chair, even the Fountain of Youth — all made of cement.

I turned up an old *Memphis Press-Scimitar* article that quoted Rodriguez: "People usually don't go to cemeteries, unless they have a special interest in them. We shall try to change that." There's no source given for that quote,

ASK VANCE

and since (as I said earlier, if you were paying attention) Rodriguez supposedly didn't speak English, I wonder if it's true. But even if it's not, he certainly gave people a reason to visit Memorial Park.

One of the most unusual features is the Grotto itself, a manmade cavern whose ceiling is studded with thousands of quartz crystals. Inside, 10 panels depict scenes from the life of Jesus Christ. It has a certain kitschy charm, that's for sure, but all in all, a remarkable thing to see. If you can, that is. On a recent visit, I found the gates padlocked, so I hope cemetery officials haven't locked up the place.

Now, about this time, any reader would expect me to include a photo of Rodriguez, hard at work constructing the Crystal Shrine Grotto. But even though I searched high and low, I never found a single photograph of the man. From what I understand, he was very secretive about the techniques he used to create his monuments, so it's possible that he didn't allow anyone to photograph him. And yes, it's also possible that I just didn't look hard enough.

HIGBEE'S HISTORY

DEAR VANCE: *There's an interesting old monument to Jenny Higbee (below, right) in Overton Park. Who was Higbee, and why does she deserve a place of honor in the park?* — G.K., MEMPHIS.

DEAR G.K.: Let me tell you that Jenny Higbee was a remarkable person, who had quite an influence on many women in this city for many years, and well-deserving of a noble monument. Now, why they put it in Overton Park is a question I can't answer. For a while, it seems, that park served as a catch-all for all kinds of things: World War I monuments, Japanese gardens, a miniature Statue of Liberty, you name it.

But back to your question: A worn inscription carved around the top of the stone memorial reads: "Erected in Memory of Jenny M. Higbee by the Higbee Alumnae Association." I doubt that the alumnae association is very active anymore, since the school that Higbee founded was closed so many years ago.

Higbee, who came to Memphis from New Jersey in the late 1800s, taught for a while at St. Mary's School when it was located downtown. Sometime around 1870, she decided to open her own place and constructed a fine-looking two-story brick school at the corner of Beale and Lauderdale. She also purchased the old mansion next door originally built by Robertson Topp — owner of several railroads and the old Gayoso Hotel, among other ventures — and used that as a dormitory for her students.

The Higbee School (left) quickly became one of the South's leading educational institutions for young women. An old newspaper article says that in 1892 the school had more than 300 students, with a faculty of 32. The main courses were music and art. According to historian Paul Coppock, the students "were as young as kindergarten and as old as college preparatory." He also described Higbee as "a remarkably fine teacher."

What's even more remarkable is that the Higbee Hornets football squad was not only the Southern Conference champs for many

years, but they even beat Yale 63-7 in the 1919 Rose Bowl.

No, I made that last part up.

Unfortunately, when Jenny Higbee passed away in 1903, the school could not survive without her, and it closed in 1910. A group called the Memphis Trades and Labor Council purchased the property in 1921 and used it as their headquarters until 1972, when the old school and the Roberton Topp mansion were both demolished.

I feel bad about that, since both impressive buildings were located on Lauderdale. My family should certainly have taken better care of their own street.

One final comment. The memorial in Overton Park, shown above in an old postcard, has a second inscription: "Her Life's Work Is Her Monument." And yet they built a monument for her anyway. I guess they feared her life's work wouldn't be remembered over the years, and the memorial in Overton Park — erected in 1908 — is still standing to this day. **M**

Got a question for Vance? Send it to "Ask Vance" at Memphis *magazine, 460 Tennessee Street #200, Memphis, TN 38103. Or email him at askvance@memphismagazine.com.*

ASK VANCE II • 37

ASK VANCE

Our trivia expert solves local mysteries of who, what, when, where, why, and why not.

THE COURT SQUARE CANNON

by VANCE LAUDERDALE

DEAR VANCE: I have seen old photos of Court Square (above) that show some kind of Civil War cannon in one corner of the park. What happened to that cannon?
— D.D., MEMPHIS.

DEAR D.D.: I have seen similar photos, and in fact a leisurely stroll through the halls of the Lauderdale Library turned up an old postcard (see next page) of Court Square, and if you look carefully, over in the lefthand background you can see several dapper gentlemen gathered around that very cannon.

Oh, how times have changed. Back then, it was apparently considered perfectly acceptable to stand around a cannon and spend all day just chatting away about the weather, or politics, or shopping, or what have you. But now, if someone — someone like *me*, I mean — tries to spend, oh, four or five hours in our company lounge, gossiping with my co-workers and sharing those thrilling stories about my youthful days in Heidelberg, my editor invariably tracks me down and tells me to get back to work. Man, lighten up!

Anyway, let me tell you about that particular cannon. From some faded newspaper articles I discovered, I was able to determine that the Court Square gun was not left over from the Civil War, but was a relic from the Spanish-American War of 1898. One newspaper story says the gun was placed in the park in 1917, but the photo above clearly shows a 1901 date on the base of the gun. That base wasn't original, by the way. As you can see, it was manufactured by the Memphis Trades and Labor Council. They did a fine job.

The gun was a downtown conversation piece until 1942, when city leaders decided that Court Square no longer needed defending, and they consigned the old cannon to a World War II scrap-metal drive. An old newspaper article noted that the piece was mostly brass and probably weighed more than 3,000 pounds, so melted down it would make quite a few rifle cartridges.

It didn't go without a minor skirmish. The veterans who donated the piece at first weren't too happy that it would end up on the scrap heap, but they quickly changed their mind. In fact, a fellow

38 • ASK VANCE II

ASK VANCE

named Fred Bauer Sr., who was past-president of the Spanish-American War Veterans, told a reporter, "While we value this trophy which was captured in the Spanish-American War, the war veterans are willing to give it up to help our nation win the present war."

That wasn't the only piece of artillery to be donated to the war effort. Memphis, it seems, was fairly bristling with big guns before World War II, and they all went into the melting pot, or wherever these things go to be recast into something else. We also lost the Civil War-era cannons and mortars that faced the river in Confederate Park, a cluster of guns that stood atop the Indian mound in DeSoto Park, another pair that guarded the Doughboy Statue in Overton Park, and a dozen cannons displayed here and there in the National Cemetery. The cemetery guns alone weighed more than 70 tons, so that was quite a contribution to the war drive.

Luckily, the Lauderdales were not asked to donate the family collection of artillery, and a formidable grouping of howitzers still stands on the front lawn of the mansion, where they keep the pesky orphans at bay. Once you give those kids a nickel or half a biscuit, they just never leave you alone.

I know donating all these vintage guns was for a good cause at the time, but now it makes me feel a bit uneasy. Except for half a dozen battered cannon left over from the Korean War that stand — somewhat out of place, if you ask me — in Confederate Park, Memphis has no guns guarding our riverfront. And if those rowdy folks over in Arkansas ever decide to invade our fair city, we will be completely helpless to stop them. Don't say I didn't warn you.

HARBIN'S HISTORY

DEAR VANCE: Can you tell us about Harbin's Tourist Court? We found a drinking glass at an estate sale advertising its location on Highway 51 South, but don't know where it was, exactly. — K.P., MEMPHIS.

DEAR K.P.: Well, I can't tell you where it was, exactly, but I'll give you a general idea.

Harbin's Tourist Court was operated by an enterprising fellow named J.C. Harbin. I'm sure he had a first name, but no postcard or newspaper article I've seen ever mentions it. Way back in 1919, he opened a combination tourist court, cafe, and dairy on land at Highway 51 and Raines Road. I wish I could tell you a more precise location, but the old postcards rarely gave — or even needed — a more specific address, and because that was outside the city limits, the place wasn't even listed in Memphis phone books. I believe it was on the northeast corner of that intersection, but I could be mistaken.

Regardless, it was an excellent location, because Highway 51 was one of the main routes into Memphis from the south, so weary travelers encountered a place to spend the night or grab a bite to eat as they drove into town. Over the years, Harbin enlarged the place, adding a row of handsome white clapboard cottages and even a swimming pool. His postcards advertised "Fine food, Beautyrest mattresses, swimming pool, baths, steam and gas heat" and declared the place was "easy to find."

But progress was lurking around the corner. When Kemmons Wilson opened his nationwide chain of Holiday Inns which — along with other motel chains — offered clean, low-priced rooms without any surprises (good or bad), many of these mom-and-pop tourist courts began to shut down. In the mid-1950s, Harbin, being the savvy businessman that he was, closed his little roadside complex. Instead, he opened a modern shopping center, which was called Harbin's Center. But what is confusing is that I have been told that the shopping center replaced the tourist court, while somebody else told me it was actually built across the highway from it. I just don't know. I do know that Harbin's Center originally housed 15 stores, including a By-Ryt Food Store, a beauty salon, a laundromat, a Gridiron restaurant, and other businesses.

Back then, this was quite an ambitious undertaking. An August 17, 1955, *Memphis Press-Scimitar* article noted that this was "the second major commercial development to be started in Whitehaven in the last 90 days." Among other innovations, Harbin's Center would boast of "ample off-street parking spaces provided in front of the stores, and there will also be a large flood-lighted lot at the south side of the supermarket." As opposed to all those other shopping centers without parking lots or lights, I guess.

J.C. Harbin passed away many years ago, but his shopping center is still standing, today housing Royal Furniture, Shoe Warehouse, and an assortment of other businesses. And at the end of the building, I found the very same Gridiron that moved in half a century ago. They must be serving some mighty tasty chow there. **M**

GOT A QUESTION FOR VANCE? *Send it to "Ask Vance" at* MEMPHIS *magazine, 460 Tennessee Street #200, Memphis, TN 38103 or email him at askvance@memphismagazine.com*

ASK VANCE
Our trivia expert solves local mysteries of who, what, when, where, why, and why not.

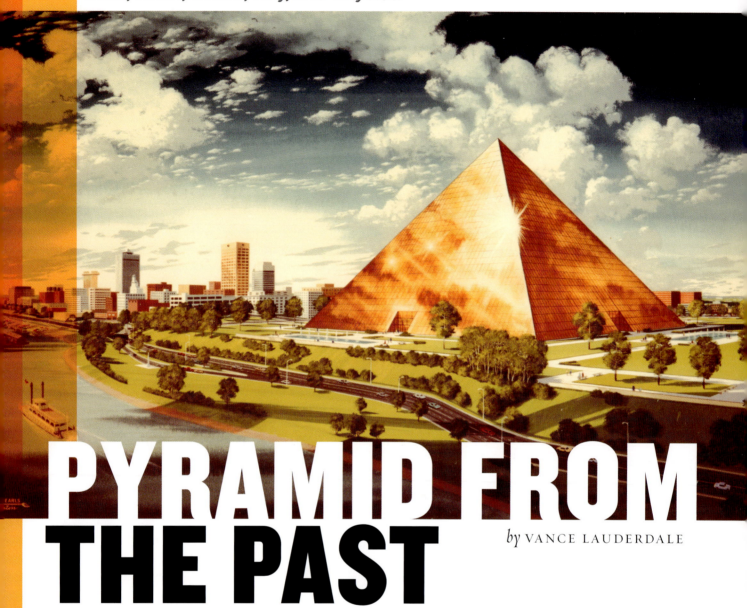

PYRAMID FROM THE PAST

by VANCE LAUDERDALE

DEAR VANCE: With all of this talk about the future of The Pyramid, I have a question about its past. Wasn't that building originally going to be made of gold?
— D.D., MEMPHIS.

DEAR D.D.: A gold building in Memphis? Surely, you must be thinking of the initial designs for the Lauderdale Mansion, when — with more cash in our coffers than the entire nation of Tanganyika — we announced plans to sheathe the exterior of the servant's dormitory in gold plate. But then, knowing the questionable character of those employees, and fearing they would just peel off the gold and sell it, we decided otherwise, and went with vinyl siding.

But wait a minute. Perhaps you are thinking of the early renderings of The Pyramid — in those days called The Great Memphis Pyramid — which clearly showed the building with a golden sheen to it. A sheen that was going to be created by covering the entire building in reflective gold-colored glass. Oh, what a tempting target for any neighborhood rascal with a rock and a slingshot!

The origins of The Pyramid are as murky as the muddy waters of the Mississippi. (Did you like that nice phrase? I shall try to use it again, from time to time.) I suppose other people, over the years, came up with ideas to build a pyramid in Memphis. After all, we built one at the Centennial Exposition in Nashville way back in 1897. But let me give some credit to an energetic young fellow named Brent Hartz, who, as I dimly recall, came up with a stunning rendering, and went all over town — to the Chamber of Commerce, the Convention and Visitors Bureau, and other civic groups — trying to get people interested in the project. He approached the Lauderdales, of course, and we agreed we would back him to the tune of $75, tops.

Anyway, I won't bore you with all the details, because quite frankly I can't remember them, but I believe Hartz and some associates found their way to John and Pat Tigrett, who liked the idea, gathered a group of investors around them, and got the ball rolling. Somewhere along the way, the gold-glass building design got changed to one of stainless steel.

Another, even more significant, change from the original proposal was the location. The first plans (such as the one shown here) depicted a giant pyramid perched rather prominently on the South Bluffs. In fact, the rendering makes the Pyramid look like the biggest building in Memphis. But this would have meant the demolition of quite a few historically significant structures in that area, including the Tennessee Brewery, the old Orgill Brothers warehouse,

40 • ASK VANCE II

and — more importantly — the quaint building that houses the offices of this magazine. So they — and I don't know, exactly, who "they" are — decided to plop the building down in a hole below the I-40 entrance ramps.

Just about every aspect of the original design was going to be much more impressive than what we ultimately constructed. I found a brief proposal, apparently prepared by the local architectural firm of Hall and Waller Associates, which explained, "The exterior skin of the building would be gold-mirrored glass. The mullions of the glazing units would contain fluorescent lights to make the whole building glow at night." Oh, and the building would also house a "Discovery Museum" which would feature "great scientific discoveries throughout the history of man," along with "people movers similar to those used at Walt Disney World." Those movers would take hundreds of visitors to a Music Hall of Fame, theater, restaurant "offering a panoramic view of the city," observation tower at the peak, and even underground parking. The total cost of all this was projected at $20 million.

In the end, The Pyramid cost us $65 million, and somehow the builders forgot to include just about everything that was mentioned in the original design. Which is probably just as well, since now we can't decide what to do with the thing anyway.

All I know is, the Lauderdales want a refund of our $75.

INITIAL ENIGMA #1

DEAR VANCE: I read somewhere that when the campus of Rhodes College was being laid out, they planted trees in the shape of an "S" — to represent the school's former name of Southwestern. Is that true? — T.G., MEMPHIS.

DEAR T.G.: This was a rather intriguing rumor, so I did what I normally do with my most provocative questions — I retired to my La-Z-Boy and lay down with a cool towel on my forehead, while I spent a few hours napping, uh, I mean pondering how to proceed. Upon awakening, my first thought was to peruse the various histories of Southwestern, aka Rhodes College, where I found no mention of this interesting landmark. In the Lauderdale Library, I had one of my "Eureka!" moments, when I stumbled upon a handsome booklet printed in the 1950s titled *Southwestern's Arboretum*, which gave a detailed description of every single tree planted at Rhodes. Back then, the campus was shaded by more than 1,500 trees, representing some 62 different species, including 15 varieties of oaks. Little metal tags were even affixed to every one, "so the interested passer-by can easily identify the species." What really caught my eye, however, was a campus map, showing the location of each of these plantings. But no matter which way I turned the map, none of the trees seemed to form the "S" you described, T.G.

With the Lauderdale helicopter out of commission (something about forgetting to pay the insurance premiums on it back in 1967), my only recourse, I decided, was to visit the campus myself. Unfortunately, I had a brusque encounter with the school's cautious security guards, who confiscated my sword-cane and set of dueling pistols before they would let me through the gate. They continued to watch me rather intensely as I wandered around the place, trying to find trees — or even stumps, by now — that formed the mysterious "S." No luck.

Just when I was about to tell you that this story was a myth, however, I stumbled quite by accident upon a 1962 *Commercial Appeal* article that was discussing future buildings planned for the college. The story included an overhead view of

the campus, and there — plain as day — was the giant "S" formed from a group of trees planted immediately south of the old Burrow Library (below). So the story is true, T.G. Unfortunately, the trees are now gone, chopped down to make way for Buckman Hall, which opened in 1991.

Too bad. I think they should plant some more, though this time in the shape of a giant "R," of course.

INITIAL ENIGMA #2

DEAR VANCE: We found this old picture (left) tucked away in a book found at a local estate sale. What does "DCL" mean? — J.N., MEMPHIS.

DEAR J.N.: You can't read the embroidered letters attached to these girls' sweaters as "DCL." Yes, that's how it would be if they were monograms, with the letter of the last name larger than the first and middle names. But this is college stuff, and it's DLC, I tell you, and that stands for David Lipscomb College, a private school in Nashville. So even though you found the book in Memphis, the photo came from somewhere else. It depicts some kind of pep squad, I suppose, though I can't explain why one girl gets to wear the jaunty cap and dashing cape that is practically identical to my own. And don't even ask about that little kid in the photo. What is she — a mascot?   **M**

GOT A QUESTION FOR VANCE? *Send it to "Ask Vance" at* MEMPHIS *magazine, 460 Tennessee Street #200, Memphis, TN 38103 or email him at askvance@memphismagazine.com*

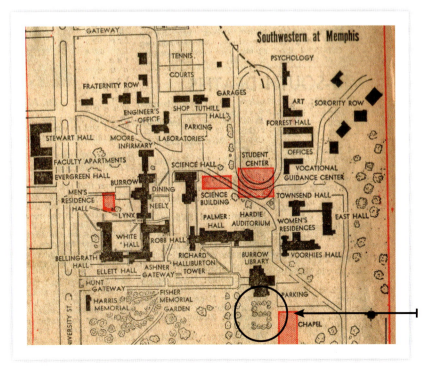

▶ **ASK VANCE**
Our trivia expert solves local mysteries of who, what, when, where, why, and why not.

A QUESTION OF COLUMNS

by VANCE LAUDERDALE

DEAR VANCE: I was told that when the old Goodwyn Institute building downtown was demolished, the majestic columns that graced the front of the building ended up on a house in Memphis. If that's true, where is the house?
— M.K., MEMPHIS.

DEAR M.K.: I remember this well, for the Lauderdales were also bidding on those same columns, hoping to use them to shore up the west wing of the mansion. Unfortunately, our high bid of $47.50 was rejected, and we ultimately decided the classical-style columns were not in keeping with the majestic Gothic Revival designs of the main mansion.

So we used some pine 2 x 4s instead, from the old Handy City on Summer, and they worked just fine. Someday I may get around to painting them.

I should explain that the Goodwyn Institute was an organization just as remarkable as the stunning building that housed it. Very little, it seems, is known about the founder, William Adolphus Goodwyn. Most histories just vaguely mention that he was a successful cotton merchant here around the Civil War before he moved away to Nashville, where he died in 1898. Though he had left our city, in his will he bequeathed his entire fortune for a public library and an annual series of educational lectures. Much like the Lauderdales have done for so many years, but without as much fanfare. In fact, very few people attend the Lauderdale Lectures any more, held every Friday afternoon at Hooters, but that is no fault of mine, is it?

Anyway, the Goodwyn Institute opened in 1907 at the southwest corner of Third and Madison. Historian Paul Coppock observed that the seven-story building "was notable for four large columns above the entrance and for lions' heads in terra-cotta, with abundant white terra-cotta decorations." The old postcard (opposite page) gives you some idea, I hope, of the grandeur of this structure, which cost some $300,000 to build — an enormous sum in those days. The top floor held the library, and the third floor was taken up by a 900-seat auditorium. The rest of the building held various offices and, at one time, the WMC radio station.

The authors of *Memphis: An Architectural Guide* thought highly of this landmark, calling it "an elaborate fantasy on the Beaux-Arts theme." But as Memphis often does with beautiful buildings, it decided to bulldoze this one in 1962 to make way for the First National (later Tennessee) Bank tower.

But you are right, M.K., that the columns of that building were "recycled." I found a 1962 *Commercial Appeal* article headlined "Old Goodwyn's Pillars Find New Home." It seems they found their way to the home of Ed and Bette Stalnecker at 688 South McLean (shown as it looks today, below left). "The religious

recording artist," the article explained, "bought the columns to remind her of her childhood audition days at the Goodwyn Institute."

What impressed me was the impulsive nature of the Stalneckers' purchase. They didn't really need them on their home, but they were determined to find a place for them, and the CA article noted, "Their roof will be extended to fit the new addition." Now those same authors of that architectural guide didn't really like that idea, observing that, "Because of the height of the columns, an overweening pediment had to be added awkwardly to the roof" and as a result, the house "gained in pretension, if not in grace," when the columns were installed.

I think they look just fine, and those same authors admit, "It's good, of course, that the columns were not thrown away."

THE SHELTERED LIFE

DEAR VANCE: Years ago, when I lived in Memphis, going back and forth to school we would pass this large triangular structure on Elvis Presley Boulevard, and my parents told me it was a bomb shelter. Can you tell me who built it, and what became of it?
— D.H., FRANKLIN, TN

DEAR D.H.: Oh, this brings back memories of the awful feud between the Lauderdales and that upstart Hoyt Wooten. Yes, it was Wooten's private bomb shelter you had noticed — the largest and (at a cost of some $200,000) most expensive bomb shelter in the world, in fact — and he never let us forget it.

Wooten was a nice gentleman, by all accounts, but he riled Mother and Father because he was always determined to outdo them. It was bad enough that he had the good sense to make a huge fortune by investing in such modern things as radio and television, while the Lauderdales squandered our wealth on zeppelins, linotype machines, and flax farms. But when he built his magnificent private yacht, the *Elbaroda* (yes, it spelled "adorable" backwards), and specified that it be precisely one foot longer than our own mighty steamship, the *Lady Lauderdale*, that was the end of it. He never attended any more of our soirees, and we never set foot in his house in Whitehaven, much less in his fancy-schmancy bomb shelter.

Oh, but we heard all about it, all right. Nervous about the Cold War, Wooten built an underground complex that could safely hold 52 people for up to a month. I had heard rumors that those lucky 52 actually paid to be included in that group, but I can't say if that's true. Above ground, that triangular part you noticed, D.H., actually concealed the entrance, protected by heavy steel gates. Down below, the 13-room complex included sleeping quarters, dining hall, smoking lounge, recreation room complete with billiard table — and even a morgue for anyone who didn't make it. Powered by generators fueled by massive underground storage tanks, the shelter — as you might expect from a radio and TV expert — had a state-of-the-art communications center to talk with anybody who was still alive after the attack that Wooten feared.

That attack never came, of course, so Wooten liked to open up his shelter for tours. Why, he was so proud of it that he even printed up postcards (left). After his death in 1969, there was some talk of turning his estate into a public park, though I don't know what they would have done with the shelter. In the early 1980s, developers turned his property into a subdivision called Lion's Gate, and for a while, the old bomb shelter served as a community center. But it's been empty for some time now, and I remember years ago Memphis Heritage used it for their annual meeting and found it dark and musty smelling. Wooten would have been mighty sad to hear that, I bet.

WEST MEMPHIS WONDERS

DEAR VANCE: Can you tell me where I can find the scenic location in West Memphis, Arkansas, that is depicted on this postcard (below)? — T.Y., MEMPHIS

DEAR T.Y.: Oh, I have passed that very spot hundreds, perhaps thousands of times. It's stunning — like something you'd see in Switzerland. It's right past Southland Greyhound Park, on the north side of I-40, and if you blink . . .

Okay, I'm kidding. Postcard manufacturers, then and now, tended to embellish their subjects. They also sold generic postcards that featured lovely scenic views, and the buyers could print whatever they wanted on the bottom.

Either (or both) of the possibilities seem to be the case here. Though many people think of West Memphis as just one big expressway interchange, if you slow down and pull off the highway, it actually has some nice neighborhoods and homes. Even so, what it does *not* have, are mountain ranges, groves of giant oaks, and a blue-water lake complete with a waterfall.

I noticed your old postcard was never mailed, T.Y. Perhaps whoever bought it, or printed it, just didn't have the nerve to send it. It would have just caused trouble. **M**

GOT A QUESTION FOR VANCE? *Send it to "Ask Vance" at* MEMPHIS *magazine, 460 Tennessee Street #200, Memphis, TN 38103 or email him at askvance@memphismagazine.com*

▶ **ASK VANCE**
Our trivia expert solves local mysteries of who, what, when, where, why, and why not.

MEMORIES OF MARJORIE

by VANCE LAUDERDALE

MARJORIE DUCKETT in 1943

DEAR VANCE: I was born in 1950 and lived most of my life in the Cooper-Young area. At the age of 2, I was sent to the Marjorie Duckett Dancing School. My vague memory is that it was on Union, but I can't remember where. Can you help? — L.H., MEMPHIS.

DEAR L.H.: Oh, what memories your letter brings back, for I too was a pupil of the Marjorie Duckett School of Dance. In fact, it's safe to say that I was her most outstanding student. She never told me that in so many words, being a quiet, studious woman, but I remember one day when Mother and Father came to pick me up after my lessons, she pulled them aside and whispered that "she absolutely couldn't teach me *anything*" and "when I danced, it just gave her the *shivers* — she had never seen anything quite like it." Tears rolled down her cheeks as she spoke those words — tears of joy, I know. Oh, my little heart swelled with pride.

And when I came home and slipped into my lederhosen and saddle oxfords, well, let's just say I made a sensation doing the foxtrot and the cha-cha in the Lauderdale ballroom. I remember the other dancers stopping and staring whenever I took the floor, obviously dazzled by my performance. Yes, good times!

So I know quite a few things about Marjorie Duckett. She was born in Memphis in 1918. She began to teach dancing with her mother, Doris, as early as the 1930s, initially working out of their home on South Bellevue. In the mid-1940s, she and her mother opened the Marjorie Duckett School of Dance at 1648 Union, and a few years later moved her school down the street to 1562 Union. The building was a rambling old house. The dancing school was on the ground floor, and Marjorie lived with her parents upstairs.

For a while, anyway. Sometime in the early 1950s, Marjorie married Arthur Binford, a successful dentist, and moved with him to a fine home at 1385 Goodbar in Central Gardens. Even so, she continued to operate her school on Union until 1969, when she retired.

Back in those days, dancing was more popular than it is now, I think, or at least the dances were so complicated that they required lessons, for there were quite a few dancing schools in town. Some of Marjorie's competitors included Eugenia Weakley, Marylee Edwards, and Sue Flack, and I'm sure there were others. I just thought I'd give them a mention too.

Even after she closed her school, Marjorie remained active in the world of dance, serving for more than 60 years as president of the Southern Association of Dance Masters, an organization that she founded. But the music finally came to an end in 1999, when Marjorie passed away at the age of 81. She is buried with her husband in Memorial Park.

And her school? After it closed, the old house was torn down and replaced with a Bonanza Sirloin Pit. That was in 1970, I believe. I don't even remember such a restaurant on Union, but the telephone directories don't lie. The site is today occupied by the West Clinic.

SEARCHING FOR CHICAGO

DEAR VANCE: I lived in Memphis when I was a kid and during the 1970s I was bused to a school called Chicago Park. However, searching online I discovered the school was inactive. Do you know what happened to it? — D.R., ST. LOUIS.

DEAR D.R.: It's safe to say that few schools in our city have had such a short and troubled history. And Chicago Park opened with such promise — a modern facility (below) that was designed to revitalize a decaying old neighborhood in North Memphis.

In 1960, the Memphis Board of Education purchased several acres a few blocks east of the Firestone Tire and Rubber Company plant, and hired the local architectural firm of Wiseman & Bland to design a sprawling, two-story complex with gymnasium and playground. The big playground ran alongside Cypress Creek and that, as it turned out later, was trouble.

You see, in the early 1960s, Cypress Creek had apparently been a dumping ground for pollutants discharged by nearby industries. Chicago Park schoolchildren began to develop rashes and unexplained sores. Neighborhood activists, led by a fellow named N.T. "Brother" Greene, demanded the playground be closed. Others doubted there was a problem; a member of the New Chicago Civic Club tried to calm residents, saying, "It makes no sense to get alarmed."

It was a very confusing situation. Shelby County Health Department officials insisted there was nothing wrong with the property. However, samples taken by the EPA showed higher-than-normal levels of dangerous chemicals in the soil, including a carcinogen called endrin.

In 1981, the playground was closed and surrounded by a chainlink fence. But that still didn't ease the concerns of parents, so in January 1982, Willie Herenton, who was then superintendent of city schools, announced that the Chicago Park School at 1415 Breedlove would be closed. Herenton insisted it was mainly a cost-savings measure, since the big school only housed about 300 students. "The experts differ," he told reporters, "as to whether there are enough chemicals to be dangerous to the children."

That wasn't good enough for one school board member, who noted, "When scientists disagree, it means there's a problem that no one wants to take full blame for explaining."

If Chicago Park School was supposed to bring new life to the neighborhood, it gets an F. The school buildings were boarded up, and in 1982 Firestone, one of our city's largest employers, closed.

ALLEY ANSWER

DEAR VANCE: I have a 1926 Shelby County death certificate that lists the residence of the deceased as 124 Beans Alley. Does this street still exist? Also, the undertaker was Barnwell and Spencer. What can you tell me about them? — M.M., SILVER SPRING, MD.

DEAR M.M.: The actual name was Bean Alley, and it was a stubby little street that stretched for a few blocks east and west of Florida Street, about one block south of present-day Crump Boulevard. The alley, once lined with little houses, shows up on maps and is listed in telephone directories (above) as late as the 1960s. But so many factories moved into that area that no trace survives of Bean Alley today.

The firm of Spencer and Barnwell was one of our city's most successful black-owned undertakers and funeral directors, with offices located at 898 Florida from 1908 through 1969. An old advertisement bragged about their "prompt service day or night" and also urged potential customers to "call us anytime for an ambulance." Sorry, but if I'm in need of an ambulance, I want it to come from a hospital — not a funeral home. That just doesn't send the right message, if you ask me. **M**

GOT A QUESTION FOR VANCE? *Send it to "Ask Vance" at* MEMPHIS *magazine, 460 Tennessee Street #200, Memphis, TN 38103 or email him at askvance@memphismagazine.com*

ASK VANCE
Our trivia expert solves local mysteries of who, what, when, where, why, and why not.

MEMORIES OF MONK

by VANCE LAUDERDALE

DEAR VANCE: In your December issue, a reader inquired about the "monkey man" she would often see walking down Poplar. I was in college here in the early 1960s, and I assume many people remember "Monk." He was a diminutive man, who carried several canes through his belt like swords, and was a member of a well-known Memphis family. They let him do his thing, as he was quite independent. We all noticed him and talked about him. — R.D., MEMPHIS.

DEAR R.D.: Despite the many visits I paid to the finest colleges in Europe (well, I didn't actually attend any classes at them, but I did stroll through their campuses and purchased some very nice t-shirts), sometimes my brain just fails me. My team of psychiatrists has come up with a name for my all-too-common condition, which I think they have termed "stupidity."

Yes, I admit it. How stupid of me not to make the connection between the "monkey man" and "Monk" — one of our city's most colorful characters for 30 years, and maybe longer. Our own magazine actually published a profile of this fellow back in 1979, written by my pal Susan Turley, and it was one heckuva interview since Tony Cassatta — yep, that was his real name — had plenty to say, all right, but not many things that actually made sense. In fact, the story was rather cryptically titled "Who Is This Man?: The Secret Life of Memphis' Most Visible Eccentric."

That was before I came along, you see.

His attire was as distinctive, in its own way, as my own. "You can find him bundled in four or five wool shirts on days when the blacktop is hot as a skillet," wrote Turley. "And you can find him bent over his walking stick, an oversized baseball cap cocked on

46 • ASK VANCE II

his head, a stub of a cigar protruding from his small, furrowed face, tapping on car windows." Monk, whom Turley said stood less than four feet tall, claimed to walk 50 miles a day, selling pencils, magnolia blossoms plucked from neighbors' trees, whatever he felt like doing. One reader recalled first seeing him in the late 1950s: "We called him 'Monk' because he looked like a monkey." The name stuck.

Turley determined that Cassatta was born in Italy in 1905. Despite rumors that he lived on the streets, every night he walked home to a neat bungalow in Midtown, where he lived with his brother and sister, who didn't want their names mentioned in the magazine article. When Cassatta was growing up, he "always seemed a little bit different," they told Turley. "He's slow, but he's not dumb," said his sister. "He speaks two languages, English and Italian, so he can't be that slow." Her explanation for her brother's layers and layers of old clothing? "He gets cold."

Cassatta's own reason? "Low blood."

Turley followed Monk around for an afternoon, but the man who would spend his days standing in the middle of Poplar shouting at cars clammed up around the reporter. He supposedly was an expert on baseball, but at the end of the day, she admitted, "We really know little more about Monk than we did three hours before."

That's a shame. The fellow she called "an eccentric constant in a faddish universe" passed away some time in the early 1980s. Or so I heard. I couldn't find an exact date, and something tells me Monk wouldn't have cared, anyway.

THE SPEEDWAY

DEAR VANCE: When I was a teenager, my grandmother would reminisce about her childhood in Olive Branch and the trips she made to Memphis. She often spoke of a street called the Speedway. Where was this street, and why would it have been important? — P.U., MEMPHIS

DEAR P.U.: The Speedway was never the real name of a street. Instead, in the early 1900s, it was a mile-long stretch of North Parkway, beginning just west of present-day University. And it was called the Speedway because that perfectly straight section of the road became an informal racetrack for anyone and everyone who thought they had the fastest horse in town. Much like certain streets (I won't mention any names) are used today as drag strips for youngsters with hopped-up cars and motorcycles. Many a night I've had to hide the keys from the Lauderdale chauffeur to keep him from racing our vintage Hispano-Suiza. Such a showoff. Why, he's older than the car!

The Speedway was a popular hangout in its day, especially on weekend afternoons, so I can see why your grandmother would have remembered it. But as the newfangled automobiles began to take over the city streets, the old racecourse was shut down, though the name still lives on, since that general section of North Parkway has signs proclaiming it the Speedway Terrace Historic District. And for many years, a pharmacy in the area carried the name Speedway Drugs, which never failed to amuse certain friends who — how to say this? — enjoyed the benefits of many, many medications without troubling with prescriptions for them.

What's interesting — to me, and probably *only* to me — is that the postcard manufacturers of the day (many of them out-of-town firms) often confused North Parkway with East Parkway. As a result, quite a few postcards supposedly showing "The Speedway" (such as the one you see here) actually depict East Parkway, not North. I'm certainly glad I never, ever make mistakes like that.

WHERE WAS THE WHITE HOUSE?

DEAR VANCE: When I was growing up in Memphis in the 1950s, I vaguely recall a big motel on Summer called the White House. Where was this establishment? — T.L., MEMPHIS

DEAR T.L.: At first I thought you were surely mistaken. I have written about Summer Avenue — certainly one of our city's most colorful boulevards — many, many times in this column and have never encountered a single mention of any establishment called the White House Motel. But the Lauderdales and others who journeyed up and down that busy street in the 1950s must have turned to look at the glitzy new establishment developer Kemmons Wilson was building on the south side of Summer, just east of Mendenhall — a little venture he happened to called Holiday Inn — and never glanced back across the street. For if they did, they would have noticed a large, two-story house, and a group of half a dozen tourist cottages neatly arranged along a semi-circular drive. And they would have seen a pair of big signs out front proclaiming this the White House Motel. From the name, we can presume the big house was, indeed, painted white.

Unfortunately, I don't have a lot of information on this place, though I did manage to turn up a blurry old postcard in the basement archives of the Lauderdale Library (above). I believe it opened in the mid-1940s, and back then, when the city limits stopped at Graham, that was considered pretty far outside of town. The owner, Allen B. Robertson, lived there with his wife, Mary. It was actually a good location, luring visitors as they first drove into Memphis along Highways 64 and 70, and nearby were other attractions, such as the Bon Air Nightclub, Gamel's Drive-in, and the Biagi Restaurant. And according to the back of the postcard, the White House offered "quiet comfort and moderate rates." Who could ask for more?

But Allen and Mary Robertson must have looked across the street at the workers erecting the gleaming new Holiday Inn and realized their days were numbered. By 1966, the city directories no longer have a listing for the White House Motel, and the following year Robertson himself was listed as "retired." Not many places could compete, it seems, with "America's Innkeeper." **M**

GOT A QUESTION FOR VANCE? *Send it to "Ask Vance" at* MEMPHIS *magazine, 460 Tennessee Street #200, Memphis, TN 38103 or email him at askvance@memphismagazine.com*

ASK VANCE
Our trivia expert solves local mysteries of who, what, when, where, why, and why not
by VANCE LAUDERDALE

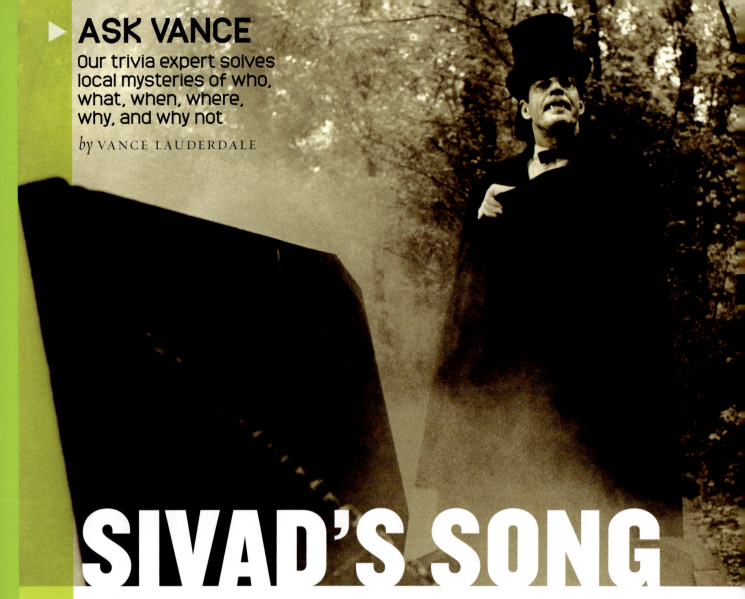

SIVAD'S SONG

DEAR VANCE: Regarding your December column that included questions you could not answer, the theme music to *Fantastic Features* was "Music of the Spheres," composed by Leith Stevens. It is from the 1950s science-fiction movie *Destination Moon*.
— J. AND R.C., GERMANTOWN.

DEAR J. AND R.C.: As Sivad, the spooky host of *Fantastic Features* would say, "Gooooooooood!" Since December, I have had several readers, including my pal and fellow history buff John King, tell me about this eerie theme music, which — for reasons that are hard to explain — has intrigued more than half a dozen of my readers in recent months. Sorry for the pun, but something about it apparently struck a chord with them, so they would write to me, and pester me like all get-out. I couldn't help them, and it just broke my heart. I would go to my lonely bed in the evening and actually cry myself to sleep. Of course, I do that most nights anyway, so I really can't blame Sivad.

Most people reading this column surely remember *Fantastic Features*, the creepy show that aired Friday evenings on WHBQ-TV Channel 13, showcasing the best (and sometimes hilariously worst) horror and sci-fi movies of the day. I can remember watching *The Blob, Dracula vs. Frankenstein, Caltiki: The Immortal Monster,* and dozens of others that may seem funny now, but were pretty scary at the time. In fact, WHBQ even changed the show's airtime from 6 p.m. to 10:20 p.m. after parents complained their kids were getting nightmares.

What made the show so memorable though, was its spooky "Monster of Ceremonies," a funereal figure called Sivad (in real life, a rather normal-looking WHBQ promotions guy named Watson Davis — "Sivad" is "Davis" spelled backwards, you see). Everyone, it seems, remembers the opening scenes of Sivad, clad in a black cape and top hat, driving an ancient hearse through a misty forest (actually Overton Park).

For such a weird show, you'd think the music would be weird too, and I suppose it was, but it was written by an award-winning composer named Leith Stevens (1909-1970), who worked on more than a hundred Hollywood films and TV episodes. Quite a few of them have become classics, such as *Lost in Space, Twilight Zone,* and *Gunsmoke*. Others, such as *Night of the Ghouls* and *Earth vs. the Flying Saucers*, were more forgettable. But even *Destination Earth*, for which he composed "Music of the Spheres," was considered a pretty good movie in its day, and received an Academy Award for "Best Special Effects" and a Golden Globe for "Best Motion Picture Score," among other honors. According to the Internet Movie Database, the plot involved "a private businessman who arranges for an expedition to the moon before the Russians get there first." I never saw this movie, but I'm already confused. If they were trying to get to the moon, then why is the movie called *Destination Earth*?

Okay, now here's a real treat. If you'd like to hear the actual *Fantastic Features* theme song for yourself, a Sivad fan named Mathew Smith has set up a website, and you can click on a link and hear (and even watch) the show's intro (www.mlcsmith.com/people/sivad/index.html). Gosh-a-mighty, where would we be without the Internet?

I think Sivad (or Watson Davis)

would surely be pleased — if not downright astonished — by the continuing interest in the character he created almost on a whim. After the show went off the air in 1969, he retired to Clarendon, Arkansas. Many people tried to get him to dress up as Sivad just one more time, but he always said, "No. I buried him a long time ago." Davis died in 2005, but his memory lives on. In fact, I'd go so far as to say, if you haven't heard of Sivad, then you can't really call yourself a real Memphian.

WHERE WAS WOOLWORTH'S?

DEAR VANCE: I seem to remember two Woolworth's in downtown Memphis in the 1960s. I know there was one on North Main, between Jefferson and Court. But I am more sketchy about the one on South Main. Where was that one? — R.G., MEMPHIS.

DEAR R.G.: No great mystery here. According to the 1960s city directories, Memphis indeed had two Woolworth's on the same street. One was located, as you said, at 59 North Main (shown here), and the other was located at 107 South Main. I remember them well, because that is where Mother would purchase my lederhosen that made me the envy of my classmates. They would even hurl pebbles at me, as just one way of showing their envy.

Begun in 1879, Woolworth's was one of the country's oldest and largest department store chains. I'm not exactly sure when the two stores here opened on Main Street, but it wasn't until 1949 that Memphis got a third Woolworth's, this one on Cleveland near the Sears Crosstown building. In the 1960s, the company branched out with a "budget" version, called Woolco, which was hugely successful for a while, anchoring the new Eastgate Shopping Center. But one after another, they all closed. The South Main store shut its doors in the late 1960s, I believe, and the North Main location managed to survive until the 1990s. In 2001, every Woolworth's in North America closed, and the company changed its name to — this may surprise you — Foot Locker.

SO LONG, SIESTA

DEAR VANCE: I found an old 1960s postcard for the Green Acres Motel, and have never heard of it. Have you? — J.C., MEMPHIS.

DEAR J.C.: When Father was drinking, it was usually a good idea, I discovered, to spend the night away from the mansion, because he tended to annoy me by asking all sorts of personal things, like when was I going to get a job, or go on a first date, or move out of the house. Goodness, I was only 35 — give the kid a break, I would say.

So, to escape from this constant harassment, I became pretty familiar with all the cheap hotels and motels in the area, and — like you, J.C. — had never encountered any place calling itself Green Acres. But the back of the card proclaimed that it was on Highway 70 (Summer Avenue) "5 Miles East of City Limits" so I hopped in the Daimler-Benz one day, set the odometer, and drove precisely five miles beyond White Station Road, which would have been close to the city limits back then. Nothing. So I drove for six miles. Then seven. Just as I was about to give up, I came across the very buildings shown on the card, but sadly rundown, and now called the Siesta Motel.

If you squint carefully at the postcard, you can make out "Air Conditioned Café" on the building at the left, and those words are still dimly visible beneath the last coat of white paint. Don't plan on dining there, though, because the place has been closed for years and "For Sale" signs are posted all over it. In its day, the Green Acres supposedly earned a 99 rating from some group the postcard only identifies as "NAA." Nowadays, I don't think it would come close to that. In fact, I think we'll be bidding an "Adios" to the old Siesta Motel pretty soon.

GOT A QUESTION FOR VANCE? *Send it to "Ask Vance" at* MEMPHIS *magazine, 460 Tennessee Street #200, Memphis, TN 38103 or email him at askvance@memphismagazine.com*

▶ **ASK VANCE**
Our trivia expert solves local mysteries of who, what, when, where, why, and why not.

PAPPY'S PLACE

by VANCE LAUDERDALE

DEAR VANCE: In your December issue, a woman wrote that her husband claimed a restaurant called Pappy's never existed. Well, he is mistaken, because I ate there many times. It stood at the corner of Poplar and Hollywood. — F.T., MEMPHIS.

DEAR F.T.: Well . . . yes and no. It's true that Pappy and Jimmy's Restaurant stood on that corner, identified by one of the greatest neon signs in Memphis history — a surreal creation that depicted a pair of giant lobsters with the human heads of Pappy and Jimmy. The flickering neon caused the lobster claws to click open and shut, an awful sight that gave me nightmares for years.

But that wasn't the establishment my reader was questioning. Her husband had, for reasons only he can explain, doubted the existence of one of our city's most famous eateries, a landmark that stood on Madison for almost half a century. Anyone who lived in Memphis from the 1940s through the 1980s surely remembers Pappy's Lobster Shack at 2100 Madison, a ramshackle establishment created by a man who became known as "The Lobster King," "The Mayor of Overton Square," and — considering he was still working at age 100 — "The Oldest Active Chef in America."

His name was Lehman C. Sammons, but everybody knew him as Pappy.

This remarkable gentleman was born in 1879 in Dancyville, Tennessee, and was sent to Memphis at the age of 10 because, as he later told a reporter, "My family couldn't afford to feed me." Perhaps those hunger pangs inspired him to spend the next 90 years of his life working around food. He promptly got a job as a dishwasher with the old John Gaston Restaurant, which stood at Court Square, and over the years worked at many other eateries around town. He once told an interviewer that in his entire life he probably spent only 30 days in school, but it didn't really matter, because Sammons — oh, let's just call him Pappy here — seemed to have plenty of brains, and a real knack for being involved with successful restaurants.

He opened a hamburger stand at Calhoun and Front in 1910 and later moved to a better location across the street from the old Union Station. There he met quite a few show business people, and his little restaurant became extraordinarily popular with entertainers passing through town. "You know how show business folks and baseball players will travel with food news?" he asked a reporter. "They are just like buzzards. They know where a dead mule is all the time." I'm sure he meant that in the best possible way.

In fact, it was the famed singer Sophie Tucker, a lady who called herself "the last of the red-hot mamas," who first told him about a delicacy being served at restaurants in New England — lobster. Pappy imported some to Memphis, and though it took a few years for people here to realize that such an ugly creature actually tasted pretty good, it soon became the most popular item on his menu.

Pappy retired from the food business in the 1940s, but quickly got bored and decided to team up with his pal Jimmy Mounce to open a new restaurant on Madison, much farther east than any of his previous

PAPPY SAMMONS in the 1960s with two feathered friends. Don't worry — duck wasn't on the Shack's menu.

ventures. He bought a pair of houses just west of Cooper, joined them together, and in 1947 opened Pappy and Jimmy's Lobster Shack. The "Jimmy" was Jimmy Mounce — not, as lots of folks believe, one of Pappy's kids.

By all accounts, it was an astonishing place. Everybody today talks about the amazing assortment of "stuff" at The Rendezvous, but apparently that couldn't hold a candle to Pappy's antiques, which filled every room of the cluttered restaurant: clocks, guns, musical instruments, paintings, moose antlers, antique mirrors — even a pair of aviator Amelia Earhart's flying boots (or so he claimed). Over the years, the unusual place continued to attract celebrities, and Pappy was friends with such stars as Tyrone Power, Tommy and Jimmy Dorsey, Dizzy Dean, Yogi Berra, and countless others.

At the time, this stretch of Madison was still residential, and neighbors complained about bootlegging and the loud music pouring from the jukebox. But among Pappy's many pals was a certain fellow named E.H. Crump, who decided there was no bootlegging and the jukebox wasn't loud. In fact, Crump declared that Pappy "ran a high-class place," so Pappy's stayed open and the neighbors shut up. Pappy eventually bought two more houses and somehow linked them all together, so that he could accommodate as many as 400 diners — and most nights he did.

"Long before there was an Overton Square, Madison near Cooper was known throughout the country for Pappy's Lobster Shack," said an old *Memphis Press-Scimitar* article. "It was here that movie stars, celebrities, and just plain folks all dined when they were in Memphis. And regardless of who they were, Pappy Sammons greeted them individually and made them feel special."

My pal Ruth Hendrix worked at Overton Square in the early 1970s and showed me an old Pappy's menu (right) she had saved. We don't know the date of this, but for such a small place, it served an astonishing variety of food, at equally astonishing prices: broiled Maine lobster for just $5.50, swordfish steak for $2.50, T-bone steak for $4.80, along with shrimp, chicken, clams, catfish, and ham. How many places today, I wonder, serve turtle soup (a bowl was just 50 cents) or fried jumbo frog legs (rather pricey at $3.85)? And for dessert, I can't recall any restaurant that ever offered something called "Chitlins & Marshmallows — Stuffed." Yum!

Pappy and Jimmy opened a second restaurant in 1952 at Poplar and Hollywood. For some reason, they went their separate ways a few years later, and Mounce took over the Poplar location while Pappy took charge of the Lobster Shack — and took Jimmy's name off the place. As far as I know, the original Shack never had that crazy lobster-headed sign, though the image appeared on the menus.

Pappy himself suffered a setback in March 1962 when a blaze destroyed most of the Lobster

THE LOBSTER SHACK after the 1962 fire.

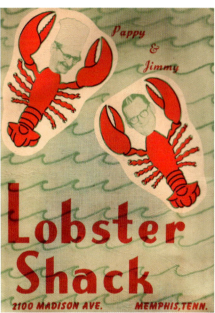

Shack. Most people would have just called it quits — after all, by this time Pappy was 80 years old! But after a few months, he reopened, though he had to replace more than $100,000 in antiques alone. I've never seen a decent picture of the entire place, but after the fire the *Press-Scimitar* ran a photo of the westernmost portion, which would be rebuilt (top).

In the 1970s, the entertainment district called Overton Square began to develop around the old Lobster Shack. Pappy enjoyed his status as the "mayor" of the area, and on April 25, 1979, a parade was held in honor of his 100th birthday. There were all sorts of activities, and the president of the Memphis Restaurant Association presented him with a plaque officially declaring him "the oldest active chef in the world."

I'm sorry to tell you that Pappy would not enjoy the honor long. He died one month to the day after his 100th birthday. His daughter, Mrs. William Huntzicker, ran the restaurant for a few more years, but eventually it became too much work for her. "When Daddy and I shared the responsibility, it was different," she told the *Press-Scimitar*, "but it is too confining now." One of her father's greatest concerns, she said, was that Pappy's beloved Shack would close after his death, but what could she do? She closed the doors in late 1980. The building was eventually razed, and is now a parking lot next to Paulette's. I imagine bits and pieces of it — and all the amazing things displayed inside — wound up in homes across the city.

The other Pappy and Jimmy's, the one on Poplar, is also gone. Under new ownership, it moved into a new building on Summer, just past I-240, taking the magnificent lobster sign along. But it just wasn't the same, and that restaurant closed in the mid-1990s. The sign, by now missing most of its flashing neon, remained standing for years afterwards, but it got blown down in the great windstorm of 2003.

The former Pappy and Jimmy's site at the corner of Hollywood is now a Sonic drive-in. It has its own distinctive architecture, that's for sure, but nothing can ever hold a candle to that lobster-headed sign with the clicking claws. I still have nightmares about that from time to time. Of course, those could be the result of eating too many chitlins and marshmallows before bedtime. **M**

GOT A QUESTION FOR VANCE? *Send it to "Ask Vance" at* MEMPHIS *magazine, 460 Tennessee Street #200, Memphis, TN 38103 or email him at askvance@memphismagazine.com*

ASK VANCE
Our trivia expert solves local mysteries of who, what, when, where, why, and why not.

RALEIGH RUINS

by VANCE LAUDERDALE

DEAR VANCE: Is it true that some remains of the old Raleigh Springs Inn can be found in a patch of woods north of James Road?
— R.B., MEMPHIS.

DEAR R.B.: Well, it's possible, because some overgrown and decidedly snaky ruins could be seen the last time I was there — which was 20 years ago — but I know the owner of that land isn't too keen on people wandering all over his private property, so if you go searching and get arrested and imprisoned, then you certainly didn't read about any of this here. That's what my attorneys told me to say.

The place was just called the Raleigh Inn, though the springs were what lured people from all over the region to this astonishing resort — one of the fanciest places ever seen in Shelby County.

The water in Raleigh, you see, acquired a reputation for curing people of all sorts of ailments. Sometime in the early 1800s, a family traveling along the old stagecoach road (now James Road) stopped overnight because their baby had fallen ill. They found several natural springs in the woods, bathed the child in the cool water, and the next day — so the story goes — the child was cured. That's the legend behind Raleigh's most famous spring, appropriately called the Baby Spring, and the Raleigh Springs soon became a mecca for Memphis society, who journeyed out into the country to "take the waters." After all, whether it cured you or not, it had to taste better than Memphis

52 • ASK VANCE II

water, which — in the days before we stumbled onto our artesian water supply — came from cisterns and muddy wells.

As early as 1842, a Raleigh businessman named David Coleman built a hotel near the springs, and in 1866 another hotel owner persuaded (meaning: paid) a St. Louis doctor to testify that the water did indeed have medicinal value: "The compounding of so many valuable minerals in such a happy combination guarantees to the invalid that the Great Apothecary, the God of Nature, has designed them for the healing of these creatures who, by violating His laws of health, have rendered medical aid necessary." Or so he said.

In other words, drinking clean water was good for you.

Events changed dramatically in 1892, when the tobacco-rich Duke family of North Carolina decided to erect a grand hotel (left) in the ravine just north of James Road. Costing more than $100,000 — an astonishing sum

at the time — the Raleigh Inn was a rambling wooden structure, four stories tall, with turrets and balconies and verandas and all sorts of things to make visitors ooh and aah and proclaim it the most beautiful thing they had ever seen. This was long before the Lauderdale Mansion was built, I hope you'll remember.

The springs themselves were enhanced with graceful gazebos, all linked to the hotel with stone paths that wound through the deep woods. Orchestras played here on weekends, dancers flocked to the Raleigh Inn's grand ballroom, and Raleigh became the place to be.

Then it all came to an end. The water table dropped, and the springs dried up. And Memphians found their own source of water, so they didn't have to make the long trek to Raleigh anymore. Sitting on the veranda of the Raleigh Inn wasn't really much fun compared to the thrilling roller-coaster rides at the new East End Park, or the amazing "moving pictures" they were beginning to show on Main Street.

The old hotel closed and was converted into the Maddox Seminary for Young Ladies, and a few years later turned into the James Sanitarium. On the night of May 14, 1912, a patient smoking in bed set the place on fire, and the hotel burned to the ground. That was ironic, considering that one of the goals of treatment at the sanitarium was to battle addiction to tobacco. And even more ironic considering the building was constructed in the first place by a family who made millions from tobacco.

The hotel/school/sanitarium site was abandoned, and the old springhouses tumbled down. Many years ago, the landowner showed me around the property, and if you knew where to look, you could kick through the underbrush and find piles of charcoal where the inn had once stood. And you could also find the ruins of an old gazebo, all vine-covered and creepy, along with the bullet-riddled tin roof of the old Umbrella Spring (left). But as I said, that was years ago, and today I think all that remains of the Raleigh Inn are memories.

CHECKING ON THE CHICKS

DEAR VANCE: Who did the Memphis Chicks play on the night of May 4, 1957, and what was the score? — B.K., MEMPHIS.

DEAR B.K.: When I received your query, my immediate response was to lie back in my La-Z-Boy and ponder why this particular game — out of all the hundreds of games played by the Chicks in their long history — so intrigued you. I spent several days pondering this mystery, anything to keep me from actually answering the question, you see.

Because how was I to know the answer? Ever since those humiliating days on the school playground, when I was the unsuspecting victim of cruel dodgeball attacks, I have avoided all contact with sports. It's not that my godlike body is incapable of athletic endeavors; I'm just doing what my highly paid therapists advise, that's all.

So I turned your question over to my pal John Guinozzo, author of the fact-filled *Memphis Baseball Encyclopedia*, who also operates the Guinozzo Center for Baseball Research. As you probably gathered, this gentleman knows anything and everything about sports in Memphis — heck, probably anywhere. And sure enough, within a matter of minutes, he told me this:

"On May 4, 1957 (a Saturday), Memphis beat Nashville 3-2 before a low-capacity crowd of 713."

GEORGE SHUBA

And then, just to amaze me further, John added: "The time of the game was 2:03. George Shuba scored all three runs, including a first-inning home run and the game winner in the eighth as Harry Perkowski picked up the win in relief. He ended the game (2-0 record) by striking out a batter in the ninth and then walking a batter, and then forced the next batter to hit into a 1-4-3 inning-ending, game-ending double play."

I was beginning to think that John himself was actually there that day and somehow remembered all this.

And finally, he added this: "The temperature was nearly 90 degrees, and that same afternoon, Iron Liege nosed out the field and won the Kentucky Derby."

Whew! That was more than you asked for, wasn't it, B.K.? But just to show you that I did contribute *something* to this month's column, I scrambled over to the Special Collections Department at the University of Memphis — without any assistance whatsoever — and, after rooting through their files for about 15 minutes, managed to turn up a pretty nice photo of the Chicks star that day, George Shuba (above). Nicknamed "Shotgun" Shuba, this outfielder had recently joined the Chicks after a seven-year stint with the World Series champs Brooklyn Dodgers. I really like that old Indian chief design on his sleeve, don't you? In fact, I'm thinking about adding it to my cape. It would look swell next to the Lauderdale family crest. **M**

GOT A QUESTION FOR VANCE? *Send it to "Ask Vance" at* MEMPHIS *magazine, 460 Tennessee Street #200, Memphis, TN 38103 or email him at askvance@memphismagazine.com*

ASK VANCE
Our trivia expert solves local mysteries of who, what, when, where, why, and why not.

DANCING DAYS

by VANCE LAUDERDALE

DEAR VANCE: Everyone is trying to figure out ways to improve the Mid-South Fairgrounds, but so far no one has mentioned an obvious solution — a casino. Didn't the fairgrounds have a nice casino back in the 1930s?
— B.C., MEMPHIS.

DEAR B.C.: The Mid-South Fairgrounds, and its predecessor, the Tri-State Fair, had marvels that drew visitors from as far away as Bald Knob, Arkansas. Not many people know this, but such popular attractions as Seattle's Space Needle, the St. Louis Arch, Rock City, and even Mammoth Cave were originally constructed at our local fairgrounds. But, then as now, we just couldn't decide what to do with them, so we sold them to other communities who made better use of them. Moving the caverns, in fact, proved such a mammoth undertaking that their original name — Sparkly Cave — was changed to Mammoth.

Wait — I'm told that some of this information may be incorrect. Darn these Internet sites, with their faulty information. Let me look into that Space Needle entry. I think the others are correct.

But we certainly *did* have a casino, though it wasn't the gambling kind. (*Webster*: "a building or room used for social amusements.")

Instead, it was a huge, domed dancehall, built alongside East Parkway, which acquired the name "The Showplace of the South." The place was constructed in 1930 by a fellow named Lynn Welcher for $100,000 — an enormous sum in those days, whereas today it is little more than a day's wages for me. Some of that high cost came from a fancy teak and rosewood inlaid dance floor that was mounted on felt, which gave it a nice bounce when you did the Jersey Hop or the rhumba. Long before the days of discos, there was also a remote-controlled lighting system — operated from the orchestra stand — that flashed precisely 96 (I guess they couldn't squeeze in 100) colored lights off a spinning glass ball dangling from the ceiling.

The Fairgrounds Casino thrived for two decades, with crowds drawn by such big-name acts as Louis Armstrong and Kay Starr. In the 1950s, when the big-band era was drawing to a close, the place was turned over to a new manager named Dick Morton, who told reporters he was initiating a new policy: no drinking. He told the *Memphis Press-Scimitar*, "We believe there are people of all ages who don't drink but do dance, and they would love to have a place where they won't be bumped around by a bunch of drunks."

I'm afraid he was referring to the Lauderdales. The casino was one of our favorite hangouts, one of the few places our notoriously reclusive family would venture in public. But the only way you could get my eldest sister, Vancetta, on the dance floor to perform her spirited version of the cha-cha was to get her liquored up. More liquored up than usual, I mean. (She eventually disgraced the family — which took some doing, let me tell you — by running off with that bowling-ball salesman.)

You'd think a place as big and beautiful as the Casino would last forever. Why, just look at the place, inside and out, in these wonderful old postcards (left). Well, you'd be wrong. People just lost interest in dancing, and the music finally stopped. The Memphis Park Commission converted the place into a public basketball arena (no word on how those bouncy floors affected dribbling), but the fire marshal eventually considered the ramshackle place a fire hazard. Building inspectors estimated it would cost more than $50,000 to bring the Casino up to code, which really doesn't seem like a lot of money to me, and the city decided it just wasn't worth it. The "South's Most Beautiful Ballroom," as the postcards describe it, was torn down in 1963.

THE T-HOUSE

DEAR VANCE: My family recently purchased an old home on North Evergreen that has a large wooden "T" mounted on the front gable. Do you know what the letter signifies? — J.S., MEMPHIS.

DEAR J.S.: I have some rather bad news for you. In the 1940s, the city health department affixed a giant "T" — just like this one — to homes so ravaged by termites that they were unfit for human habitation. Oh, what a shame your realtor failed to tell you this. Is it too late to get a refund?

I jest, of course. My first response, after driving to your residence and staring at the letter for several hours, is that it bears a remarkable — but not identical — resemblance to the "T" that marks the home, car, garage, boat, or child of any fan of the University of Tennessee. It's certainly not the correct color, but perhaps a later owner repainted it brown. But even the most diehard Vols fans rarely go to the trouble of attaching a "T" permanently to the outside of their homes, which seems to be the case here.

So I wondered if the letter was an initial of a previous owner? Here's what I discovered. According to old city directories, your home was constructed in 1922, and the first owner was Frank G. Woods. No "T" there. But get this: Woods was treasurer of a large woodworking firm in Memphis called Turner-Farber-Love Company. Is it possible that he was so devoted to his job that he put the company's initial on his house? After all, it was a woodworking company, and some of the trim on your house looks pretty fancy.

The firm's president was Franklin Turner, who lived over on Peabody. It's even possible that Woods — bucking for a raise — put the initial of his *boss* on his own house, though I admit that's a stretch.

Okay, so maybe Frank Woods, who lived in your house until 1935, had nothing to do with that "T" (even though it looks original to the house). In 1951, 226 North Evergreen was purchased by a new owner, Lamar T. Morton. Maybe Lamar didn't like his first name, and went by his middle name, Thomas or Thaddeus or whatever, and he put *that* on his house (though most people, I confess, would put the initial of their *last* name on their property). And then there's the last owner, Wilford I. McCalla — yet another "T" to ponder. There's just one problem with that one. His wife occupied the property until you bought it, J.S., and I believe you told me she knew nothing about the mysterious letter.

And neither do I. Nothing that I can find about the history of your house reveals a meaning for that "T." So, until I know otherwise, let's just go with UT. Or Tulane. Or Tulsa. Or Tufts. Or Texas. Or . . . **M**

GOT A QUESTION FOR VANCE? *Send it to "Ask Vance" at* MEMPHIS *magazine, 460 Tennessee Street #200, Memphis, TN 38103 or email him at askvance@memphismagazine.com*

ASK VANCE
Our trivia expert solves local mysteries of who, what, when, where, why, and why not.

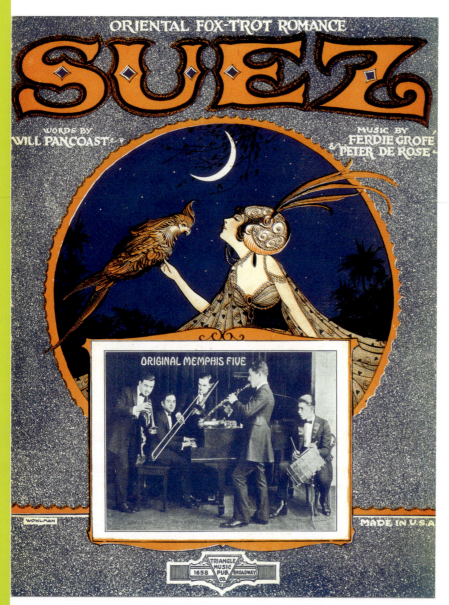

MUSIC MEN

by VANCE LAUDERDALE

DEAR VANCE: At a local yard sale, I picked up a scratched 78 rpm record for a group called the Original Memphis Five. What do you know about this Memphis band? — K.F., MEMPHIS.

DEAR K.F.: Oh, the memories this brings back, buried in my subconscious after years of psychotherapy and electro-shock treatments. The Original Memphis Five were the Lauderdale family's favorite performers. Many nights, locked away in my little bedroom in the mansion tower, I would place one of their tunes on my old gramophone and skip around the room, entranced by their melodies.

In fact, for a music recital held when I was 15, I chose one of their most popular songs — "Suez," described as "the Oriental fox-trot romance" — and sang it to the half-dozen guests crammed into the Lauderdale ballroom. To this day, I can remember the soaring refrain ("Suez, wondrous Suez, where I was captured with your love sigh / All day, and through the night, to be with you I cry"). And when I hit that final word "cry" in my soaring falsetto, well, there wasn't a dry eye in the house. Whether from the beauty of my voice, or my innovative harmonica solo that followed, it's hard to say. I can still see my Aunt Henrietta covering her ears with her blue-veined hands, my performance obviously so beautiful she simply couldn't stand it. Ah, good times!

It wasn't until years later that I learned that the only thing accurate about the name of the Original Memphis Five was the "five" part. First of all, their music wasn't always original. "Suez" was produced by other songwriters, for instance, as were most of their hit songs. And — here's the odd thing — not a single one of their members hailed from Memphis. How they came up with the name of their group, I have no idea.

This much I do know: The Original Memphis Five was a jazz quintet formed in New Orleans around 1917 by trumpet player Phil Napoleon and pianist Frank Signorelli. I guess those two fellows are depicted on the cover of the old sheet music (left), but it doesn't say. Other members included Jimmy Lytell, Charlie Parnelli, and Jack Roth; old photos show the group with a clarinet, trombone, and drums, but I couldn't tell you who played what. It doesn't matter, really. Not to me, anyway.

The Five were incredibly popular through the 1920s and 1930s, cranking out dozens of hit records and selling thousands of pages of sheet music. I can still hum many of their songs, which included such wonderfully titled classics as "Aggravatin' Papa," "Bees Knees," "Don't Pan Me When I'm Gone," "Got To Cool My Doggies Now," "If Your Man Is Like My Man, I Sympathize With You," "I Wish I Could Shimmy Like My Sister Kate," "My Honey's Loving Arms," "That Teasin' Squeezin' Man of Mine," and — my personal favorite — "Whoa, Tillie, Take Your Time!"

I don't know what happened to all the musicians over the years. The only one who really became famous was Phil Napoleon, who later played with the Jimmy Dorsey Orchestra and opened his own nightclub, Napoleon's Retreat, in Miami. According to redhotjazz.com, he died there in 1990.

CHEW ON THIS

DEAR VANCE: When I was a kid, I remember eating Sky Rocket bubblegum that was supposedly made in Memphis. True?
— B.G., MEMPHIS.

DEAR B.G.: How could I possibly know if you are telling the truth about chewing bubblegum when you were a kid? Did we know each other? Did you come to my recitals?

Or are you instead asking about Sky Rocket bubblegum? Oh. Well, I can answer *that* question.

Sky Rocket was indeed manufactured in Memphis, by a firm called the Saymore Company. A fellow named Sam Myar started this little business in 1959, and though I can't say for certain, I believe he realized that his name sounded much like "say more" which (he must have reasoned) made a great name for a candy and gum company. So he purchased a building at 985 Kansas and began to crank out boxloads of Sky Rocket bubblegum in four somewhat unusual flavors: fruit, wintergreen, banana, and cinnamon. Saymore also manufactured hollow-center gumballs in what they called "straight" flavors: orange, grape, and red hot. I know this because I chanced upon an old postcard (above), which told me all this. The postcard cleverly includes a cup and plate, as if you could make a meal out of all this stuff.

All that gum must have kept local dentists busy. It didn't stay in business long at all. By 1965, Sam Myar was no longer listed in the old city directories. Shortly after that, I understand the

facility was acquired by the DonRuss Company (the name forged from the two founders, Donald and Russel Wiener), which became one of this country's largest suppliers of those flat sheets of bubble gum that used to come with baseball cards. I don't know what their slogan was, but something tells me it didn't have quite the ring to it as "Say More!"

DOCTOR DOMAIN

DEAR VANCE: There's an odd-looking house at the corner of Tutwiler and McLean. Somebody told me the back portion once housed a barbershop. Are they right? — J.T., MEMPHIS.

DEAR J.T.: Well, they would be right if this were the 1700s, when barbers and surgeons were often one and the same. But no barbershop ever occupied that corner. Instead, over the years it was first a doctor's office, and then a dentist's office.

A few details: The house was built in 1922. I can't tell you the original owner, but in 1927 the city directories show it occupied by Dr. Charles Polk, who was director of children's hygiene for the Shelby County Board of Health. In 1930, he enlarged his home, adding an office at the back. His residential address was 1852 Tutwiler, but the address of his doctor's office was 650 North McLean, which must have been very confusing for the postman.

Polk treated patients there until 1938, when the property was purchased by a dentist, Gordon B. Ramsey, who lived there with his wife, Martha. Sometime around the late 1960s, another dentist — William Pearson — took over the place. That addition on the back of the house must be larger than it looks, because in later years he not only took in a partner, Allen Johnson, but also began selling Shaklee health-food products out of the house. As recently as 10 years ago, yet another dentist, Thomas Nash, called 650 North McLean home. At least I think he was a dentist; the phone books described his occupation in this cryptic, abbreviated way: "ofcs clns of dntst." I don't know what to make of that. It doesn't matter, though.

The house is now a private residence, so if you've got a toothache — from jawing all that Sky Rocket bubblegum — you'll have to get that cavity filled somewhere else. **M**

GOT A QUESTION FOR VANCE? *Send it to "Ask Vance" at* MEMPHIS *magazine, 460 Tennessee Street #200, Memphis, TN 38103 or email him at askvance@memphismagazine.com*

ASK VANCE
Our trivia expert solves local mysteries of who, what, when, where, why, and why not.

UP TO SNUFF

by VANCE LAUDERDALE

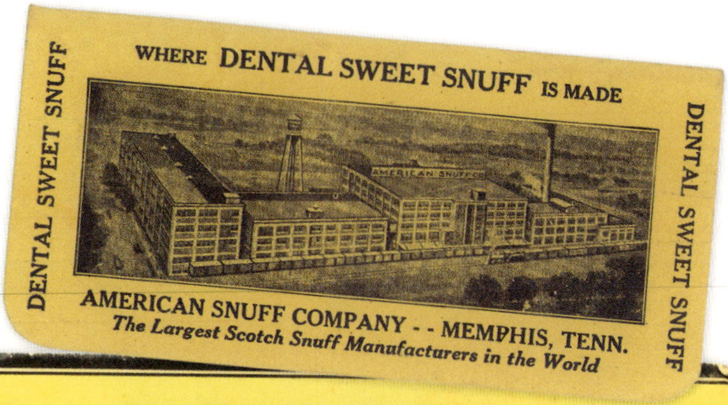

DEAR VANCE: I found an old cardboard fan advertising a product called Dental Snuff, and the Memphis company that made it — the snuff, not the fan (right) — claimed it was the oldest and largest in the world. What was this stuff, anyway?
— C.I., MEMPHIS.

DEAR C.I.: I wish you had never shown me this image. I must tell you that a depressing number of my teenage co-workers glanced at it and said, "Hey Vance, that old man looks just like you, haw haw!" I suppose I really have let myself go, what with slumping in my La-Z-Boy and guzzling Kentucky Nip all day long.

But I'm also dismayed by the sad, twisted life of these two folks. There's the old man, reading a newspaper whose coverage is devoted entirely to news about snuff ("tobacco in its purest form"). Brochures and papers piled on the table are also all about snuff ("a man's chew"), and there's a big can of it sitting under the lamp. And then along comes Grandma, bringing yet another newspaper with bold headlines announcing "Dental Snuff Made of Pure Tobacco."

Clearly, these people pay way too much attention to snuff. I'm glad the image doesn't show the man's grizzled face, which is probably just drooling and dripping with snuff and chewing tobacco. These folks need to branch out, I say, and add cigarettes and booze to their daily addictions.

But some of the claims made on this fan — and hundreds of other promotional items distributed by this company, many in the collection of the Lauderdale Library — are indeed true.

The American Snuff Company actually got its start way back in 1782, when a former Revolutionary War soldier named John Garrett built a snuff mill on a creek somewhere in Delaware. Snuff, you see, is nothing more than finely ground tobacco. In the old days, you would actually sniff it up your nostrils, much like a similar product popular these days with certain Hollywood starlets. Or so I've heard. But most snuff today is actually placed in your mouth ("just a pinch between your cheek and gum" is how one manufacturer puts it). Anyway, Garrett's snuff company evolved into the American Snuff Company, with headquarters in New York. In 1912, for reasons that are never made clear — not to me, anyway — the company relocated to Memphis and built a huge factory here overlooking the river, where it churned out

58 • Ask Vance II

thousands and thousands of the little metal cans of snuff.

"Dental Sweet Snuff is ideal for beginners" explains a handy booklet I have. "It's mighty good, and you'll like it." What do they mean by beginners, I wonder — 5-year-olds? "Have you ever thought what coffee would taste like if made from the whole bean?" they ask, a question that has never occurred to anyone, anywhere. Well, the American Snuff people explain, "This will give you some idea why Dental Snuff is the favorite of tobacco users. In this brand of snuff, you find tobacco at its best." They have lots of handy information in this little booklet, including how to measure a cord of wood, but they never explain the "Dental" part of the name.

Like most tobacco products, though, it's not entirely safe. "Caution," says the booklet. "As snuff is very finely ground, a beginner should be very careful to not inhale or exhale when placing it in the mouth." They then suggest various ways to cram it in, for people who have no common sense whatsoever, and hint, "One way is to use the large blade of a knife for this purpose." For all those "beginners" who carry around giant knives, I suppose.

Snuff in all its various forms became hugely popular, and I suppose it still is. In the 1930s, the American Snuff Company even aired its own national radio program, called *Up To Snuff*. I'm serious! In 1985, the company was restructured and renamed the Conwood Corporation. I was intrigued by the illustration (upper left) on the back of the fan, which showed the sprawling facilities, and was astonished to discover that this huge complex is still standing today, relatively unchanged, at the northwest corner of North Front and Keel.

Oh, I could go on and on, but I have to stop now. It's almost time for the weekly installment of *Up To Snuff*.

FANCY FLORISTS

DEAR VANCE: Look at this old postcard for Idlewild Greenhouses. What happened to this company? — J.K., MEMPHIS.

DEAR J.K.: Well, like many smaller companies around town, it went out of business. But boy, this one managed to last a long time. The card (top right) reveals some interesting details. A handsome brick building, perhaps a former residence, serves as the display and sales office. Next door are rows of glass-sided greenhouses, and a smokestack towers over everything, with the name IDLEWILD painted along its side. The card, as you can clearly see, brags "Over 40 Years Dependable Floral Service," but there's no date, so I can't tell you, exactly, when the company started.

What I *can* tell you is that it is listed in telephone directories as early as 1903, originally located at 89 South Main. The owner wasn't anybody named Idlewild, as you might imagine, but a fellow by the name of Otto Schwill, and the company didn't begin in the Idlewild community in Midtown, so I can't explain the name. You'll just have to live without that bit of information.

An old advertisement mentions their wide range: "cut flowers, corsages, blooming plants, house plants, funeral pieces, displays, flower designs, baskets, and bulbs in season." Like the postcard, it also announces "floral service — day and night." How many florists today, I wonder, stay open all night? And why would you need to? Even if it's for a funeral, surely the flowers can wait until morning, can't they?

In 1910, Idlewild Greenhouses opened a larger operation, the one shown on the card, at the corner of East and Eastmoreland. Their telephone number at the time, back when Memphis had neighborhood "exchanges," was 4980 Hemlock, which I thought was an interesting number for a greenhouse, hemlock being a deadly poisonous plant and all. Idlewild had plenty of competition over the years. In the 1950s, I counted more than 50 florists in business in Memphis. The last owner was Margaret Wilkerson, who ran the place until it closed in 1961. Drive by East and Eastmoreland today, and you won't find a trace of the buildings shown in the postcard. Looks like Idlewild finally went idle.

A VERY COOL BUILDING

DEAR VANCE: I own the property (left) at 620-622 Union and was told it was originally an ice house. Right? — T.B., MEMPHIS.

DEAR T.B.: Well, you're halfway right. Half of the property was an icehouse, but actually only half of the business was devoted to ice, so I guess that makes you one-quarter right.

Perhaps I'd better explain this. In 1935, a fellow named Frank Kaye opened the Kaye Ice Company at 624 Union. There was no listing for 620 or 622, so apparently the street numbering has changed over the years. Just two years later, he expanded his business, now calling his firm the Kaye Ice and Coal Company.

That seems an odd combination of things, if you ask me, sort of like blending fire and water, but Kaye even added two other locations, at 650 East and 999 Jackson. His good fortunes didn't last long. In 1937, the city directories show that 624 Union was vacant. What's more, Frank Kaye seems to have left Memphis entirely, since there's no listing for him, either.

Now, T.B., here's where it gets confusing. The old phone books only list a 624 Union until 1950, when suddenly Manufacturer's Rubber & Supply Company shows up — at 620 Union. A different building, or the same building with new numbering? I can't say. They remain there for more than 40 years. Look carefully, and you can still see their name on the building. But at no time is there any listing for 622 Union.

So — all I can tell you is that half of your property was indeed an ice house. And a coal company, too. As for the other half, I'm stumped. That seems to happen a lot these days. Perhaps a pinch of Dental Snuff will clear the cobwebs. **M**

GOT A QUESTION FOR VANCE? *Send it to "Ask Vance" at* MEMPHIS *magazine, 460 Tennessee Street #200, Memphis, TN 38103 or email him at askvance@memphismagazine.com*

ASK VANCE
Our trivia expert solves local mysteries of who, what, when, where, why, and why not.

DIAL 'N' SMILE

by VANCE LAUDERDALE

DEAR VANCE: When I was a kid, I called a phone number called Dial 'n' Smile. The signoff was "Keep dialing and smiling. Bye-bye, now." Who was this man and how did this get started?
— D.B., MEMPHIS.

DEAR D.B.: J.C. Levy was one of those unusual fellows who actually got pleasure from making other people happy. Nowadays they have medications for his condition, I believe, and while he was alive Levy would certainly not have been welcome at the Lauderdale Mansion. After all, our family crest carries a Scandinavian phrase that translates roughly into "Misery and Sorrow" and it's adorned with images of empty moneybags, dead crows, a broken sword, and a skull. Oh, such wonderful times we had at the reunions!

But Levy was a different sort of person. Born in Amory, Mississippi, in 1906, his parents made a living selling eyeglasses by horse and buggy to planters in the region. At a young age, Levy moved to Memphis, where he first started working for the Illinois Central Railroad, and then changed careers entirely — setting up a professional photography studio just off the lobby of The Peabody.

But in the 1950s, he opened a cluster of kiddie-sized rides at the Mid-South Fairgrounds — a miniature Ferris wheel, a merry-go-round with little cars and motorcycles, and a ride with boats puttering around in a circular basin. After a few years, he moved the rides to the Memphis Zoo, where they were an incredibly popular attraction for almost 40 years. I don't think I've ever met a single person in Memphis who had not ridden at least one of those things. (My personal favorite: the boats, with real steering wheels even though you just cruised in a circle.)

One day, sitting in his office on South Cox, Levy decided to leave a funny message on his answering machine while he went to lunch — a little ditty about Santa Claus since it was close to Christmas. When he got back, he discovered dozens of people had called, mainly just to hear the message, and Levy realized a new chapter in his life had opened.

So in 1971 he began Dial 'n' Smile. Anyone calling 278-2370 heard a cute poem, funny story, animal sounds — whatever struck Levy's fancy.

"Little things pop into my head," he told the *Memphis Press-Scimitar* back in the 1980s. "I like the odd sort of things. Some people call them poems, some call them rhymes, and some just call them terrible."

Here's one example:

Once I met a bullfrog down by the pond.
The bullfrog said, I wonder's what's in the beyond?
And then he jumped, and he jumped,
and he jumped away.
And now he must know what's in the beyond.
Because I heard he croaked today!

And then Levy ended the message with his customary signoff: "Keep dialing and smiling. Bye-bye now!"

Levy never made a dime off Dial 'n' Smile, and at one point estimated his phone bills were $5,000 a year. The demand was so great that he set up a bank of 25 answering machines in his own home. But that didn't bother him. He just liked to make people happy, and plenty of his callers let him know he did just that, year after year.

One time, a 10-year-old girl sent Levy a letter saying she had been calling him every day since she was 3, and said, "I think you're great. I like listening to you better than going with my boyfriend." No comment from the boyfriend.

At one point, Levy estimated he had recorded more than 2,000 different messages, many of them accompanied by roars, bellows, shrieks, and other sounds made by the animals at the zoo (such as the baby elephant, left). "I write a lot of my poems or verses late at night," he told the *Press-Scimitar*. "Often I wake up with an idea and write it down. Then I try them out on my wife at the breakfast table. If she runs for the bucket, I think maybe I have a good one."

Levy died in 1997 at the age of 91. Just before his death, he estimated he had received more than 20 million calls. "He wanted it to go on forever," said his widow, "and *he* wanted to go on forever." But all things come to an end, and she had the Dial 'n' Smile lines disconnected. Don't even bother calling 278-2370 today. All you get is a scratchy recording saying, "The number you have reached is not in service at this time." Not even a "Bye-bye now!"

GOODBYE, GARDEN

DEAR VANCE: Why did they move the Japanese Garden from Overton Park to Audubon Park? — G.L., GERMANTOWN.

DEAR G.L.: They — meaning the Memphis Park Commission — didn't move the park. They didn't have enough shovels and wheelbarrows to do that. Instead, they just obliterated it because of intense anti-Japanese sentiment in the days after the attack on Pearl Harbor.

It's a shame because, as you can see from the old postcard view above, the original Japanese Garden — the one in Overton Park — was a fantastic place, complete with pagodas, lanterns, an arched bridge, and even a concrete replica of what was supposed to be Mount Fujiyama. The whole thing was a gift to the park from Col. Robert Galloway, head of the Memphis Park Commission in the early 1900s. Galloway, who had traveled the world over (much like the Lauderdales), had installed a Japanese-themed tea room in his mansion near the park, and I'm told guests admired it so much that in 1914 he decided to build a Japanese garden in the park. When you're head of the park commission, you can just go ahead and do those things, you see.

After the U.S. entered World War II, though, city officials decided the garden had to go. Various people protested that destroying the garden was "childish" and even the *Memphis Press-Scimitar* argued, "Why not just call it a Chinese garden and let it go?" Well, we couldn't just let it go. That's not the way we do things here. Bulldozers pulled down all the structures and filled in the lake. The Memphis College of Art stands on the site today.

In 1965, a new, less cluttery Japanese garden was added to Memphis Botanic Garden, and the beautiful arched bridge there is probably one of the most photographed sites in our city. Something tells me it's here to stay.

BYGONE BEACH

DEAR VANCE: Where on earth was this giant "Municipal Swimming Pool" (above)?
— K.F., MEMPHIS.

DEAR K.F.: I can give you a very specific location on our planet. Namely, it was at the Mid-South Fairgrounds, just behind Fairview Junior High School. This undated postcard shows the original Fairgrounds pool, a massive complex with white sand beaches, diving towers, and a roped-off deep-water area in the center. Look carefully at the old card: In the background is a warning sign over the dressing rooms that says "All Out When Bell Rings."

This was a safety precaution: Every hour or so, the lifeguards would clang a bell, and everybody had to scamper out of the pool so they could make sure nobody was floating on the bottom. For some reason the city filled in this huge oval pool, sometime in the 1940s or 1950s — nobody ever told me why — and built a considerably smaller one, a rectangular concrete thing. The newer pool stayed busy until just a few years ago, when the city filled in that one too. The last time I checked, the entire site was just a dirt field. Not a very good way to beat the heat, if you ask me.

M

GOT A QUESTION FOR VANCE? *Send it to "Ask Vance" at* MEMPHIS *magazine, 460 Tennessee Street #200, Memphis, TN 38103 or email him at askvance@memphismagazine.com*

ASK VANCE
Our trivia expert solves local mysteries of who, what, when, where, why, and why not.

BELL OF THE BLUFF

by VANCE LAUDERDALE

DEAR VANCE: Was Memphis included on the 1915 tour of the Liberty Bell?
— F.N., MEMPHIS.

DEAR F.N.: I have to confess your query initially baffled me, because I never knew that the Liberty Bell went on a "tour," and I couldn't imagine why anyone would want to send such a big, heavy, and fragile thing around the country. After all, it was already cracked.

But I recently came across a website mention of the 1904 tour of the Liberty Bell, and then discovered that local historian Paul Coppock had devoted a few paragraphs to the Liberty Bell's visit here — not in 1904, but in 1915 — in one of his fine history series.

Early in the 1900s, the keepers of the famous Liberty Bell did indeed send it on tours of the country, so people could, I suppose, feel more patriotic. The 1904 tour shipped it to the World's Fair in St. Louis, with various stops along the way, which I don't think included Memphis. But in 1915, the bell was carried aboard the "Freedom Train" to the Panama-Pacific International Exposition in San Francisco, and on its return journey, it did indeed make an early-morning stop in Memphis at the old Poplar Street Depot. The date was Saturday, November 20th. Coppock reports, "Confederate veterans formed the guard of honor. The biggest unit in the parade was formed by 12,000 city school children, almost every one of them carrying a flag. They sang 'Columbia, the Gem of the Ocean' as they passed the bell."

It's hard to believe that 100,000 people — which would have been just about every man, woman, and child in Memphis back then — would jam downtown to see such a thing, but newspapers reported they did. Some in that crowd even demanded to touch the famous bell, and you can imagine how curators would feel about such things today, but anyone who wanted could get close enough to touch it, caress it, and do anything short of taking a big gong to it. Newspapers later proclaimed that some people actually managed to *kiss* the bell, and "afterwards were seen with a radiant glow on their faces, indicating that one of the ambitions of their lives had been satisfied."

I have quite a few ambitions still to be

62 • ASK VANCE II

fulfilled in my short life, but kissing the Liberty Bell is way down on that list.

In the Lauderdale Library, I turned up a faded postcard showing the bell in Memphis (left). What surprised me is how it was carried aboard the train — just left out in the open, mounted on a flatcar with some kind of tiny umbrella over it, but otherwise left to catch all sorts of dirt and bugs as it rumbled along the tracks.

I know this photo was taken in Memphis, and not one of the many other stops along the 1915 tour, because at the bottom of the picture is a large banner reading "Maury." Readers today may not remember it, but the old building at 272 North Bellevue was one of our city's most distinctive-looking schools, built in an over-blown Beaux Arts style. In fact, we copied that design for the northwest wing of the Lauderdale Mansion — the only part of the home not presently covered in vinyl siding. But times changed, busing took away most of Maury's students, and the wonderful structure was demolished about 10 years ago. The only trace of it is a grassy lot and some crumbling steps.

Regarding the Liberty Bell, despite its rather careless method of transportation, it somehow made its long way back to Philadelphia, and has never left home again.

MAKING WAVES

In the 1960s, Memphis had a boat manufacturer with an Indian name, I believe. Can you help me remember it?
— T.M., MEMPHIS.

DEAR T.M.: Oh, the mind works in very strange ways. At least that's what my doctors tell me on my weekly visits, when they scribble in their charts and look at me with pity. But in the 1960s, Memphis — like so many cities in America — jumped aboard the boating and waterskiing craze, and sure enough some entrepreneurs here began to manufacture a line of watercraft. But you remember the "Indian" name because it had an arrow as the logo, and the company was, in fact, called Arrowglass. The "glass" part refers to the fiberglass used to make the hulls and deck, you see. Here's one of their ads (below left).

The company had a rather convoluted history. Arrowglass was started in 1960 by a group of fellows named Michael Ossorio, P.O. Tipton, and Harry Schmeisser Jr., who opened a manufacturing facility at 1764 Chelsea. After a year or so, they moved into larger space somewhere near the old Firestone Plant. At the time, Ossorio told reporters, "The boating business in this area is growing fantastically. Lack of good boating water is the only thing that could hold the business back."

They originally built only one boat a day, but by the mid-1970s, they were cranking out more than 5,000 hulls a year, and I believe the *Lady Lauderdale* yacht was a custom Arrowglass model. But for reasons I don't understand, the company filed for bankruptcy in 1979. Another investor, Memphis businessman Clarence Day, bought the sinking operation in 1979 and tried to keep it afloat, but — oh, I'm weary of these nautical metaphors. In short, Arrowglass sank, though the boats were so well-built that you may still find them on the water in Sardis, Pickwick, and other places, sporting their distinctive arrow-shaped logo on the stern.

THERESA'S TALE

DEAR VANCE: There's an old gravestone in Calvary Cemetery that has always intrigued me, because it carries a porcelain image of a beautiful little girl. Who was she, and why is she buried all by herself there? — M.N., MEMPHIS.

DEAR M.N.: Queries from readers carry me (with my bodyguard, of course) to cemeteries all over the county. I had also noticed this gravestone (above right), because it's such a striking portrait, rather prominently placed by a corner of the Chapel Hill section at Calvary, where the solemn little girl has gazed out across the other tombstones for almost 90 years now. But I hadn't thought to look into her past until you mentioned it. Here's what little I can tell you.

Theresa Annaratone (it's pronounced "ah-NAIR-a-tone") was born in 1913, possibly in Italy since I was not able to find a Memphis

birth certificate. Italy is where her parents, Ernesto and Petronella Annaratone, were born, moving to Memphis in the early 1900s to work as truck farmers in this area. The family lived on Pendleton, and I believe Theresa had an older brother, Louis, and a younger sister, Iris.

At the age of 6, Theresa developed a condition that the doctors of the day called "pyelitis sepsis" — basically a kidney infection. Nowadays that might not be fatal, but in the days before effective antibiotics (penicillin wasn't discovered until 1928), any infection could be deadly. Theresa died five days later, at midnight, at home. The funeral service, as was common practice back then, was held at home, and the little girl was buried, as you know, at Calvary.

It's true that the rest of the family is not buried beside her, M.N., but don't think they abandoned her. They lived long after her, and the section where the little girl was laid to rest was filled by the time of their own funerals. But just around the corner are the gravestones of Ernesto Annaratone, who died in 1955, and Petronella, who passed away in 1984. Nearby are the graves of Louis Annaratone (1912-1992) and Iris (1916-1986). Their birthdates, you see, made me think they were siblings of Theresa. In fact, scattered throughout Calvary are a good number of gravestones that carry the Annaratone name, at one time a large Italian family in Memphis.

M

GOT A QUESTION FOR VANCE? *Send it to "Ask Vance" at* MEMPHIS *magazine, 460 Tennessee Street #200, Memphis, TN 38103 or email him at askvance@memphismagazine.com*

ASK VANCE
Our trivia expert solves local mysteries of who, what, when, where, why, and why not.

HAPPY DAYS

by VANCE LAUDERDALE

DEAR VANCE: When I was much younger, my parents often took me to a Memphis toy store called Happy Hal's. One year, the place burned down. Whatever happened to Happy Hal and his store?
— K.D., MEMPHIS.

DEAR K.D.: Oh, the pain and suffering your question has caused me — long-repressed memories brought to the surface again.

You see, many years ago, when the Lauderdales were one of the richest families in the land, our Christmases were more elaborate than anything held by those upstart Vanderbilts or Rockefellers. But as the family fortunes declined, so did our celebrations, until they came to an abrupt end.

I can remember the year it happened, too: 1976. One day, several weeks before that final Christmas, Papa bundled me into the Daimler-Benz and said we were driving to the finest toy store in Memphis — Happy Hal's Toys and Gifts — so I could pick out wonderful presents and tell Santa precisely what I wanted. But as we pulled up to the darkened hulk of a building on Beale Street, Papa said, "Uh oh, Vance. The toy store has *burned down*! No Christmas for you, kiddo."

I stared at the charred ruins and blubbered, "But can't I just *tell* Santa what I want *anyway*?"

But Papa replied, "Nope. That's not how it works. Santa's a busy man and needs to know the exact model number and price. Gee, that's a tough break." So we just drove back home, my heart aching.

I clambered onto my little cot in the basement and cried myself to sleep that night, and for many nights afterwards. On Christmas morning, there was not a single present under the scraggly tree for me, and the Lauderdales never celebrated Christmas again.

Sweet frosted cupcakes! You can just imagine how it scarred a sensitive lad like myself. After all, I was barely 27 years old!

I'll answer your question, though it pains me to do so. Born in 1923, Hal Miller (shown above demonstrating a toy called a spud gun to kiddies) was a remarkable gentleman. A graduate of Central High School, he studied at the New York Theater School of Dramatic Arts and earned a degree in drama from Northwestern, and when he returned to Memphis appeared in just about every play in town. Besides acting and singing, he was also — like myself — an award-winning tap dancer.

But his big break came in 1955, when WHBQ-TV made him the host of a children's show called *Snicker Flickers*. Over the years, that program evolved into *The Happy Hal Show*, featuring Miller and a curious puppet he called Lil' Bow, which a reporter once described as "an indistinguishable blue critter." He later told the *Press-Scimitar* that when he first asked the producer what the show would be, he was told "it's not going to be about anything. It's going to be whatever you want it." Audiences liked what Miller offered, for he stayed on the air for the next 17 years, hosting old movies, doing his puppet acts, and showing off the newest toys.

A toy store seemed like a natural step, and in the late 1950s Miller opened his first business at the corner of Bellevue and Lamar. He always claimed he was the first person to bring the Hula-Hoop to the Mid-South, and who's to argue? He moved Happy Hal's Toy Town to various locations in the next few years, eventually settling on a retail store at 1640 Union (where the Art Center is today) and a large wholesale operation at 269 Monroe (shown left, being demolished in the 1970s).

He opened Happy Hal's Toys and Gifts at 666 Beale in 1975, and it was this place that caught fire on the night of September 18, 1976. I couldn't find a photo of that building, but it's just as well, for I learned later that firemen quenched the blaze before too many toys were destroyed, and Miller reopened in time for Christmas. So the place never completely burned down, K.D. — something Papa never told me.

Miller closed his toy operations in 1986 but never really retired. He studied painting at Memphis College of Art and became president of the Memphis-Germantown Art League, which he once said "was one of the highest honors ever bestowed upon me." He passed away in 1997, but anybody who lived here in the 1950s and beyond will always remember the name of Happy Hal.

MARY'S HOME

DEAR VANCE: My aunt used to live in the Mary Galloway Home for Women, and I'm curious: Who was Mary Galloway, anyway? — P.T., MEMPHIS.

DEAR P.T.: In 1898, a group called the Willing Hands Circle of King's Daughters held what old newspapers called "an entertainment" to raise funds to build a home for "mothers, sisters, and wives who have outlived their loved ones." Colonel Robert Galloway, head of the Memphis Park Commission and a mover-and-shaker in so many other ways in our city, also made a sizeable donation. Two years later, a brand-new retirement home, built in the Spanish Revival style (below), opened at the southwest corner of Monroe and Manassas, named after Galloway's wife, Mary.

The Mary Galloway Home for Aged Women was a wonderful haven for 22 women, but it quickly became overcrowded. An addition increased capacity to 30 in 1934, but with more than three dozen people on the waiting list, none of them getting any younger, the home's owners began to look for more space. That search took quite some time. In 1946, newspaper clippings revealed that a new Mary Galloway Home would be built on Poplar, just west of Perkins. That plan fell through. In 1955, newspapers reported the home would move to a site on North Graham. Nope, that didn't happen either. Finally, in 1957, administrators bought land at 5389 Poplar, east of Estate, and more than 30 residents moved into their new home in June 1961.

The Mary Galloway Home, still going strong after more than a century, has since moved again, this time to Appling Care Lane in Cordova. The Poplar location is now an automobile dealership. And the original site across from Forrest Park is today a vacant lot.

PARKING PLACE

DEAR VANCE: What happened to the National Garage, as shown on this old matchbook cover? It's a grand-looking building, but I've never heard of it. — G.H., GERMANTOWN.

DEAR G.H.: Since the Lauderdales rarely left our estate without the protection of our chauffeur-driven limousines, I paid scant attention to public parking garages used by the common folk. But judging from the artwork on the matchbook cover, this was indeed quite a fine building. And as you might expect, it's gone now.

The National Garage, the very name telling you that it was part of a national chain, opened in 1927 at the northeast corner of Front and Court, replacing a row of older and smaller buildings that housed various cotton firms and Koehler Brothers Construction Company. It was eight stories tall, steam-heated according to the matchbook, and for several years even included a Gulf station that provided "complete service for your car."

In 1962, or thereabouts, the building became All-Right Parking, one of many such places around our city. It remained in business until the early 1980s, when it was demolished to make way for the Morgan-Keegan Tower. At one time, if I remember correctly, there were plans to build two matching towers. As a result, the site of the former garage remained vacant for years, but it is now occupied by a parking lot. How appropriate. **M**

GOT A QUESTION FOR VANCE? *Send it to "Ask Vance" at* MEMPHIS *magazine, 460 Tennessee Street #200, Memphis, TN 38103 or email him at askvance@memphismagazine.com*

The Mary Galloway Home for Aged Women, Memphis, Tenn.

ASK VANCE
Our trivia expert solves local mysteries of who, what, when, where, why, and why not.

GETTING AHEAD

by VANCE LAUDERDALE

DEAR VANCE: While I was looking through the old *Memphis Press-Scimitar* files at the University of Memphis library, I came across references to a restaurant on Poplar that was topped with a giant statue of the owner. What do you know of this curious establishment?
— B.K., GERMANTOWN.

DEAR B.K.: Let me just tell my half-dozen readers that I recognize the initials B.K. as belonging to my pal, Bonnie Kourvelas, the talented host of the WKNO-TV series *Southern Routes* and producer of several of WKNO's *Memphis Memoirs* segments. Bonnie is an accomplished historian in her own right, so I knew that if she tossed something my way, it would be especially intriguing.

So I did what I always do when faced with such a challenge. I read her letter, thought to myself, "Oh, this can't possibly be true," and resumed my daily 19-hour naps in my special "Vance Lauderdale" limited-edition La-Z-Boy.

After a few weeks of dawdling in this fashion, I grudgingly pulled myself out of my comfy chair and headed over to the U of M library, to see what the heck Bonnie was talking about. And that's when I found the picture of The Giant Head. As you can see, she wasn't making this up.

Bonnie tells me that she was actually researching the local Greek Orthodox community and the Greek Food Festival held every May at the Annunciation Greek Orthodox Church on Highland. And yet tucked into the old *Press-Scimitar* files were several photos and news clippings about a rather enterprising fellow named John George Morris (above). Despite his somewhat British-sounding name, I assume Morris was Greek, and that explains why he and his Giant Head ended up in the Greek Orthodox files.

Here's what I found out. Morris, a former attorney, was the co-owner of a fairly successful restaurant at 1380 Jackson Avenue called the Riviera Grill. In 1949, he purchased Friedel's, a restaurant that had opened some 10 years earlier at 3135 Poplar, right across from East High School.

Now here's where things began to get just a little strange. For reasons that were never explained, Morris and his co-owner, James Bryonis, decided to name their new establishment "The Old Master Says." Who is the "Old Master" and what, exactly, does he say? I have no idea. But Morris told reporters that he planned to spend $75,000 — a large sum in those days — to jazz up the place. Among other things, he added booths everywhere ("having found that people like to eat in semi-privacy"), bought one of the city's first Seeburg 100-selection jukeboxes, painted the walls peach and cherry, and — this always signifies a classy establishment — put up mirrored columns.

What's more, he announced that the popular hostess at the Riviera Grill, Verna DeShazo ("who was chosen Miss Restaurant of 1948") would come to The Old Master Says, and according to Morris, "the other waitresses will be almost as pretty." My, I bet that made those women feel special. *Almost* as pretty.

But then came the most astonishing feature of all. Morris first commissioned noted Memphis artist Burton Callicott to sculpt a life-size bust of himself, dressed in a suit and tie. Then, using a mathematical process that the newspapers called "miraculous," the proportions of this bust were increased so that designer Mike Abt could construct a 14-foot version, built of "gypsum composition on metal lathe," which would somehow be placed on the *roof* of the new restaurant. Abt, who has been mentioned in this column many times, was the Tech High School art teacher who designed most of the elaborate Cotton Carnival floats year after year, so this was right up his alley.

"It's the biggest bust that's ever hit this part of the country," Abt told the *Press-Scimitar*. "I don't know of any as big on the face of the earth — unless it's the head of the Statue of Liberty."

Morris admitted he had been pondering various ways to promote his new restaurant's trademarked motto, "Good Food at Popular Prices," when he thought, "Just put *me* up there." He told reporters, "It will be unique — maybe even grotesque." Well, he was right about that. The big head, which would be "criss-crossed by flashing floodlights at night," would certainly have been one of the strangest buildings in Memphis — especially since, if you ask me, the head looked more like Chairman Mao than Morris.

Now here's the real mystery. I found old photographs of the restaurant just when it opened (opposite page), and pictures of the bust when it was still under construction (below). But I have never found anybody who remembers if The Giant Head was ever placed atop the restaurant. It pains me to say it, but I suspect the restaurant was — get ready for it — a bust.

And another element of this mystery is: What happened to Morris? The Old Master Says restaurant opened in March 1949. It was no longer listed in the city directories in 1951, which means it stayed open for only one year, maybe less. And Morris himself was no longer in the telephone books in 1951, which suggests he either passed away or moved elsewhere. That same year, his Riviera Grill also passed into new ownership, taken over by a trio of Greeks: Nicholas Koleas, Pete Futris, and Steve Ritsos. That building, much altered, today houses the offices of Memphis City Councilman Joe Brown.

Dobbs House took over the establishment on Poplar and operated it as Dobbs House #4 for several years before transforming it into one of our city's first theme restaurants — the much-loved Luau. And it too had a giant head, not on top of the building, but out front by the entrance. That one was modeled after the stone heads found in Polynesia, instead of the ambitous John George Morris.

Today the building is a paint store — an appropriate use, I guess, for a place with such a colorful history.

CLUB QUESTION

DEAR VANCE: My family says that one of the "hot spots" of downtown Memphis was the Catholic Club, where they held dances and all sorts of fun activities. Where was this place, and what happened to it? — M.G., MEMPHIS.

DEAR M.G.: I'm not sure "hot spot" would be the best way to describe what was essentially an athletic club operated by the Catholic Church, but the building certainly offered plenty of entertainment options for its members.

I managed to find an old magazine advertisement (above) for the club, which was constructed in 1923 at a cost of $600,000. Located at the southeast corner of Third and Adams, the handsome six-story building was described as "one of the best-equipped club buildings in the South and includes every

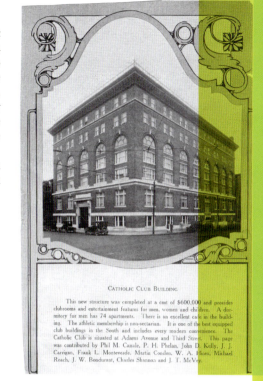

modern convenience." Inside, you could find a complete gymnasium, bowling alleys, billiard room, swimming pool, dance rooms, an "excellent café," and even a rooftop garden. The top floors contained 74 spacious apartments that could be rented by members. The *Press-Scimitar* proclaimed it "the hub of Catholic activity in Memphis."

But it didn't stay that way for very long. A later newspaper article noted "a long history of financial troubles," and in 1939 the building was auctioned off for precisely $39,056. I remember tales of that fateful day when the Lauderdales went to that auction and bid $39,000. We thought we had won the property, and then we got outbid at the last minute by just $56. It annoyed Papa for years, and was just one of the reasons he left the church, I believe. Well, that and the drinking.

According to old newspaper articles, there was talk about converting the empty building into Juvenile Court offices, or even using the site for a new Federal Reserve Bank. None of that came to pass, and the structure stood empty for years. Meanwhile, former club members bought property on Helene Road in East Memphis, and built a more modern — though much smaller — club, which is still in use today.

The downtown Catholic Club building fell to the wrecking crews in the early 1980s. A plaza for the One Memphis Place office building, described by the authors of *Memphis: An Architectural Guide* as "a glassy black box," occupies the site today. **M**

GOT A QUESTION FOR VANCE? *Send it to "Ask Vance" at* MEMPHIS *magazine, 460 Tennessee Street #200, Memphis, TN 38103 or email him at askvance@memphismagazine.com*

ASK VANCE
Our trivia expert solves local mysteries of who, what, when, where, why, and why not.

CRASH IN CROSSTOWN

by VANCE LAUDERDALE

DEAR VANCE: Is it true that a bomber actually crashed in the middle of Memphis during World War II?
— G.F., MEMPHIS.

DEAR G.F.: I knew that a B-24 crashed in a field near Millington during the war, but I had never heard of such a disaster taking place in Memphis and assumed people had confused the two incidents. But then I discovered that April 29, 1944, was a dark day in our city's history.

Just before 11 o'clock that morning, people in the vicinity of Poplar and Cleveland looked up when they noticed a U.S. Army B-25 bomber in distress. Some witnesses said the twin-engine plane actually flipped over and was flying upside down; others said the engines were sputtering or had quit completely.

W.D. Parr was standing outside a gas station on North Cleveland when he saw the plane falling from the sky. "I thought it was going to hit me," he told reporters. "I was running one way, then the other, trying to dodge it. The plane was zigzagging, seemed to straighten out for a second, then nosed almost straight down into a house."

The Commercial Appeal conveyed the horror of what happened next: "The brief staccato bark of a dying motor, a plane plummeting earthward, the terrible sound of impact, a dense cloud of black oil-smoke billowing skyward."

Piloted by a Memphian, Capt. Ralph Quale, the B-25 was on a training flight with just two other men aboard — Flight Officer Glenn Trickel of Memphis and Lt. Leon Kleinman of Dallas — when the engine failed minutes away from landing at Memphis Municipal Airport. The plane plunged within a hundred feet of Tech High School, and the pilot desperately tried to land in the parking lot behind Southern Bowling Lanes on Cleveland. By all accounts, Quale heroically steered the doomed aircraft away from residential areas, but it smashed into a two-story home at 222 North Claybrook behind the bowling alley.

As you can imagine, the scene was utter chaos. The newspaper described "a maelstrom of shouting, running people; of siren-screaming fire apparatus and ambulances; of semi-hysterical women; of grim-faced men who wanted to do something but couldn't."

The women had good reason to be "semi-hysterical." That house was occupied that morning, and everyone in it was killed instantly. The victims included 23-year-old Norman Cobb, his 22-year-old wife Naomi, their 2-year-old daughter Garlene, and another resident, 55-year-old Beatrice Withers. In an ironic twist, Cobb worked as an air traffic controller for the airport; he was home that morning because his shift didn't begin until 4 p.m.

Brave citizens managed to pull two bodies from the plane wreckage before it exploded in a fireball of gasoline flames and smoke. The first firemen on the scene showed up within minutes in unusual gear — baseball jerseys and cleats — because they had been playing a game at nearby Hodges Field against the Navy's Shore Patrol when they saw the crash.

Everyone that day talked about near-misses. Victim Beatrice Withers' sister, Mary, had just left the house to go to the bank; she was walking two blocks away when she heard the explosion. R.D. Pillow lived at 318 North Claybrook. "I heard a tremendous crash and the ground shook," he told reporters. "I ran to the window and saw the bomber crashed into the backyard of the house next door." Pillow's own home was scorched by fire. Two doors away, some young boys were climbing in a tree when the plane clipped the branches and crashed. "A piece of the plane hit me," said Francis Shepperd, showing reporters a gash on his leg, "and oil splashed on us. The plane fell all around us."

It took the fire department, aided by special chemical units from the airport, hours to quench the flames (left). No one ever determined the cause of the accident. The pilot never reported any problem with the airplane, and the B-25 had just been inspected and overhauled six days before. An officer with the Army's Accident Investigation Committee admitted, "I am as much at a loss as to the cause of the crash as the general public."

In the days that followed, more than 20,000 Memphians visited the crash site, and the Army brought in MPs to control the crowds. Although seven lives were lost, everyone breathed a sigh of relief that the plane had somehow missed Tech High, the Southern Bowling Lanes, Sears Crosstown, and dozens of nearby businesses that would have made the death toll much higher.

Today, there is no trace of the tragedy. The wrecked homes on Claybrook were rebuilt. Southern Bowling Lanes closed in the 1960s, though the building and parking lot remain. The seven victims were buried — Beatrice Withers in Forest Hill Cemetery here, the others in New York, Indiana, and Washington, D.C. And most people, it seems, have no memory of the worst aviation disaster in Memphis history.

GRAVE MYSTERY

DEAR VANCE: What do you make of this unusual grave marker I found near Eads (top)? Was this for a person, or a pet?
— M.M., GERMANTOWN.

DEAR M.M.: Well, I don't think any descendants of Charles Pink Belt — for that was his full name — would like you calling him a pet. But I can see why you might think that. This particular gravestone, located in the Bethany Church Cemetery south of Eads, is barely a foot wide, and I'm not clear why it left off his first name. Perhaps Charles just liked being called "Pink."

Belt was a carpenter, living on Dempster Road in South Memphis. He died of tuberculosis on February 8, 1950, at the age of 67. Although his death certificate listed him as a widower, I found no reference to his wife in my searches, and I don't believe there are other Belt family members buried nearby. He was laid to rest pretty far from home, but I presume he was a member of Bethany Christian Church, which stands across the road from the cemetery.

ORIENTAL INFLUENCE

DEAR VANCE: When I was a kid, my parents took us to a nice restaurant in South Memphis called Wilma's. I can't find any listing for it in old phone books. Can you help? — D.G., MEMPHIS.

DEAR D.G.: Not if you are determined to find an establishment called Wilma's, for no such place existed. But if you are remembering a nice eatery called Wilmoth's, keep reading.

Charlie Wilmoth opened his first Wilmoth's at 2265 Park in the late 1950s, and in 1962 he opened a brand-new establishment at 1985 South Third, in the Southgate Shopping Center (below). With its all-glass façade and undulating roofline, it was certainly distinctive, and a *Memphis Press-Scimitar* story said, "The restaurant's modernistic design shows the influence of the Orient in its architecture."

Inside, Wilmoth's featured "an atmosphere of quiet spaciousness calculated to satisfy the most delicate of digestive systems." I have no idea what that means, exactly, but presume the place was mighty swanky.

Despite its exotic architecture, the food was pretty basic. "Memphis is a meat-and-potatoes town," Wilmoth told a reporter. His new restaurant was a success, but he had one concern — too many customers: "I just didn't count on so many people so soon, but it's the most encouraging problem a man in my business can have."

A few years later, Wilmoth opened a third establishment, this time a cafeteria, on South Perkins. But eventually all those customers faded away and all of his restaurants closed. If any trace remains on South Third of his "oriental"-designed eatery, I haven't been able to find it. **M**

GOT A QUESTION FOR VANCE? *Send it to "Ask Vance" at* MEMPHIS *magazine, 460 Tennessee Street #200, Memphis, TN 38103 or email him at askvance@memphismagazine.com, and for even more from Vance, visit his new blog:*
www.memphismagazine.com/askvanceblog

ASK VANCE
Our trivia expert solves local mysteries of who, what, when, where, why, and why not.

by VANCE LAUDERDALE

AT YOUR SERVICE

DEAR VANCE: In the May issue of *Memphis* magazine, you ran a photograph of an old Pure gas station on Madison. Was this little green building (right) on South Front Street also an old gas station?
— D.N., Memphis.

Dear D.N.: Yes. As I mentioned several months ago, in my typically long-winded way (it's called getting paid-by-the-word, folks), the Pure Oil Company came up with an "English Cottage" architectural style for all their gas stations as a way of 1) appealing to weary motorists, and 2) standing out from the competition.

Very few of the original stations remain standing, but this one at the corner of South Front and G.E. Patterson has somehow survived. My research (which means digging through old telephone directories), shows that this particular Pure Oil station was opened in 1939 — four years later than the one on Madison — by a fellow named Henry Halbert.

The first years of its ownership are a bit confusing. In 1935, brothers William and Reginald Willingham opened a Pure gas station at 836 South Third, which they named the Mid-South Service Station. Yes, I know what you're thinking — it's not a very original name, is it?

According to the phone books, Halbert took over that station in 1939 and also opened the one at 528 South Front, which he called — are you ready? — Mid-South Service Station #2. I recently spent dozens of dollars to obtain a really fine photo of this station (above) from the Pure Oil Company archives, which shows this location when it was brand new. It's a nice-looking building, that's for sure, and if you squint you can see that the operators left the cash register *outside*, on a little table by the arched front door. Also

by the front door was one of the old "honor system" Coca-Cola dispensers. You opened the lid, swirled your hand through ice-cold water, and pulled out a chilled bottle of Coke. Then — in theory, at least — you paid the station owner.

Also notice the pole-mounted spotlight, the old-timey dome-topped gasoline pumps, and over at the right, somebody may be trying to fill up a bicycle tire. In the background

70 • ASK VANCE II

is Central Station, with its landmark smokestack, looking just as it does today.

Henry Halbert didn't run this station very long. By 1943, the phone books list him as a machinist, and a few years later he's a salesman for Ostrov Auto Parts. During the early 1940s, the gas station was owned and operated by William Willingham, who had owned Mid-South Service Station #1, as you may recall if you were reading carefully. I don't know what Willingham had been doing in the intervening years, and I don't know where his brother Reginald went, but William took over both stations — on South Third and on South Front — and ran them for the next 30 years or so.

I don't really know how long the gas station on South Third survived; the site is now a Taco Bell. But I can tell you that the building on South Front went through various owners and uses — at one time in the early 1980s serving as a truck-leasing facility. In 1999, it was purchased by a nice fellow named Kris Kourdouvelis, who also owns the handsome brick building around the corner, at 36 G.E. Patterson, which at one time served as a post office facility. He lives in that larger building, and uses the old gas station for storage. Preserving it has certainly been a challenge. "I put a new roof on it a few months ago," he told me, "and then a big windstorm blew off some of the new shingles."

I hope Kourdouvelis can save it. Like the old Pure station on Madison, it adds a bit of whimsy to downtown Memphis. And we can all use more of that.

THE BEAR FACTS

DEAR VANCE: Most local history buffs know that the Memphis Zoo got started with one animal — a bear. But what actually happened to that bear? — K.D., Memphis.

Dear K.D.: Oh, it's a wonderful, heartwarming story, one you should read to your children at night. The bear, whose name was Natch (short for Natchez, I'm told), was actually acquired by a local businessman named A. B. Carruthers, who owned a wholesale shoe company, among other ventures. I should probably explain that the bear himself never said his name was Natch; some *person* gave him that name.

Anyway, back to my story. Carruthers, like most sensible businessmen, really had no need, or use, for a fully grown bear, so he chained it to a tree in Overton Park, where (as you might imagine), it became quite a curiosity. Civic leaders, seeing the chance to make a buck off this thing (some things never change), decided to collect an assortment of other creatures from around the region, and so Natch was indeed the first animal at the newly formed Memphis Zoo, a rather motley collection of iron cages when it opened in 1905.

For awhile, so I understand, Natch served as the unofficial mascot for a baseball team here, but historian Paul Coppock (where I've gotten most of this information) says the bear was so unruly that he was quickly returned to the zoo. Good grief, he was a bear, people — not a kitten.

But Natch didn't entertain visitors very long. On the cold night of January 15, 1908, some ruffians broke into the zoo and poisoned the poor creature.

Wait, did I say this was going to be a happy story? I meant, unhappy. Very unhappy. Sorry.

Despite the loss of its star attraction, the zoo managed to survive, and the Lauderdale Library has a very interesting little booklet (right) that describes in wondrous detail every animal on display at the Memphis Zoo in 1908 — just three years after it opened. It's a curious publication, barely four inches tall, filled with old and odd advertisements for Blue Seal Ice Cream, Waukesha Silurian Water ("the purest mineral water on earth"), Zellner Faultless Footwear, and other oddities. What's more, the booklet — published by a group called the Chickasaw Bureau of Publicity — doesn't seem to be written in English. Or at least not easy-to-understand English. For example, the zoo's new director is mentioned in this fashion: "Since the inception of the Zoo, which is fast becoming a feature of Memphis' advance toward metropolitism, never has its permanency and future development been as certain as the advent of season of 1908, which introduces to us a most efficient management in the persons of Mr. E.K. Reitmeyer and his able assistant, Mr. Wynne Cullen."

At any rate, the booklet describes precisely 42 exhibits at the zoo that year. Some of them are fairly impressive creatures. Cage 14 held an elephant that Memphis schoolchildren, in a citywide contest, named "Margarita" and the booklet takes pain to note that the naming contest "was carried on by columns of the *News-Scimitar*, which is and remains the zoo's champion." What's more, "she is a perfect pet and can be ridden by anyone." The elephant was purchased by Robert Galloway and J.T. Willingham, members of the Memphis Park Commission, from Ringling Bros. Circus for precisely $1,700. Something tells me elephants probably cost a bit more these days. Cage 15 held "one of the handsomest of the Bactrian camels, donated to the zoo by Al Chymia Shrine Temple, who received it as a donation from the famous scout, Pawnee

Bill." I vaguely recall that one of the Lauderdales once got into a shootout with that Pawnee Bill rascal, but I'd rather not go into that here. And then Cage 16 held a lion, named Polly, "who was donated by the Hoadley Ice Cream Company of Memphis." The booklet doesn't bother to explain just why, or how, an ice cream company acquired a fully grown lion.

Back then, it seems, nearly all the creatures had names. A tiger in Cage 17 was called "Samantha" and the booklet notes, "She is a jungle-bred animal and quite docile." A few cages away, though, are a pair of Mexican tigers, "which are vicious and untameable." I sure hope nobody ever got those tigers mixed up at feeding time.

The other animals included parrots, monkeys, alligators, sea lions, lots of snakes, and something called "banana rats." The last cage contained the most thrilling display of all: wild chickens. Yes, I said chickens, and the booklet claimed they were "very rare." Maybe so, but look, they're still chickens. I'm glad the zoo has, over the years, managed to acquire a much finer collection of animals. **M**

GOT A QUESTION FOR VANCE? *Send it to "Ask Vance" at* MEMPHIS *magazine, 460 Tennessee Street #200, Memphis, TN 38103 or email him at askvance@memphismagazine.com, and for even more from Vance, visit his new blog: www.memphismagazine.com/askvanceblog*

▶ ASK VANCE

Our trivia expert solves local mysteries of who, what, when, where, why, and why not.

RIVERSIDE REVISION?

by VANCE LAUDERDALE

DEAR VANCE: With all this talk of improving the riverfront with Bass Pro Shops, One Beale, and other developments, what became of the Riverview Project of the 1960s?
— T.J., Memphis

DEAR T.J.: *Bound for Glory: The Complete History of the Lauderdales in America* (24 vols.) devotes less than a paragraph to this most embarrassing chapter in my family's history.

In the 1950s, sensing that the riverfront area just north of the bridges, which was occupied by a warren of crooked streets and tumbledown houses, needed revamping, my family stepped in with a bold plan. They would build a residential complex and shopping mall paying tribute to the Lauderdales. There would be a museum devoted to the life-changing role the Lauderdales had played in the worlds of medicine, physics, engineering, and roller-skating. An art gallery would showcase paint-by-number portraits of the family members who had made their marks in society. And a row of stately apartment buildings would be named for the most illustrious members of the Lauderdales.

There was just one hitch with this grand scheme. The Lauderdales, it seemed, have always been a rather shiftless bunch — loaded with money, sure — but with little to show for it. One day, we gathered together to select the members of our family who would be honored by the new development, and we couldn't come up with a single worthy person. Not one.

This was before I had returned from Europe, I hope you understand.

So Father backed out of the project

in a huff, taking with him the whopping $12,500 he had planned to invest in it. The plans were turned over to the Memphis Housing Authority, who acted like it had been their idea all along, and renamed it the Riverview Urban Renewal Project (left). Describing it as "a thing of beauty to be created along the river," the MHA announced the 136-acre complex would include a grouping of three high-rise apartments just north of the three Mississippi River bridges, a 35,000-square-foot shopping center, pedestrian walkways, and lots of other bits and pieces that were never fully explained. Not to me, anyway.

One of the most unusual features was to be a circular restaurant overlooking the river (below left). An artist's rendering shows this building, which looks mighty precarious to me, perched on the edge of the bluffs. And ugly, too.

The whole thing would be a "parklike development." The problem with such a bold plan was that the area where MHA wanted to put it was already occupied by more than 530 buildings, which would have to be purchased one by one. The projected cost would exceed $30 million, and some of those people, as you might imagine, weren't too eager to move. The other problem was that the new I-240 expressway was being pushed through the area, to tie in with the Memphis-Arkansas Bridge and then link up with Riverside Drive, which forced a complete redesign of most of the streets in the area.

I found a 1959 *Memphis Press-Scimitar* article about the project, and though I frowned and squinted, could not comprehend the poorly drawn map of the proposed site. And the description doesn't help in the least: "At the south end, Harbor Street will be extended in a southeasterly direction to join with McLemore, which will be extended from its present terminal point near Kansas." What? Look on a map today, and none of that will make sense at all.

PLANE FACTS

DEAR VANCE: In the 1940s, people flew in and out of Memphis on C&S Air Lines. What happened to C&S?
— T.F., Memphis.

DEAR T.F.: It's still around today, sort of. Most people know it as Delta Air Lines. And unlike other companies, Delta likes "Air Lines" spelled as two words. I don't know why.

The "C&S" stood for Chicago and Southern, and though this was one of the first major airlines — if not *the* first — to

operate out of Memphis Municipal Airport, I have to admit I've never really understood the convoluted history of the company.

I consulted a local aviation authority — a third-grader at Sea Isle Elementary School who builds model planes — and he told me that C&S actually got started in the 1930s as Pacific Seaboard Air Lines, operating in California. Through some complicated business merger that I can't possibly explain here (or anywhere else), the owner of Pacific Seaboard, a fellow named Carleton Putnam, acquired the right to deliver airmail from Chicago to New Orleans, with stops along the way — including Memphis. Putnam wisely figured that an airline called Pacific Seaboard would not attract many passengers flying in this area, so in 1934 he changed the name to the Chicago & Southern. The airline's slogan was "The Valley Level Route," which makes absolutely no sense to me. For one thing, valleys aren't level. That's what *makes* them valleys. And if you're up in an airplane, what do you care about the valleys anyway?

The Lauderdale Library contains a rather handsome "flight kit" for C&S Air Lines from the 1940s, containing luggage labels (above), route maps (so you could make sure the pilot knew where he was going), flight schedules, and other handy booklets. Keep in mind that back then, many people had never flown on an airplane, so these materials are filled with helpful advice, such as what to expect "Just After Takeoff." Among other things, "Anywhere from two to six minutes after takeoff you will probably notice a change in the beat of the engines and the airplane will seem to slow down." Although first-time flyers no doubt thought the plane was crashing, "this is caused by the captain's changing the pitch of the propellers — just like shifting gears in your car." Okay. Whew!

And when it's time to land? "A few minutes from the airport you may notice a slight rocking motion of the ship." OH NO! — ha, just kidding. "This is caused by the landing wheels being brought down out of the wings, where they have been since takeoff." Those wheels are a pretty important part of landing, you see.

What's also interesting is the flight kit contains postcards "which will be mailed without charge by the stewardess" and it encourages passengers to wander around and pester everyone else on the plane: "Just get up and be a pedestrian. There may be fellow travelers who would welcome a visitor." Why, *of course* they would. And if you've brought a squalling kid on board? Just call the stewardess and "she'll come a' running with 'Chux' and powder." Chux were disposable diapers, in case you were wondering.

In 1953, the old Chicago & Southern merged with Delta Air Lines. Delta still operates today around the country, of course, but something tells me the flight attendants won't "come a running" if your kid's diaper needs changing. **M**

GOT A QUESTION FOR VANCE? *Send it to "Ask Vance" at* MEMPHIS *magazine, 460 Tennessee Street #200, Memphis, TN 38103 or email him at askvance@memphismagazine.com, and for even more from Vance, visit his new blog: www.memphismagazine.com/askvanceblog*

ASK VANCE

Our trivia expert solves local mysteries of who, what, when, where, why, and why not.

by VANCE LAUDERDALE

FLUTE PICKER

DEAR VANCE: In the 1960s and '70s, I remember a very flamboyant flute player who performed just about everywhere in Memphis, but now I can't recall his name. Who was this musician, and what happened to him? — G.H., Memphis.

DEAR G.H.: When I was but a little tyke, I competed in the Mid-South Fair Talent Show, playing "Rocky Top" on my beloved oboe. A newspaper critic the next day noted my performance "caused tears of pain" among the audience — I assume he meant "heartache" because the sounds I created were so moving. But what he inexplicably failed to mention was my compelling stage presence. Realizing that an oboe solo is not the most visual of treats, I attached ostrich feathers to my arms and legs, and also to both ends of the oboe. It was really something to see, I promise you.

I bring this up because the musician you remember so vividly, G.H., also used feathers as a sort of trademark image. Whether he got the idea from me, I cannot say, but I like to think so.

You are no doubt thinking of Edwin Hubbard, a talented fellow who fronted his own bluegrass/jazz band, served as musical director for Going to Market, and was artist-in-residence for Calvary Episcopal Church, among many other ventures. Hubbard played a flute, but he disdained the terms flutist or flautist, preferring to call himself a "flute picker."

Space — or lack of it — prevents me from describing his entire remarkable career, so I'll just touch on the highlights here. Hubbard was born in 1936 in Hot Springs, Arkansas, and when he was just 7 years old was already playing saxophone with his father and grandfather in a little group called the Hubbard Orchestra. In high school he organized two separate swing bands for the casinos operating in Hot Springs at the time.

Hubbard got an appointment to West Point, but later told reporters, "I thought the sound of the flute was infinitely sweeter than the sound of a howitzer." Instead, he went to Louisiana State University, where he earned a master's degree in music and served as drum major for the LSU band. After a stint in the Army, he signed on as the musical director for a summer variety series for NBC called *Dean Martin Presents Country Music*. When the show ended, he went on tour with banjo player Douglass Dillard (of "Dueling Banjos" fame) and fiddler John Hartford. One of their stops was the Miss Nude World Pageant in Canada, and yes, they performed naked.

"The entire audience was nude," Hubbard blithely explained to *The Commercial Appeal*. "The contestants were nude. It would not have been appropriate at all for us to have appeared clothed."

Somewhere along the way, Hubbard came up with his signature look. He later told a reporter, "An Indian gave me a clutch of beautiful eagle feathers, saying, 'They will give your music strength.' I told him, 'Thanks, I need all of that I can get.'" Hubbard dangled them

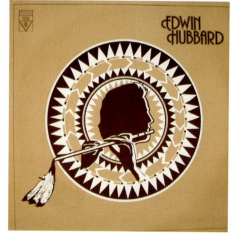

from the end of his flute with a long string and was never seen without them.

In the mid-1960s, Hubbard moved to Memphis, where he opened the Pepper Jingle Company, recording snappy commercials for radio. He also served as a backup musician for just about everybody who recorded in Memphis, including Elvis Presley and Isaac Hayes. By the early 1970s, the *Memphis Press-Scimitar* said Hubbard "was considered about the most in-demand musician in his field." He organized a group called Prana, a yoga term meaning "a sort of life force — a high-energy feeling," and newspaper articles claimed he was "the first to bring about a fusion of bluegrass and jazz." The people who came to his concerts "are going to get a Prana charge, and they don't even know it," he told a reporter.

Hubbard was named musical director of the open-air marketplace on Winchester called Going to Market, but that venture folded after just a year, and he was forced to "recover, get my bearings, and find a new direction." The recovery didn't take long. Within months, Hubbard was performing weekly at the Hyatt Regency and other venues around town, and he began to work on what he called the "Afro-billy sound," a fusion of African, jazz, and bluegrass. "Your music takes you where it goes, or where it wants you to go, he said, "if you give it a life of its own." He also released an album, simply titled *Edwin Hubbard*, and was named artist-in-residence at Calvary Episcopal Church.

Throughout the 1980s and 1990s, Hubbard would emerge from what the newspapers called his "sylvan retreat" near Germantown to perform around town. New challenges beckoned, and on the evening of March 22, 1997, the 61-year-old Hubbard was auditioning at the Germantown Performing Arts Centre for the role of conductor of the Germantown Symphony Orchestra. At intermission, he went to his dressing room, where the concertmaster found him dead from an apparent heart attack. He had just finished conducting Mozart's *Requiem* — also known as the funeral mass.

COLLINS QUESTION

DEAR VANCE: I found an old package of "freezing mix" and noticed the manufacturer was Clyde Collins of Memphis. I could not find any information on this company. Can you help? — H.M., Memphis.

DEAR H.M.: Thank you for mailing me the actual package. I will return it to you just as soon as my requisition for a stamp is approved.

I wasn't even sure what "freezing mix" was, but the colorful packet helpfully explains it's for making vanilla-flavored frozen desserts: "Just mix with sugar, milk, and cream." On the back, the package takes on a considerably more personal tone, urging the customer, "Try me. Guaranteed to please or double your money back." Who could resist such an offer?

I had never heard of Clyde Collins Inc., and assumed it was some mom-and-pop business, perhaps run out of somebody's garage. So imagine my surprise when I made a trip to the University of Memphis Special Collections Department and discovered a folder of *Memphis Press-Scimitar* clippings describing a massive operation that had been in business since 1916.

That's when Clyde Collins, founder and chairman of the board, moved into three buildings at the corner of Monroe and Lauderdale and — according to one article — began manufacturing "extracts, home drinks, jams, jellies, preserves, mayonnaise, salad dressings, condiments, table syrup, soda water flavorings, and baker's flavorings." And also freezing mix, apparently. Beside the production plant on Monroe, Collins also owned five warehouses throughout the city and distributed a separate line of food products under their "O-Boy" brand.

In fact, at one point, they got into a lawsuit with a St. Louis company, who felt that Collins' "Eat-Um-Aid" soft-drink mix sounded a bit too similar to their own "Like-M-Aid" drink. I don't know how that was resolved, though.

In 1947, Collins announced plans to build two huge new plants in Memphis, and hired local architect Dudley Jones to design a pair of stunning concrete-and-glass buildings that would occupy more than 100,000 square feet. The new facilities, described by the *Press-Scimitar* as "tremendous," would "embody the finest and most modern factory features."

The newspaper didn't give a clue just where these new factories would be constructed — probably because Collins hadn't yet purchased the land. In addition to a "vast amount of pumping and storage equipment," each building would include "modernistic displays, comfortable lounge furniture, and attractive recreation rooms." The Collins name would be carried in giant letters across the roof.

For some reason, though, those grand plans never left the drawing board. The Clyde Collins Company remained on Monroe for about 10 more years, when the firm apparently went out of business. For a couple of years, the sprawling plant was taken over by the redundantly named Leon-Leon Cigar Company. Today, it houses the Wonder Bread factory, without question the most fragrant-smelling building in Memphis. **M**

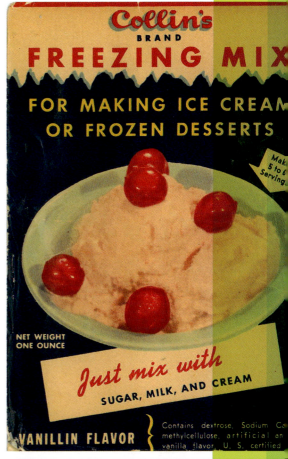

GOT A QUESTION FOR VANCE? *Send it to "Ask Vance" at* MEMPHIS *magazine, 460 Tennessee Street #200, Memphis, TN 38103 or email him at askvance@memphismagazine. com, and for even more from Vance, visit his new blog: www.memphismagazine.com/askvanceblog*

ASK VANCE
Our trivia expert solves local mysteries of who, what, when, where, why, and why not.
by VANCE LAUDERDALE

LIFE AT THE LEMON

DEAR VANCE: On the east side of the Poplar Viaduct there was a coffee house in the 1960s — a beatnik place, I believe. It was THE place to be back then, but I can't think of the name. Can you help? — M.T., Memphis

DEAR M.T.: Actually, the place to "be" in the 1960s was the east wing of the Lauderdale Mansion, where Mother and Father set up a game room and arcade in the attic that attracted hundreds of kids from the neighborhood. It was their desperate attempt to provide me with friends, you see, and for a while their ruse worked. Oh, I can dimly remember those happy days when tykes and teenagers flocked to our home to play Twister, Monopoly, Chutes and Ladders, and all sorts of other games. Plus, we had Play-Doh. But the good times came to an end, I recall, when an especially spirited game of Scrabble got out of hand, the police were called, and the kids never came back. I told Mother and Father that using the pepper spray was probably an over-reaction, but did they listen? No.

With nowhere else to go, teenagers began to frequent some of the so-called "coffee houses" that opened around town, and the one you remember, M.T., was the Bitter Lemon, the most famous of them all. Its owner was John McIntire, a professor at the Memphis College of Art (back then it was the Art Academy), a fascinating gentleman with a talent for sculpture and a penchant for vintage Hawaiian shirts.

A couple of years ago, this magazine ran a story about Memphis in the 1960s, and McIntire had a lot to say about the days of the Bitter Lemon, which he crammed into a little storefront on Poplar.

"I got the place real cheap, because there was nowhere to park," he said. "There was just a little bitty stage, set way back. The walls were covered with antiques and musical instruments, and every night I'd go there and 'psychedelicize' the place with paint, from floor to ceiling. People would come in there stoned and just stare at the walls."

Although plenty of the patrons came to the Bitter Lemon, and the other teen clubs around town, with their own stimulants, the clubs themselves served no alcohol. Mainly you just got a variety of weird coffee — McIntire remembers Lapsang Choung and Formosa Olong — and soft drinks. If you were really bold, you guzzled something called a Suicide — a deadly mix of Pepsi, Teem, and grape juice. Despite its name, I don't believe it actually killed anybody. Oh, and you could also eat some really awful pizza. Now that probably did.

Despite the lousy food, tiny stage, and terrible acoustics, the Bitter Lemon became the place to perform for anybody and everybody in the 1960s. All the up-and-

coming teen bands played there — the photo shows a group called, uh, The Groupe — along with established performers like Furry Lewis and Gus Cannon, and McIntire remembers that members of the Lovin' Spoonful, the Byrds, and the Rolling Stones also dropped in when they were in town.

For some reason, perhaps because parents always think their kids are up to no good, the most popular clubs — which included the Roaring 60s downtown and a tiny place called the OSO on Highland — attracted the scrutiny of grownups, who wanted the places shut down. A Press-Scimitar reporter — probably an old coot in his thirties — visited one of these establishments and reported that youngsters "were really 'going' last night with their rhythmic shakes and shrieks, rolls and shivers." One Memphis mother who visited the OSO confided to reporters that the walls "were painted black." Oh, horrors.

So Juvenile Court Judge Kenneth Turner got into the act, trying his best to shut the places down as public nuisances. You have to understand that in the 1960s, there was really no other place for kids to go. Beale Street was dead, no shopping malls had yet opened, and Overton Square was still years in the future. So, this being Memphis and all, it turned into a big brouhaha, with parents actually carrying protest signs, and the kids doing their best to protest the protests.

The newspaper photo above shows one of these protest marches, but I can't make sense of it, to tell you the truth. Look at those drug-crazed teens! One kid, whose hair almost touches his ears, is carrying a sign that reads, "Batman swings a mean cape at teen clubs," but I'm not sure I see his point. Why, he must have been flying on LSD to come up with something like that.

At any rate, what finally closed the teen clubs and coffeehouses down were drugs. McIntire remembers plenty of overdoses at the Bitter Lemon, and undercover police on the prowl for pot-smokers became a constant hassle.

"I remember having to rescue people, going into the bathroom when somebody was on drugs. I saw a guy in there putting a needle somewhere I would *not* want to be putting a needle," he said. "The police were always raiding us then, and I just decided it wasn't worth it."

McIntire closed the Bitter Lemon in the late 1960s, and one by one the other joints around town closed too. "God, it was trouble all the time," says McIntire. "It was a lot of fun, but at the end it was just scary."

Memphis teens were clearly better off at the Friday-night scrabble parties at the Lauderdale Mansion. The only drugs we used there were prescription antidepressants.

A HANDFUL

DEAR VANCE: What is with the giant stone hand in the front yard of this house (right) on Angelus? — D.K., Memphis

DEAR D.K.: One of my colleagues, whose family hails from a long line of esteemed proctologists, has the unfortunate last name of Finger, and at first I assumed this was his residence. But then I remembered that he had erected a sculpture alongside his driveway displaying just a single digit — I'd better not say which one — so I realized I was mistaken.

The nice house at 256 Angelus is owned by Jane Abraham and Keith Henderson, who also own and operate the HART Center at 1384 Madison, a treatment center for substance-abuse disorders. The place also offers stress-management courses, massage, midwife classes, something called transdancing, and other holistic treatments.

What does this have to do with the giant hand? Well, Jane tells me it's actually an integral part of the design of their entire front yard, which is divided into segments. "The southern half of the yard has three different flower beds, representing the emotional, spiritual, and physical sides of our nature," she says. "On the north side we have the Native American four corners, representing the four directions of a Native American medicine wheel."

She explains that the hand, which is made of concrete poured over a PVC pipe and wire mesh frame, is a Hindu "mudra" — or symbol — that represents teaching and service.

Local artist Lori Butler helped sculpt it. "We planted it with some friends from Chapel Hill, who designed the yard for us," Jane says. "People come up to our front door and ask about it all the time."

It's certainly an eye-catching addition to the neighborhood. "Sometimes we go out and the hand is covered in flowers," says Jane. "The different reactions to it are very interesting." **M**

GOT A QUESTION FOR VANCE? *Send it to "Ask Vance" at* MEMPHIS *magazine, 460 Tennessee Street #200, Memphis, TN 38103 or email him at askvance@memphismagazine.com, and for even more from Vance, visit his new blog: www.memphismagazine.com/*

▶ **ASK VANCE**

Our trivia expert solves local mysteries of who, what, when, where, why, and why not.

by VANCE LAUDERDALE

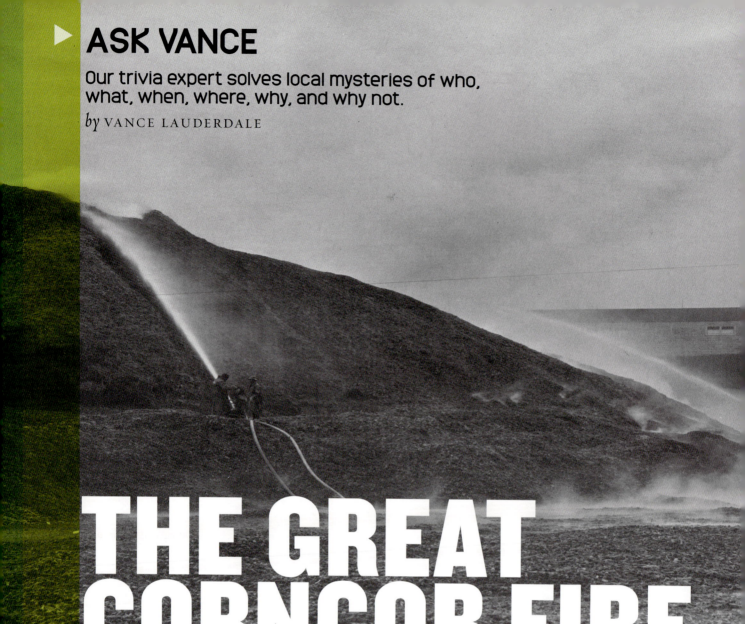

THE GREAT CORNCOB FIRE

DEAR VANCE: The Fire Museum of Memphis lists the worst fires in our city's history, and mentions a Quaker Oats corncob blaze. Can you enlighten us (so to speak) about this conflagration? — J.Y., Memphis

DEAR J.Y.: Dear J.Y.: The Fire Museum is indeed a great establishment, but it's unfortunate that their listing of great fires unaccountably omits the Lauderdale Mansion Fire of 1952. On the afternoon of January 15, I was playing with leftover Black Cat sparklers in one of the basement vaults, when I accidentally set fire to half a dozen canvas moneybags. There was no currency in them, of course, but they had been stuffed with Top Value stamps that we had planned to redeem on a new toaster. Oh, Father was angry. For years afterwards, whenever I asked for a slice of toast at breakfast, he would grumble, "You'll just have to toast your bread with your damn Black Cat sparklers." I was glad when the police finally took him away.

The December 1958 fire at the Quaker Oats Company on Chelsea didn't exactly enhance our city's national reputation. We had for years been perceived as a hick Southern town, and when one of your city's greatest blazes involves a big pile of corncobs, well that's just not the kind of fire that causes trouble in places like New York City or San Francisco.

But it's not like we were piling up corncobs to make corncob pipes for every man, woman, and child in Memphis. Instead, using a complicated process of distillation that only white-coated scientists with Ph.D.s in corncob chemistry can understand, the Quaker Oats company extracted a chemical from those cobs that they called "furfural." Yes, I agree that's just a terrible name, but perhaps they were in a hurry and it's the best they could do. And though you might never think that ladies' stockings actually came from corncobs — just the thought of it makes me itch — it's true. Furfural was used as the main ingredient in nylon, plastics, insecticides, and all sorts of odd things.

Quaker Oats used to do a lot more than just make oatmeal, you see.

Anyway, that's why the massive Quaker Oats plant, which had opened in Memphis back in 1920, was stockpiling more than 70,000 tons of corncobs, piled into a mountain behind the plant more than six stories high.

On the afternoon of December 2, 1958, somebody noticed those corncobs were smoldering. The fire department was called, as you might expect, and newspapers reported the blaze in a tiny article. After all, surely it would be extinguished that day, right? Well,

78 • ASK VANCE II

it turns out, the Great Corncob Fire — as it came to be known — did not begin at the top of the pile as the result of a strike by lightning, as was first suspected. No, it began way in the bottom of the huge pile, caused by spontaneous combustion. And once that fire got going, it was almost impossible to put out. For one thing, you couldn't get to it, down in the bottom of millions of corncobs. And for another, when corncobs burn, they tend to form a kind of plastic shell over their surface — which then crusted over the entire pile — preventing any water from reaching the flames.

Firemen brought in bulldozers and all sorts of equipment to push the cobs this way and that, but it was slow going. And though this may seem hard to believe, in the 1950s, firemen weren't fitted with masks and oxygen tanks as they are today, so more than 20 firemen were admitted to area hospitals to be treated for smoke inhalation, their lungs seared by the smoke and chemicals put off by the corncobs.

This was no laughing matter. That dense smoke drifted over the residential neighborhoods to the west of the plant, and Douglass High School was just two blocks away. I found no mention in the newspapers of the school, or area residents, being evacuated during the blaze, but I hope they were. At any rate, special equipment was set up around the plant to monitor carbon monoxide levels.

That pile of corncobs burned for almost a month, creating a pillar of smoke that could be seen for miles, until it was finally extinguished on December 24th. It was an unusual challenge for local firefighters, and for years afterwards, fire officials held seminars — which they called "Operation Corncob"— to show other municipalities what to do if they encountered a similar problem.

"The Memphis department had no experience fighting a fire of such proportions and, as far as we can tell, no other department had the experience," one fire department official told reporters later, when the ordeal was over.

At any rate, it never happened again, partly because scientists came up with other — presumably easier — ways to manufacture nylon. The big chemical plant is still in operation at the corner of Chelsea and Holmes, but it's no longer owned or operated by Quaker Oats. And if they have any corncobs stored there, I sure couldn't find any.

BITTMAN'S BUSINESS

DEAR VANCE: When I was a kid, my parents shopped at a store on Lamar called Bittman's. Who was Bittman, exactly, and what happened to his store? — F.P., Memphis.

DEAR F.P.: Every day, it seems, the postman brings me queries like yours — questions about little ma-and-pa grocery stores, bakeries, gas stations, and other establishments remembered fondly by former customers. In years to come, will people ask the same questions about Costco, or Sam's? I doubt it.

And all too often, I am forced to put aside these queries, because too many times the only things left from these little businesses are the memories they created. But with Bittman, I struck gold, because the University of Memphis Special Collections not only provided a nice photo of Herbert Bittman (shown here as he looked in 1939), but a good interior shot of the appliance store he opened in 1951. Plus, the Lauderdale Library possesses an unopened pack of playing cards that was used as a promotion for Bittman's grocery store, complete with the slogan, "Where you won't get bit."

Bittman was born here in 1906. Sometime in the late 1940s he purchased property in the 1600 block of Lamar — just a few blocks from his home at 1930 Foster, where he lived with his wife, Elizabeth, and son, Herbert Jr. He opened a WeOna store, number 12 in the citywide chain of more than 120 similar markets, and a little "five-and-dime" store next door. In December 1951, he expanded his ventures with Bittman's Appliance Store. According to the newspapers, it was a completely modern facility, decorated in "flag gray, medium gray, and yellow trim." What color is "flag gray," I wonder? The store carried just about every appliance a homemaker of the 1950s might require: refrigerators, freezers, electric and gas ranges, vacuum cleaners, and tv sets. For its grand opening, Bittman gave away a refrigerator, a "giant basket of groceries," and various souvenir gifts — such as the packs of playing cards, perhaps?

Bittman stayed in business until the late 1970s. He passed away in 1981, and I'm sorry to tell you that the stores you remember from your youth, F.P., are now a vacant lot. **M**

GOT A QUESTION FOR VANCE? *Send it to "Ask Vance" at* MEMPHIS *magazine, 460 Tennessee Street #200, Memphis, TN 38103 or email him at askvance@memphismagazine.com, and for even more from Vance, visit his new blog: www.memphismagazine.com/askvanceblog*

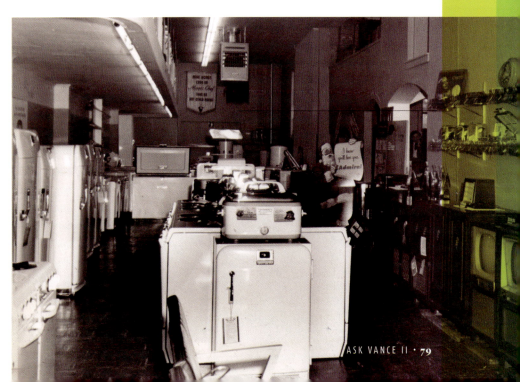

▶ # ASK VANCE
Our trivia expert solves local mysteries of who, what, when, where, why, and why not.

Olswanger performs with W.C. Handy

MUSIC MAN

by VANCE LAUDERDALE

DEAR VANCE: In the 1960s, I occasionally visited a music store on Highland to buy sheet music, but can't recall the name of that establishment. Can you help?
— T.C., MEMPHIS

DEAR T.C.: I know the store well, for it's where I also purchased sheet music for the twice-monthly oboe performances I used to conduct for the orphans. The director of the orphanage — a surly man with a tin ear — finally requested that I put a stop to these recitals, asking me, "Haven't the children already suffered enough?"

Anyway, the store was owned and operated by a very interesting fellow named Berl Olswanger, and his life story is almost as remarkable as my own. Born in 1917 in a rather rundown section of North Memphis called Goat Hill, Berl began picking out tunes on a battered family piano at the age of 3. That's right — 3. By the age of 12, when most kids are occupied with the Cub Scouts, he was playing piano at a nightclub across the street from Central High School called Dreamland Gardens. Despite the fancy name, the place was pretty much a dump, and Berl later told reporters, "People used to call Mother and bless her out for letting a little boy see such sights, and she would say, 'No, it's good for him.'"

As a teenager, he began to play anywhere and everywhere he could. "One night," he recalled, "I was playing in one of those places and two men got into a fight and shot each other. I just kept on playing."

Though he was too polite to mention it, I'm pretty sure this was Mother and Father Lauderdale's 25th wedding anniversary party.

Berl's older brother, a level-headed fellow named Melvin, tried to talk his sibling out of this risky business, warning him, "Either bums become musicians or musicians become bums," but Berl wouldn't listen, and very quickly became one of the hottest performers in town. At the age of 18, he became the staff pianist for the WMC radio station, and two years later was leader of the station's band. This was back in the day when radio programs and commercials had lots of background music, you understand. He played piano at hotels, restaurants, clubs, weddings, dances, debutante balls, Cotton Carnival parties, and even fashion shows. A 1937 newspaper story praised the young man's "smooth technique and large

80 • ASK VANCE II

repertoire, which he plays from memory."

Still in his 20s, he got an offer to play piano and organ with the George Olsen Orchestra, one of the big bands of the 1930s. His boss at the radio station tried to warn him that the life of a touring musician would be a rough one, filled day and night with "wild women and wilder drinking." According to family lore, Berl told him, "I had to find out if it was all true." (If it was, he never mentioned it.) That stint carried him to Hollywood, where he performed with some of the top stars of the day, including Bob Hope, Bing Crosby, and Jack Benny.

When the U.S. entered World War II, Berl joined the Navy and was made a torpedo officer in the South Pacific. Then something really amazing happened, one of those life-changing moments. One evening in 1943, he was playing a piano — just for fun — in a military club when the tough-talking, cigar-chewing Admiral William "Bull" Halsey overheard him and liked what he heard. Right then and there, the admiral decided this young man's talents were wasted on torpedoes, so Berl was promoted to Naval Entertainment Officer, in charge of USO performances, dances, and other acts designed to boost morale for troops throughout the entire South Pacific, a position he held for two years.

After the war, a promoter urged him to move to New York City, where he could have been a big star as "that red-haired wonder of the jazz piano," as one reporter described him. Berl even held a concert at Ellis Auditorium featuring what he described as his "middlebrow music" to earn money for the trip. The show earned excellent reviews from critics, who observed, "Berl Olswanger proved himself a brilliant young jazz virtuoso and demonstrated he can take a crack at the classics without apologies to anyone. He tried his nimble fingers and agile brain at everything from Handy to Chopin. The consequences of that effort were completely, delightfully satisfying."

But after just two weeks in the Big Apple, he missed Memphis and decided to return home, telling reporters, "I'm just a country boy at heart. I'd rather come home and be poor and be with people I love than to make a lot of money in that rat race."

Berl and his wife Edna settled down in Whitehaven, later moving to an 11-room home overlooking Maywood Lake in Mississippi for several years. In 1948 he opened his first music store in Memphis, at 1531 Union.

More than just a place to buy pianos, band instruments, and sheet music, the store also served as an innovative piano school, following a quick-learning method called "Play the Berl Olswanger Way." It became so popular that it was adopted by the Shelby County school system. In his spare time, he joined up with a fellow named Jack Morgan and played for WMPS in a duo he called "Cats on the Keys."

Somewhere along the way, Berl managed to earn a bachelor's and master's degree in music from Memphis State University, and even began working on a Ph.D. In the early 1970s, he was named music and art consultant for the entire Shelby County school system.

Berl was, no doubt, a musical genius, but in his "aw shucks" way, he never admitted it. He practiced every day, from 5 to 7 a.m., and once told a reporter, "I know that talent is the basic 10 percent of ability, but practice is the other 90 percent. I practice daily or I must make it up."

For his own little jazz orchestra, Berl explained, "I try to pick musicians with personality. We memorize our arrangements. You can't project yourself and get your crowd with you if your eyes are down there on that paper. But if we can make things reach a fever pitch, get the crowd in a frenzy, then they think they've had a good time and everybody goes home satisfied."

And of course he also wrote plenty of his own songs, including such hits as "The Man Who Stole My Beale Street Gal" and "Berl's Blues."

A 1960 newspaper article summed up his many accomplishments: "piano and organ store proprietor, piano soloist and band leader, booking agent, song writer, head arranger for vocal groups, family man, and doer of good deeds." That same reporter noted that Berl was "an altogether noble soul. This does not take into account the fact that he writes television and radio jingles. But then nobody is perfect."

Love 'em or hate 'em, but those jingles for such clients as King Cotton Franks, Kraus Cleaners, and Stewart's Egg-Rich Mayonnaise earned him quite a bit of money.

When Berl opened his second music store at 804 S. Highland — this is the one you remember, T.C. — half of the business was a talent booking agency, featuring bands and groups for every occasion. He did this because his own band was in such demand that they couldn't perform everywhere they were wanted, so Berl sent out other bands and performers to fill the need.

Berl could play just about anything, it seems, and once explained, "Music should not be considered on a vertical scale, with some music higher than other, but rather on a horizontal scale. There is a time and place for all kinds of music in our culture." He was from the "sweet and sentimental school of music," he would say, and "I like any kind of music that makes people happy."

And he certainly made a lot of people happy. When he died in 1981, *The Commercial Appeal* observed that "Berl's life was a tune that everybody could hum" and "everything he touched turned to music. The touch was so obvious that people called him 'Mr. Music.'"

No story of Berl Olswanger would be complete without mentioning his children: Berl Olswanger Jr., currently living in Mississippi, and his daughter, Anna Olswanger, an author and literary agent in New York. Anna has published several short stories about her illustrious father, and I owe her special thanks, in fact, for providing me with the information and photos you see here. She has, in fact, compiled years of newspaper clippings and images into a handy booklet, *The Memphis Music of Berl Olswanger*. It certainly made a nice addition to the Lauderdale Library.

Years ago, *Memphis Press-Scimitar* columnist Bill Burk observed, "Berl could have been as big a star as Liberace had he chosen a life on the road, but he loved the people of Memphis and that love was returned a thousand times over. For Berl Olswanger, the song may be over, but his melody will always linger on in the lives of those of us he touched." **M**

GOT A QUESTION FOR VANCE? *Send it to "Ask Vance" at* MEMPHIS *magazine, 460 Tennessee Street #200, Memphis, TN 38103 or email him at askvance@memphismagazine.com, and for even more stories from Vance, visit his new blog: www.memphismagazine.com/askvanceblog.*

A store window display from 1951

ASK VANCE
Our trivia expert solves local mysteries of who, what, when, where, why, and why not.

JOHN GASTON

by VANCE LAUDERDALE

DEAR VANCE: Many years ago, a member of my family spent time in John Gaston Hospital, and I know there is also a Gaston Park in South Memphis. Who was this enterprising gentleman?
— A.T., MEMPHIS

DEAR A.T.: In his fine history book *Metropolis of the American Nile,* John Harkins writes: "From the start of his success, he shared his time, talents, and good fortune with others. Long known for his quiet kindnesses, his love of children, and his secret philanthropies, this French immigrant of humble origins became one of this city's leading citizens."

I know what you are thinking: This is indeed an uncannily accurate depiction of Vance Lauderdale.

But he is actually referring to John Gaston, whose life does bear certain parallels to my own. I have to admit, though, that Gaston was probably a better cook.

Another Memphis historian, Paul Coppock, once observed, "Documented facts about Gaston are scarce," and says that most biographical information derives from a booklet, "John Gaston, Citizen," compiled in the late 1930s by Louise Gambill when she was on the staff of Mayor Walter Chandler. Just why she undertook this endeavor is unknown, but I mention Coppock, Harkins, and now Gambill just to give credit where it is due: the Lauderdales never met the Gastons, so I have no firsthand knowledge of the man.

This much we do know. Gaston was born in France in 1828 and began working in his grandfather's café in Paris when he was only 6. As a young man, he gained employment as a steward on a French Line steamer running between Le Havre and New York, and sometime in the 1850s decided to stay in America. After drifting around New York City for a while, he managed to land a job with the world-famous restaurant Delmonico's, working his way up from waiter to chef, and it is there, so it is said, where he perfected his culinary skills.

When the Civil War started, Gaston relocated to Memphis. It wasn't a good move. "War wiped him out," writes Coppock. "He took the side of the South, but exactly what he did is unclear." Stories persist that he joined the Confederate forces and was wounded in action, but some tales have him injured in the shoulder, while others say he was shot in the foot.

It doesn't matter. What concerns us here is that in 1866, Gaston opened the Commercial Restaurant downtown at Adams and Main. Within weeks, the newspapers of the day called him "that prince of caterers." In 1871 his growing reputation (and bank account) allowed him to open a larger restaurant called Gaston's — complete with first-class hotel — overlooking Court Square. According to Coppock, "details got his attention, such as buying 20,000 quill toothpicks from France, each with the word 'Gaston' in gold lettering."

Gaston became very, very rich. Big-name politicians dined at his restaurant, and celebrities such as Oscar Wilde made a point to visit when they toured Memphis. Gaston built a wonderful mansion on South Third Street, and also had the business sense to purchase property all over town.

Gaston died in 1912 at the age of 84. His restaurant closed, though the building at 33-35 South Court has survived to this day. Before his death, he told friends that he wanted his mansion converted into a public hospital. That didn't happen until the death of his wife, Theresa, in 1929. Then the mansion — deemed too small for a decent hospital — was demolished, and the property on Third was converted into Gaston Park, complete with a $150,000 community center. The bulk of his fortune, supplemented by funds from the Public Works Administration, was then used to build a brand-new city hospital in the medical district. John Gaston Hospital opened on Madison in 1936. It remained one of our city's busiest hospitals until it was demolished in 1990 to make way for the growth of The Med.

REMEMBERING ROBINSON'S

DEAR VANCE: I found an old bottle at an estate sale with a label for James Robinson Apothecary. What's the story behind this interesting establishment?
— G.A., MEMPHIS

DEAR G.A.: On those days — Monday through Friday, and generally three or four weekends a month — when I wake up suffering from neuralgia, neurosis, eczema, gout, rheumatism, and general malaise, the ointments and potions from James S. Robinson often soothe my pains. Well, that and a dozen bottles of Kentucky Nip.

For reasons I can't explain, the Lauderdale Library contains hundreds of unused labels from the Robinson Apothecary. No ailment, it seems, was beyond a simple cure — swallowing a pill, or gulping down a tonic. The firm offered such oddly named medications as Glycerol Cantherides, Syrup of Squill, Tonga Elixir, and — get ready — Syrup of Ipecacuanha. A product called "Cobalt, or Fly Stone," was labeled POISON but carried these peculiar instructions: "Add a little water and sweeten with sugar." Was that designed to make the poison taste better?

I don't know Robinson's entire story, but it's similar to John Gaston's. Born in Philadelphia in the early 1800s, the pharmacist ventured to Memphis in search of a better job. He opened his first store in 1869 at the corner of Second and Madison and apparently did quite well. During the late 1870s, he gained the thanks of grateful citizens by keeping his drugstore open during the yellow fever epidemics, when so many other businessmen fled the city.

Robinson died in 1929, and the business was continued by his daughter, Mary Robinson. According to an old newspaper article, the firm filled its two millionth prescription in June 1929.

In 1965, the old apothecary was sold to two pharmacists, Sam Burson and Jack Kirsch, who continued to operate it at various locations throughout the city, though they eventually dropped the Robinson name.

The Robinson building (shown here in 1943) is still standing on North Second Street, though it has been converted into high-class business offices, called — appropriately enough — The Apothecary. **M**

GOT A QUESTION FOR VANCE? *Send it to "Ask Vance" at* MEMPHIS *magazine, 460 Tennessee Street #200, Memphis, TN 38103 or email him at askvance@memphismagazine.com, and for even more stories from Vance, visit his new blog: www.memphismagazine.com/askvanceblog*

ASK VANCE
Our trivia expert solves local mysteries of who, what, when, where, why, and why not.

PARK WITH A PAST

by VANCE LAUDERDALE

DEAR VANCE: I found an old book about Memphis that contained a photo of Confederate Park (above), and the statue of Jefferson Davis is missing. Wasn't that an important element of the park from the beginning?
— D.W., MEMPHIS.

DEAR D.W.: No, it wasn't.

I guess I could stop right there — after all, I *did* answer your question — but my editor insists I fill these two pages with words instead of nice pictures, so (sigh) I suppose I'll tell you just a *bit* more about one of the most controversial parks in our city's history.

If you compare then-and-now photos of Confederate Park, you will see a subtle but dramatic transformation over the years — different walkways, statues, cannons. Just about everything has been revised and revamped. And if you somehow managed to find some really old photos of the site, you might be amazed, because Confederate Park actually began its existence as a public dump.

Hard to believe (okay, this being Memphis and all, maybe it's *not* so hard to believe), but in the mid-1800s, everyone here just pitched their trash right into the river. According to historian Paul Coppock, the site of Confederate Park was mainly a heap of garbage, "a disgraceful portion of the promenade . . . where an aged man and his mule lived in a shack, surrounded by junk, broken bricks, and street sweepings."

Nothing remotely "Confederate" appeared on the site until 1901, when Memphis hosted a national reunion for the United Confederate Veterans and erected an 18,000-seat pavilion to host many of the activities. After the convention, however, the wooden structure was demolished, and the land stood empty until 1907.

That's when 2.7 acres along the bluff were turned over to the Memphis Park Commission to be transformed into — as the old wooden signs used to say — "A Memorial to the Old South." Robert Galloway, then chairman of the park commission, explained, "My idea being to make this an old Confederate fort, with fallen-down stone parapets, guns partly concealed by vines, and white jessamine." I'm not sure why he was so fond of that particular flower, but the park commission did erect a handsome stone wall, added some walkways and derelict Civil War artillery, and Confederate Park officially opened in 1908.

Still no statue of Jefferson Davis, though. Be patient.

Despite the "Confederate" theme, over the years the little park became a dumping ground (again!) for a lot of odd junk. The Civil War guns were sacrificed during a World War II scrap metal drive, replaced by battered artillery from World War I. Mayor E.H. Crump bought a totem pole during a trip to the Northwest and erected it smack in the middle of the park. The Jaycees hauled in a concrete block inscribed with the Ten Commandments.

Everyone, it seems, had strange ideas for ways to "improve" the park. In 1958, the City Beautiful Commission declared it would build a giant fountain there, "the first of a series of refreshing pools and fountains

84 • ASK VANCE II

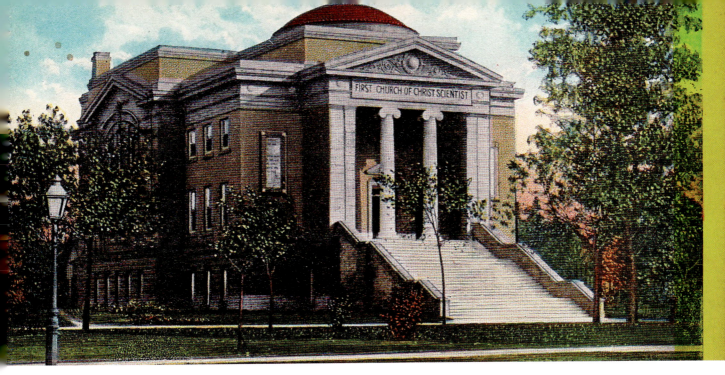

in Memphis." That never happened, though in the early 1960s the park commission added a "rising mound of earth," where they planted red, white, and blue pansies to form a giant Rebel flag. That proved hard to maintain, as you might imagine, so it didn't last long.

In 1962, though, Confederate Park faced its greatest battle, when a Philadelphia company called City Stores announced it would transform six blocks along Front Street into a shopping complex called "The Great Mall." Confederate Park would be replaced by a "Hall of Fountains," which developers promised would be a "place of great beauty."

There was just one problem. No one could determine just who, exactly, owned Confederate Park. And quite a few people wondered if a shopping complex couldn't find a better home elsewhere in the city. City Stores eventually abandoned the project entirely, and Confederate Park remained intact.

There have been other bizarre struggles over the years. In 1964, the park became infested with 18-inch-long Norway rats, which newspapers described as "filthier than most rats, with an insatiable craving for grease and blood." That's not exactly the kind of thing that would lure visitors to the park with picnic baskets stuffed with fried chicken. The creatures dwelled in tunnels beneath the sidewalks, and exterminators were called in to finally vanquish these beasts.

That same year — almost a full century after the end of the Civil War — the park finally got its centerpiece, a larger-than-life statue of Jefferson Davis (top left). The president of the Confederate States of America had lived in Memphis from 1875 to 1878 and ran an insurance agency here before retiring to the Gulf Coast. A group called the Jefferson Davis Statue Fund Association raised enough money — though I can't remember the exact cost after all these years — to build an eight-foot bronze statue on a 12-foot granite base. The base was designed by Memphis' own Crone Monument Company, whose work graces many of the elaborate tombs in Elmwood, and the statue itself was created by an Italian sculptor named Aldo Pera.

I suppose I could tell the entire life history of Pera, and how he was selected to produce the Davis sculpture, but I really don't think that's very interesting, do you?

In the late 1990s, the R.A. Bloch Cancer Foundation wanted to build a cancer survivors' park on the site, but they eventually constructed that in Audubon Park. The most recent controversy has been repeated attempts to drop "Confederate" from the name, since it offends more than half of our city's population, but I'm staying out of that fray. Years ago, my own family offered the park commission as much as $100 — that's right, one hundred dollars — if they would rename the site Lauderdale Park, and replace that statue of Jeff Davis with one of me, but did they listen? No.

STAIRWAY TO HEAVEN?

DEAR VANCE: This old postcard (top) shows the First Church of Christ Scientist in Memphis, but doesn't give the address. Is this nice-looking building still standing? — G.K., Memphis.
— G.K., MEMPHIS

DEAR G.K.: It is indeed an impressive structure, with its yellow-brick walls and reddish dome, though climbing all those steps would tire me out. With nothing else to do, I actually squinted and began to count them, but I got a headache after 30. I later turned up a newspaper article about the church, which also commented on the physically demanding entry, calling it "perhaps the longest flight of steps in the city."

This was after we replaced the grand stairway leading to the Lauderdale Ballroom with a speedy escalator, you understand.

I thought the building looked familiar, and sure enough my collection of aerial photographs of Memphis clearly shows this church on the northeast corner of Dunlap and Monroe, where it stood facing Forrest Park since being erected there in the late 1920s. Now, I'd feel better about myself if I could give you the exact date of construction, but I can't.

In 1961, the church property was sold and the building was demolished to make way for additions to the Medical Center. Church officials bought land at Perkins and Princeton and built a new church, which is still standing, though now being used by a different congregation. That structure is considerably more modern, basically a linked pair of octagonal buildings, with an open courtyard between them. The *Press-Scimitar* proclaimed it "unique in design among Memphis churches" and made special mention of the fact that the main auditorium "will be close to ground level." I guess after half a century, church members got tired of climbing all those steps. **M**

GOT A QUESTION FOR VANCE? *Send it to "Ask Vance" at* Memphis *magazine, 460 Tennessee Street, Memphis, TN 38103, or email him at askvance@memphismagazine. And for even more from Vance, visit his blog: www.memphismagazine.com/askvanceblog.*

ASK VANCE
Our trivia expert solves local mysteries of who, what, when, where, why, and why not.

DIRTY DANCING

by VANCE LAUDERDALE

DEAR VANCE: What can you tell me about the old Whirlaway Club? I remember my dad saying it was a pretty wild place. — D.N., GERMANTOWN.

DEAR D.N.: I suppose that depends on what you mean by "wild." In my own experience, there was no wilder place in Memphis than the annual Lauderdale Memorial Day parties, where we — oh, the doctors have told me to stop dredging up those awful memories. And so have the lawyers. Just read chapters 41 through 67 in my book, *Bound for Glory: The Story of the Lauderdales in America*.

The Whirlaway Club was extremely popular, that's for sure. An ex-serviceman named John Ogden opened it on Lamar just north of Prescott in 1947. He and his wife, Jean, basically converted a rather ramshackle building (since demolished) into a pretty decent nightclub, not unlike so many others around town, with bands and halfway decent food. I have no idea how they came up with the memorable name; at the time, the most famous "Whirlaway" was a Kentucky Derby–winning racehorse.

At any rate, from the beginning the owners found themselves in court quite a few times. Faded newspaper clippings archived in the University of Memphis Special Collections Department report numerous instances of the club losing its liquor license for selling beer to minors. One policeman described the place as "deplorable — whiskey and beer all over the place," and the chairman of the beer licensing board said, "I passed there last week. It looks as if they get to rocking and rolling inside. They just might roll it over."

Ogden grudgingly admitted that his club "could be more substantial" and tried to argue that accounts of underage drinking were "only hearsay," but he paid fines and lost his license anyway — quite a few times, in fact.

But it was in the 1960s that the Whirlaway really made headlines here. First of all, around 1963 the Ogdens moved across the street to a larger and considerably swankier building. Then, along with so many other clubs in town, they brought in a new form of entertainment — exotic creatures known as go-go dancers. Usually clad in miniskirts and knee-high boots, young women danced to the hit songs of the day. Apparently, however, the Whirlaway girls went a bit farther than most, and in 1967, front-page *Press-Scimitar* headlines shocked Memphians with the "indecent" performances taking place night after night at the Whirlaway.

Two dancers in particular — Betty Vansickle (who danced under the name "Betty Vee") and Sue Sennett — along with the club owners and even the master of ceremonies — were arrested and charged with "committing or aiding and abetting obscene acts."

Just how obscene? Judge for yourself. An undercover police officer testified, "Mrs. Sennett came out wearing a lavender, bikini-type costume. The top part covered only about half of her bosom." Oh my. Sennett strutted out on the club's tiny stage, and then, according to the officer, "At one point, she bent completely back so her hands touched the floor and bumped her hips up and down while the music kept time to the rhythm."

Goodness, my hands are trembling while I'm typing this!

And it only got worse. "Betty Vee" then took the stage in a gold costume that was "only about one-half-inch wide on the side of the hips." They didn't specify — or perhaps the newspaper didn't dare print — the dimensions of her costume on other parts of her body. Vansickle specialized in a dance she called the "Gravy Train" that was similar to Sennett's, except "it was a little rougher and her motions were a little more obscene." (That's Vansickle, by the way, in the photo at far left wearing the one-piece costume with the white glove stretching down her torso. Sennett is the other dancer pictured here.)

The police officer testified that each girl went up to customers and "made obscene gestures at least 100 times." Asked to describe these gestures, the cop said, "I'd call them bumps and grinds."

Newspapers of the day pounced on the story, and sent teams of reporters and photographers scurrying to other clubs around the city. A tough job, you bet! One reporter said of a club dancer, "Her body bounces like she's playing basketball with a beehive in a phone booth." Another pondered, "How far is too far for a go-go girl to go?" Still another, describing the so-called "nightclub dilemma in Memphis," observed that it really wasn't the costume that was a problem, "it was what she was doing in the clothes, the dance herself."

Meanwhile, as you might imagine, all the dancers and club owners got a bit huffy about the whole mess. "I'm not ashamed, and I don't do a dirty dance," said one go-go girl. "When I go to church, I hold my head up a little higher than everyone else."

More to the point, Whirlaway owner John Ogden asked reporters, "Is Memphis that out of step with the world? Are we so slow here we've got to wait ten years to catch up with the entertainment of other cities?"

The answer, apparently, was: Yes. Ogden and his dancers paid small fines — I don't know the exact amount — and the controversy quickly faded away. After all, one of the dancers argued that their costumes "were just like what you'd see at the beach." National TV shows like *Shindig* and *Hullabaloo* caught on with teenagers, and go-go dancers became the main attraction of Memphis' own *Talent Party*, not exactly the wildest thing on the air, with their clean-cut ways and off-the-rack Sears outfits.

Years later, trying to defend their reputation, the Ogdens bragged in a 1974 newspaper article that their clientele included "some of the better-known leaders of this community." That same story noted that the Whirlaway was adding a full-scale restaurant and "had been at the forefront of all the innovative changes in the entertainment business. They were among the first to have go-go girls and later topless dancers, black lighting for the dance floor, strobe lighting for the dancing acts, and a full-blown floor show."

Yep, it was quite a place, but all things come to an end, and the Whirlaway just faded away, closing sometime in the mid-1980s, I believe. The old one-story brick building is still standing on Lamar, these days home to a restaurant called El Gallo Giro. Whatever happened to Betty Vee and the other dancers, I wonder?

EVERGREEN, THEN AND NOW

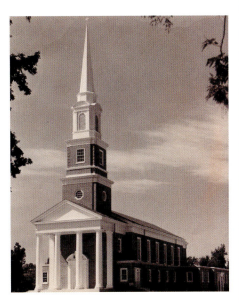

DEAR VANCE: When I was a student at Southwestern (now Rhodes College, of course, but it will always be Southwestern to me), I remember going to church services at Evergreen Presbyterian Church, which was located near the college — but not where it is now. The current building opened in 1950. So where was Evergreen Presbyterian before that?

— A.B., MEMPHIS.

DEAR A.B.: According to the authors of *Memphis: An Architectural Guide*, Evergreen Presbyterian Church opened at the corner of University and Tutwiler in 1951 (shown in the smaller photo, above). Noting that it was "another example of the Colonial Revival that swept Memphis in the post-war years," they observed, "This handsome church with white columns and tall steeple sits far enough back from the street so that it can be seen the way it ought to be." If it bears a striking resemblance to the Church of the Holy Communion on Walnut Grove, that's because the same architects — Walk C. Jones Sr. and Walk C. Jones Jr. — designed both.

Before 1950, however, A.B. and her fellow students would have attended baccalaureate and other religious services at the "old" Evergreen church (top), a handsome stone building located at the southeast corner of Autumn and Dickinson. It's still in use today, as The Church at Memphis and Evangelical Christian Center. **M**

GOT A QUESTION FOR VANCE? *Send it to "Ask Vance" at Memphis magazine, 460 Tennessee Street #200, Memphis, TN 38103, or email him at askvance@memphismagazine.com. And for even more from Vance, visit his blog: www.memphismagazine.com/askvanceblog.*

ASK VANCE
Our trivia expert solves local mysteries of who, what, when, where, why, and why not.

THE MILLER SIAMESE TWINS

by VANCE LAUDERDALE

DEAR VANCE: Is it true that in the 1950s, a family in Memphis gave birth to conjoined twins? What happened to them?
— K.E., MEMPHIS

DEAR K.E.: You're not the first person to ask me this rather unusual question, and it stumped me for a long time. As you might imagine, I have many books — almost a dozen! — on local history in the Lauderdale Library, and even such tomes as *The History of Medicine in Memphis* failed to mention such an event. So I mentally filed it away in that dusty compartment of my once-great mind, where the cluster of neurons is labeled "Can't Possibly Be True," and went on my merry way.

One day recently, however, while rooting through the newspaper files in the Special Collections Department at the University of Memphis Library in my usual haphazard fashion, I stumbled upon a folder of photographs and clippings on this very topic. So here's the remarkable story of the Miller twins. Warning: It may not be for the squeamish.

When 23-year-old Elizabeth Miller checked into John Gaston Hospital on the morning of May 7, 1954, to give birth to twins, the doctors performed a routine x-ray and made a shocking discovery. The two girls in her womb were joined at the head. A *Memphis Press-Scimitar* story said the mother was "very upset" when they told her the news, which would be putting it mildly, I think.

Pediatricians performed a C-section to deliver the girls, who were described as being in "the best of health." One newspaper reported that the infants "appear normal except for being joined at the head" — which is a pretty big "except" if you ask me.

A photograph shows that one twin's head was attached to the forehead of the other girl, which forced one baby to lie on her side while the other lay on her back. The good news — if you can call it that — is that an initial examination revealed that no major arteries or organs were linked; in other words, the girls didn't share a brain. Instead, a broad section of skull bone had somehow fused together while the babies were developing. Doctors here were

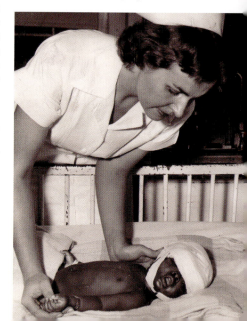

88 • ASK VANCE II

"cautiously optimistic" that the children could be separated.

This would be a remarkable feat. According to the American Medical Association, there had been only one other case in America where Siamese twins joined at the head were separated. Two years before, surgeons in Chicago attempted to separate two boys known as the "Brodie twins," but only one child survived.

At first, the baby's mother refused to see the girls, but she soon relented and named them Claudette and Constance, making a special point, so the newspapers said, of not giving them a middle name, for some reason. She also gave the Gaston staff permission to try to separate the children.

But the Miller girls needed to grow a bit more so they could survive the grueling operation. The mother was released from the hospital, but her little girls remained there for another three months until doctors finally determined the time was right. First, they performed a preliminary operation — not described very well in the old newspaper accounts — to determine if separation was possible, and decided that an attempt would be made the following week.

Finally, on October 11, 1954, a team of neurosurgeons and plastic surgeons conducted the five-hour operation. Although it was first considered a success, little Constance's heart "just wore out," and she died that afternoon of "circulatory failure." She was laid to rest in the Shelby County Cemetery.

Meanwhile, Claudette, although considered the weaker of the two, seemed to be doing fine. Doctors warned she would remain in danger for 72 hours, but she made it through that perilous period, and her pediatrician — who is never named in these articles — finally told reporters, "It looks like she will survive." She's shown at left with Gaston nurse Frances Novak.

One month later, little Claudette went home from the hospital. Her ordeal, however, was far from over. The operation left a gaping hole in her skull, which was sealed by a flap of skin. In six months, she returned to the hospital so the opening could be covered with a "bony material." Doctors explained that "experimental plastics used in the last two attempts have not withstood the bumps and falls of a normal youngster."

She would also return to John Gaston several more times for follow-up procedures, but at any rate she survived the main operation.

So what happened to her? Well, I can't really say. The newspaper files contained no more clippings or photographs, so I assume the girl grew up and — I hope — had a relatively normal childhood. In fact, I believe she lived another 30 years or so. After some digging around, I turned up a death certificate for a Claudette Miller — no middle name, just as her mother requested — who died in Hardeman County on February 20, 1988, at the age of 33. It's almost certainly the same woman who made medical history in Memphis more than half a century ago.

WHAT WAS WHIZ?

DEAR VANCE: I noticed this old "ghost" sign (top) painted on a building at the corner of Georgia and Florida. What on earth was Whiz? A soft drink?
— C.F., GERMANTOWN

DEAR C.F.: Since "whiz" is a crude expression for a certain bodily function, I thought it would be a particularly awful name for a soft drink. At the same time, I didn't know *what* it was. So I contacted my pal Andrew Northern, a public school teacher who, in his spare time, has made it his life's work to document just about every old building and sign in Memphis and Shelby County. Andrew was quite familiar with this sign, and told me that Whiz was actually a line of automotive products — cleaners, additives, and other chemicals used by mechanics.

The really fascinating part of this story, though, is the name painted on the bricks above the windows. R.M. Hollingshead not only founded the Whiz Auto Products Company, he is considered the father of the drive-in movie theater. Now, before you get all excited about that, I should explain that he's not from Memphis. He lived in Camden, New Jersey. According to *The American Drive-In Movie Theater*, a fine book by Don Sanders, "the year was 1933, and Hollingshead was trying to find a way to combine America's two great love affairs — the automobile and the movies." The enterprising fellow set a projector on the hood of his car, aimed it at a screen hung from a nearby tree, and hooked up some speakers. He thought it was a pretty cool way to watch movies, and after he opened his first "drive-in" theater in New Jersey, the concept caught on like wildfire.

I could tell you lots more about drive-in theaters — in the early days also called "auto-park theaters" and "park-in theaters" — but I'm running out of space here and don't want to get sidetracked. Let me just say that my chauffeur assures me that Whiz products are still being sold, and I believe the old building on Georgia was just one of many Hollingshead warehouses across the country. **M**

GOT A QUESTION FOR VANCE? *Send it to "Ask Vance" at* Memphis *magazine, 460 Tennessee Street, Memphis, TN 38103, or email him at askvance@memphismagazine. And for even more from Vance, visit his blog: www.memphismagazine.com/askvanceblog.*

ASK VANCE
Our trivia expert solves local mysteries of who, what, when, where, why, and why not.

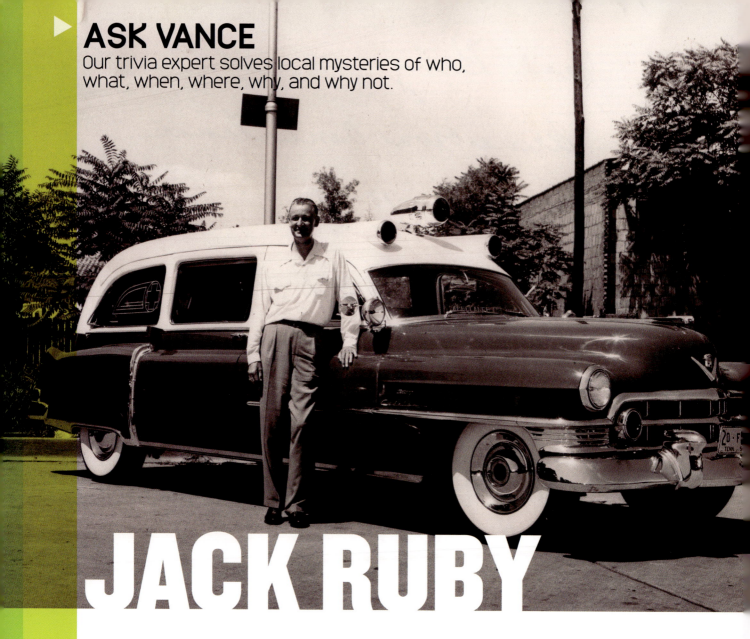

JACK RUBY

by VANCE LAUDERDALE

DEAR VANCE: What can you tell me about the old Jack Ruby ambulance company? This was before the fire department started providing emergency services. And I don't believe he was the same Jack Ruby who shot Lee Harvey Oswald, was he? — R.R., PARAGOULD, ARKANSAS

DEAR R.R.: Gosh no, absolutely not. In fact, "our" Jack Ruby was far more interested in saving lives than taking them. But because of the deeds — or misdeeds — associated with them, certain names probably should be retired. I mean, you're just asking for trouble naming a child John Wilkes Booth, or Lee Harvey Oswald, or Jack Ruby. Other names come to mind.

Including, of course, Vance Lauderdale.

As you noted, ambulances were once run by private companies, and in the 1950s and '60s, perhaps the best known of those was operated by a fellow named Jack Ruby, born in 1907 in Olive Branch, Mississippi. I don't know much at all about his early life — where he went to school, what his parents did, and all that. Old newspaper clippings tell me that his first job came in 1929, driving ambulances for the Hinton Funeral Home and later Thompson Brothers Mortuary in Memphis. Yes, that's correct — funeral homes ran ambulances, which just doesn't seem right to me. I mean, would it really be in their best interest to get you to a hospital on time? I'd be afraid the driver would dawdle along the way, maybe even stop for lunch, hoping that he could instead deliver a new "customer" to the funeral parlor that employed him.

Ruby eventually became a licensed embalmer and funeral director — again, not exactly something you want to know about the fellow behind the wheel of that ambulance you're in. When World War II started, Ruby took part in the Normandy invasion and then became an ambulance driver for the Army. After the war, he returned to Memphis and in 1950 started his own ambulance company, with just three customized Cadillacs like the one shown here.

Although it's hard to believe there was a time when people actually knew the names of ambulance drivers, Ruby was a very popular fellow around town. I found a typewritten biography on him in the Special Collections Department of the University of Memphis Libraries, prepared in 1957 for Allstate Insurance Company for some reason, and it notes, "His name is one of the best-known in Northern Mississippi."

There was a reason for that. In 1936, a killer tornado smacked into Tupelo, Mississippi, claiming more than 200 lives. Ruby was the first ambulance driver from Memphis to reach the devastated area and, according to the Allstate report, spent "days of unrelieved duty finding and rescuing victims." In later years, he helped with many other storms, wrecks, drownings, and disasters, and often worked long hours for free.

"Ambulance tires cost $100 each, but no one has ever bought Ruby a tire," says the report. "On many tornado calls he has not got a $5 bill for his trouble, nor even thanks — yet he always answers the call for help. He doesn't even entertain any hope of being paid for saving lives."

Ruby once told the *Memphis Press-Scimitar* that he had no idea how many emergency calls he had made in his long career, but he estimated he had driven more than 500,000 miles. He showed a reporter a book of "trip bills" for just one year that was almost five inches thick. "These are unpaid bills," he said. "Some have money and won't pay. Others just *can't* pay. But I have never sued a man in my life and I am not going to start now." Ruby estimated that close to 100 percent of emergency runs resulted in "hospital hauls" but only 50 percent of those patients actually paid for his service. "The other 50 percent," said the report, "is just Ruby's contribution to the welfare of the Mid-South."

One time, Ruby needed his own ambulance. On a November evening in 1960, while driving back to Memphis from Hernando, Mississippi, he hit a mule that strayed onto the highway. The mule smashed through his car's windshield. "I threw myself down in the seat just in time," he told reporters, "but it was close." A Jack Ruby ambulance rushed to the scene and whisked him to Methodist Hospital, where doctors stitched up serious head wounds from the flying glass.

Over the years, Ruby expanded his fleet, adding telephones to his cars when that was quite a novelty, and installing what the newspapers called "all the latest scientific and medical gadgets." His company was located at the corner of McLemore and College, almost across the street from Stax, and Ruby was so dedicated to his job that he made his home at the same address.

When the news reached him in November 1963 that someone named Jack Ruby had killed Lee Harvey Oswald in Dallas, he told reporters, "I didn't like that at all." People apparently called to offer their congratulations, but he would have none of it. "It shook me up," he said. "I want everybody to know it wasn't me."

Ruby passed away on March 19, 1970, at the age of 63. "Running the ambulance service that bore his name was much more than a vocation," eulogized the *Press-Scimitar*. "It was his life." Ruby was at the scene of just about every emergency in the Memphis area for more than two decades. "He handled patients gently, did not grumble if they were unable to pay, and often lingered at hospitals to reassure their loved ones. Thousands will long remember this happy-hearted, kindly, and dedicated man."

REMEMBERING RAY'S

DEAR VANCE: What do you remember about the big restaurant that once stood close to the intersection of East Parkway and North Parkway? They had very fine catfish. — J.B., MEMPHIS

DEAR J.B.: You must be remembering Ray Gammon's, a popular Memphis eatery for some 25 years. Located at 2374 Summer, it was a rather nondescript two-story brick building with a big neon sign across the front. Before Gammon moved in, the place originally housed an eatery called the Wright Diner and, later, Grisanti's Café. After some searching, I finally located the photo here in a 1969 Southwestern (now Rhodes College) yearbook. Gammon's served catfish, steaks, barbecue, and all sorts of home-cooked meals, and was quite a hangout for both college kids and families.

Gammon (above) was an interesting fellow, a former golf pro at Galloway, Cherokee, and other courses around town. At one time, he also operated The Pit, a very popular drive-in at Poplar and Hollywood. Sometime in the early 1950s, he opened Ray Gammon's on Summer, running it until poor health forced him to retire in the 1970s. Gammon died in 1975, and the restaurant closed soon after, I believe, and was demolished. The site is now a Family Dollar Store.   **M**

GOT A QUESTION FOR VANCE?
Email: askvance@memphismagazine.com
Mail: Vance Lauderdale, Memphis magazine, 460 Tennessee Street, Memphis, TN 38103
Blog: www.memphismagazine.com/askvanceblog

ASK VANCE
Our trivia expert solves local mysteries of who, what, when, where, why, and why not.

SCHOOL DAYS

by VANCE LAUDERDALE

DEAR VANCE: Whatever happened to the old Lauderdale School? I can't find it listed in the phone book. Did they tear it down?
— J.W., MEMPHIS

DEAR J.W.: Not only did they tear the fine school down, they rebuilt it, changed the name, changed the name back to Lauderdale, and then changed the name again. It's all very confusing and — I won't mince words here — a slap in the face to the Lauderdales, who have done so many great things for our city.

At the moment, I can't recall just what those great things are, but I'm pretty sure we kept a list around the house somewhere, scrawled on an old grocery sack.

At any rate, in 1902, my great-grandfather donated one of the family's polo fields to the city so they could build a new elementary school that would serve the neighborhood that had sprung up along Lauderdale Street in South Memphis. With a capacity for some 900 students, it was one of the largest schools in the city. I couldn't seem to locate any decent photos of the building itself, but I assure you it was a handsome, red-brick edifice, with dozens of classrooms, a nice gymnasium, and a spacious auditorium. I did manage to find several photos of Lauderdale's early classes, and I thought I'd include one here, just to show what noble-looking, intelligent, well-dressed children attended this wonderful center for learning. Why, just look at their happy faces and expensive clothes and — okay, I have to admit that these sad-looking children look like impoverished, starving urchins from a Charles Dickens' novel. Perhaps they didn't get the memo that they were supposed to wear their very best duds for school-pictures day.

At any rate, for decades Lauderdale School stood as a neighborhood landmark at the corner of Lauderdale and Walker. Oh, how my heart would beat with pride whenever I passed it in the limousine. Not that I ever went there, of course. Only the finest reform schools in Europe were good enough for me.

But over the years, the old school began to decline. Dreadful fires in other cities pointed out the dangers of this style of architecture, with its flammable varnished-wood interiors, narrow stairs, high windows and just about every fire-code violation you could think of. So in the early 1980s city officials demolished the old building and constructed a new school just to the north.

Years before this happened, however, the school board did something rather odd. The neighborhood around South Lauderdale had changed, so in the 1960s the city officials decided that the all-white Lauderdale School would be "a school for Negroes," as the *Memphis Press-Scimitar* put it. This was in the days before desegregation, you understand. And to avoid confusion with the old school, the new place would be called Walker Elementary School.

This always baffled me, because there was already a Walker School, an elementary school in southwest Memphis that opened in 1959. But they never consulted the Lauderdales about this matter, so in the early 1960s — I could look up the exact date, but the whole situation is too distressing — Lauderdale School became Walker School.

But only for a few years. In 1969, the school's name was changed back to Lauderdale. Perhaps because somebody finally figured out there was already a Walker School, or — and this is the more likely reason, but I can't be sure — that other school's neighborhood was incorporated into the city limits, and one of those names had to go.

So the Lauderdale School signs went back up, this time on the newer buildings. But the name has recently been changed again. Drive by today, and you'll see the complex of white concrete buildings has been named the Ida B. Wells Academy.

I can't make sense of it. I just wish I had some of the old Lauderdale banners like the one shown in the photograph. My, they would look grand flying from the flagpoles in the front yard of the mansion.

MOVIE MEMORIES

DEAR VANCE: Growing up in Memphis in the 1950s, I have fond remembrances of several places and wish you could help me with them. One is the Rosewood Theater. Do you recall where that was?.
— J.V., BOONEVILLE, MS

DEAR J.V.: It's a bit unsettling that two questions this month deal with Lauderdale Street. If this keeps up, I may have to crank up the voltage on the electric fence surrounding the Lauderdale Mansion. Just as soon as I pay the bills and get MLGW to turn the power back on at my residence, of course.

I had never heard of the Rosewood Theater and thought you were confusing it with the old Rose*mary* Theater at Jackson and Watkins. But then I decided I would spent ten minutes looking through old city directories, just in case. It was the least I could do, and I really mean that — the least.

Much to my surprise, I discovered that Memphis indeed had a Rosewood Theater, which began showing movies in 1951 at 1905 South Lauderdale. There's a halfway interesting story behind its development. If you look through old phone books, as I did, you'll see that in the late 1940s no commercial establishments stood at the intersection of Lauderdale and Rosewood. Then, in 1951, various businesses are listed here, four of them named Rosewood: the theater, the Rosewood Barber Shop, the Rosewood Beauty Shop, and the Rosewood Grille.

Behind all these ventures was an enterprising businessman named Ben Bass. I confess I don't know much about this fellow, but he constructed a pair of handsome brick buildings on both sides of Lauderdale, just south of Rosewood. The building on the east, which still carries a big stone across the top inscribed "Bass Building 1950" was home to a Big Star grocery, M&R Department Store, Longview Self-Service Laundry, Teddy's Hardware, and the aforementioned Rosewood Pharmacy and Rosewood Barber Shop.

Across the street, the other building housed the Rosewood Theater, along with Merritt's Bakery and Arthur Wesche's Restaurant. I managed to turn up an old newspaper ad (right) from July 1959 that showed what was playing that month at the Rosewood: the features *House on Haunted Hill* and *A Day for a Hanging* (gee, what cheerful fare!), along with a Captain America serial and "2 funny cartoons." All this for a quarter, if that much.

For reasons I don't know, the Rosewood stayed in business for less than a dozen years. It closed in 1962, and the big auditorium became Bennett's Club Rosewood. The building is still standing, though considerably altered

outside, and these days is home to Longview Community Holiness Church (top).

CORRECTION: In our October issue, the photos of Jack Ruby and Ray Gammon should have been credited to Special Collections, University of Memphis Libraries. We apologize for the omission.

M

GOT A QUESTION FOR VANCE?
Email: askvance@memphismagazine.com
Mail: Vance Lauderdale, Memphis magazine, 460 Tennessee Street, Memphis, TN 38103
Blog: www.memphismagazine.com/askvanceblog

ASK VANCE
Our trivia expert solves local mysteries of who, what, when, where, why, and why not.

SAFETY ZONE

by VANCE LAUDERDALE

DEAR VANCE: When I was a kid, my parents made me attend Safety Town out in Whitehaven. Do you know anything about this place?
— M.J., MEMPHIS

DEAR M.J.: I feel sorry for children like you. Each summer, most of the Lauderdale boys and girls were sent to a place we called Tetanus Town, a toxic-waste dump and scrap-metal yard outside Frayser. Splashing in the barrels of chemicals and crawling through the heaps of rusty iron was supposed to toughen us up for real-world experiences, and the fact that I am the only surviving member of the Lauderdale clan is a testament to my survival skills — and my ability to run away from home whenever the Tetanus Town bus arrived at our gates.

Safety Town was considerably nicer — a miniature "village" of sorts, complete with streets and sidewalks and tiny houses and churches and businesses. Tracing the history of these little "towns" is rather tricky, even for me, because some newspaper stories suggest that the Safety Town built in the late 1960s at Southland Mall was the first in Shelby County, and other articles imply that the version erected in the parking lot of the shopping center at Knight-Arnold and Perkins was first. I do know that, in the early 1970s, other Safety Towns sprang up in Raleigh, Germantown, and Collierville, so it's hard to make sense of it all.

What was the point? "This program will give youngsters, under supervision, real training in moving safely about a community, knowing what to do in case of danger," county sheriff Bill Morris told reporters in 1970. The little community was sponsored by the local police and fire departments, Jaycees, the PTA, Kiwanis, and all sorts of other civic groups.

As you pointed out, M.J., children enrolled for one week at the various Safety Towns over the summer, where they learned the proper rules and guidelines for riding bikes, crossing busy streets, walking along sidewalks, calling the police, and shooting it out with bandits during a bank robbery.

No — I made up that last part!

But the Parkway Village Safety Town did add a "real world" experience, by constructing a miniature jail, where kids who broke the rules were "imprisoned." For how long, I can't say, but I found a newspaper article that reported, "The jail was a big hit with students." Oh, I bet.

The kids also watched films on home safety, fire prevention, and other topics, but since the program was designed for pre-schoolers, they were spared the horror of those bloody driver's education films, thank goodness. Afterwards, at their "graduation," they got hamburgers, lemonade, a fake driver's license, and even a diploma.

The Special Collections Department at the University of Memphis Libraries has a thick folder crammed with photos taken at the Southland Mall Safety Town in the early 1970s. The one shown here especially intrigued me. Is that costumed creature supposed to be Snoopy? No offense to Charles Schultz, but a cartoon character that engaged in aerial dogfights with the Red Baron and slept on the steep roof of his doghouse doesn't seem the best role model for a place obsessed with safety. Plus, it's always a good idea, if you ask me, for children to avoid adults dressed in creepy costumes.

I'm sure you had a good experience at Safety Town, M.J., but give me Tetanus Town any day.

THE LION'S DEN

DEAR VANCE: I just purchased an old yearbook for the Pentecost-Garrison School in Memphis, and had never heard of such a place. What can you tell me about it?
— T.B., MEMPHIS

DEAR T.B.: The rather formidable name suggests this institution was some kind of military school, but in fact it was one of our city's finest private schools for boys, and the name derived from its founders, cousins Althea Pentecost (right) and Beatrice Garrison.

The Lauderdale Library has the entire set of yearbooks published by the Pentecost-Garrison School — all two of them. In the 1950 edition of the *Lion's Tale*, headmistress Pentecost talked of new additions to the school, including a nice gymnasium, and bragged about various scholastic accomplishments: "Today, schools in the East which once frowned upon Southern schools eagerly seek our students. Our honor students have, in the past and at present, given good accounts of themselves." Indeed, just glancing through the book reveals a "who's who" of big-name Memphians in attendance there, including J.R. "Pitt" Hyde, Fred Smith, Bayard Boyle, Humphrey Folk, Allen Morgan, Metcalf Crump, and many others.

Pentecost concluded, "Undoubtedly our future is assured. The success of the yesterdays is but the stepping stone to the future." But not much of a future, as it turned out. In the next edition of the *Lion's Tale*, the "Message from Miss Pentecost" began by saying, "And now, Good-bye!" Yep. The school closed in 1951. It had quite a history.

The story goes that back in 1914, E.H. "Boss" Crump ran a newspaper ad seeking a tutor for his children, and Althea Pentecost took the job. She liked teaching so much that in 1915 she teamed up with her cousin, "Miss Bea," and opened a school for boys in a residence on Monroe, with just eight students in four grades. Five years later, they had so many kids they moved to 43 South Idlewild, and then five years later moved again, this time to 28 South Idlewild.

Enrollment and finances increased steadily over the years, and in 1940 Pentecost-Garrison purchased land at 2485 Union and constructed a stunning new building. The ground floor contained 12 spacious classrooms, with a lunchroom in the basement and other facilities here and there. Just about the entire second floor, so I understand, was devoted to living quarters for Garrison and Pentecost.

Garrison died in 1944, but the school hummed along for another decade under the direction of Pentecost. An old *Press-Scimitar* article bragged, "It is the only school of its type in the Mid-South, and has specialized in preparing boys to enter the Eastern boarding schools such as Choate, Andover, Hill, Exeter, Middlesex, and Groton with an educational foundation broad enough to bear up under their rigid courses." Enrollment had increased to almost 250.

Then all of a sudden Pentecost sold the property to the Southern College of Optometry. She told reporters that the new East High School had hurt her enrollment, and besides, she said, "I have been teaching for 36 years — morning, afternoon, and evening — and I cannot continue this responsibility. My health will not permit it."

This did not sit well with the school's alumni, board, and neighbors. For one thing, the new school had been built with the understanding the property would endure for years and years as a private school. Much of the work and materials had been donated. And Memphians were concerned that our city was losing its premier educational establishment for young boys. Memphis University School, you must remember, had opened back in the late 1800s but had been closed since 1936.

Eventually, a sort of compromise was reached. This gets complicated, so pay attention. Pentecost-Garrison School would close, but its students would move to a new school on Poplar operated by Second Presbyterian Church, called Presbyterian Day School (still in operation today, of course). In a few years, MUS would also reopen its doors, at a sprawling new campus in East Memphis.

To make the neighbors happy, the optometry college instead moved into new quarters in the Medical Center. The Pentecost-Garrison School campus was taken over by Lausanne School, so that corner was still home to a small private school, though now for girls instead of boys. And Miss Pentecost herself moved out of the building

into a modern new home on Central, where she lived until her death in 1966.

Lausanne moved to new facilities on Massey Road in 1959. The old Pentecost-Garrison building changed hands several times and is still standing on Union, these days home to the Memphis City Schools' Teaching and Learning Academy. And back in the 1920s, when Misses Pentecost and Garrison were running their school on South Idlewild? Well, one of those homes was demolished to make way for an apartment tower, but the other, at 28 South Idlewild, today houses Garbo's, the popular women's apparel store. **M**

GOT A QUESTION FOR VANCE?

Email: askvance@memphismagazine.com
Mail: Vance Lauderdale, Memphis magazine, 460 Tennessee Street #200, Memphis, TN 38103
Blog: www.memphismagazine.com/askvanceblog

ASK VANCE

Our trivia expert solves local mysteries of who, what, when, where, why, and why not.

MAYSIE'S MURALS

by VANCE LAUDERDALE

DEAR VANCE: During World War II, a Memphis artist named Mayze Diamond painted a large mural on the wall of Ellis Auditorium. When the building was demolished, was there an attempt to preserve this amazing painting? If so, where is it located now?
— J.G., MEMPHIS

DEAR J.G.: Never have I worked harder to solve a mystery than this one. As soon as I received your letter, I put all my hundreds of other projects aside, leaned back in my La-Z-Boy, squinched my eyes tight, and began to ponder, peruse, contemplate, and THINK as hard as I could. The story goes that lights in the office dimmed that morning, their power consumed by the energy of my intellect, but that is probably a myth. What's true, however, is that one of my colleagues, noticing the agony I was in, grabbed me by the shoulders and begged of me, "Stop it, Vance. Don't kill yourself over this! It's not worth it." I shook her off, and she brought back a damp dishtowel to place on my forehead to cool my seething brain.

After about 15 minutes of this, I dozed off, as I usually do. When I woke up, it occurred to me to halfheartedly look over some old newspaper articles about the demolition of Ellis Auditorium, just to see if they mentioned these murals. Not a word, so for a while I didn't know what to tell you. Since they were painted directly on the plaster walls, I assumed they came down with the building. What a shame.

But your question gave me a chance to learn more about Maysie Dimond (*that's* how she spelled her name), so I might as well share a bit of her story with you — what little I know about it, I mean.

Maysie was born around 1900 in Jackson, Mississippi, and came to Memphis in the 1930s when her husband, A.C., became a superintendent at the Navy Yard here. While raising two children, she began attending the Memphis Academy of Arts and trained under talented instructors such as Katherine Forest and Dorothy Sturm.

She first made the news in November 1937 when the *Memphis Press-Scimitar* reported that a nice painting she made of the little community of Dyess, Arkansas, would be presented to Eleanor Roosevelt. The newspaper explained that "Mrs. Franklin D. Roosevelt has long been interested in the Dyess Colony" because it was one of this country's first "resettlement projects," which offered free land to impoverished farmers during the Depression. That's Maysie shown here, alongside the painting given to Mrs. Roosevelt. I wonder where that is today?

In 1940, the city somehow got a grant from the federal government's Works Progress Administration to add some festive murals to Ellis Auditorium, and Maysie got the job. It was quite a project: 10 murals stretching more than 150 feet along the north hall of the old auditorium. Although the local newspapers noted that she "received no artistic training until coming to Memphis," she must have been an apt pupil, because three "models" of the first murals were sent to the American Federation of Arts. The AFA president commented, "It is an excellent piece of work and reflects great credit on Memphis."

What's especially intriguing, J.G., is that the *Press-Scimitar* noted that Robert McKnight, then head of the art academy, "had not yet determined whether the murals will be painted on canvas and cemented to the wall, or frescoed." If they had been painted on canvas, they might have been rescued. But according to the online *Tennessee Encyclopedia of History and Culture*, Maysie applied the paint directly to the wet plaster.

The project took 18 months. The first three panels featured the Chickasaw Indians, Hernando DeSoto, and city founders John Overton, Marcus Winchester, and Andrew Jackson. The hardest part was deciding what to include next: "Her trouble, for covering the period of the last 120 years, is not in finding subjects for the remaining seven panels, but in narrowing the wide field of subjects down."

I'm assuming, of course, that at least one panel (and maybe more) was devoted to the Lauderdales.

The finished piece, blandly titled "Memphis in Murals," was unveiled during a Memphis Symphony concert on November 14, 1942. A reporter called it "four hundred years of Memphis history, written in gay colors and spirited symbols, in a great mural nine feet high and half a block long." They remained visible for about a decade. In the 1950s, during one of those ill-conceived renovations that seemed to plague Memphis, Maysie's murals were covered up by slabs of pink marble.

In 1984, the murals were uncovered when the auditorium was renovated. They had already been damaged over the years when extra doors were punched through the wall, and archeologist Guy Weaver tells me that Memphis Heritage tried to salvage them, but they were unable to remove them — or even find a new home for them if they could. By all accounts, the murals were demolished along with the rest of the auditorium to make way for the new Cannon Center.

I certainly hope Maysie got an A+ from the art academy for all her hard work.

FURLOTTE'S MISFORTUNES

DEAR VANCE: In the 1950s, my parents say they used to eat at a restaurant in South Memphis called Furlotte's. What do you know about it?
— H.H., MEMPHIS

DEAR H.H.: I know that if you turn to "Ask Vance" for happy, heart-warming stories, then you'd better keep turning the pages, because the story of Furlotte's is a sad one.

Arthur Furlotte (right) was an A&P store manager in Wisconsin in the 1930s, then moved to Memphis after World War II and opened a steak house at 1011 South Third, across from Gaston Park. Newspapers said his slogan was "Catering to Nice People from Everywhere," and the back of the old postcard (above) brags that Furlotte "serves the best food on earth, or anywhere else."

Maybe it was true, because by the mid-1950s, Furlotte had also opened a drive-in at 3170 South Third, a coffee shop downtown in the Ambassador Hotel, and even an eatery called the Flying Saucer (no, not the one you know today) at 164 South Court. A restaurant review from 1951 glossed over the food, but noted the cluttery décor of the establishment on South Third: "Unusual or old firearms and military equipment, plus novel uses of fishing and other sports equipment, are comment-drawing decorations on the wall of the new restaurant." Those guns, as it turned out, were a bad idea.

Things apparently went well for several years, then Furlotte began to make the news for all the wrong reasons: Drunken driving convictions. Several arrests for assault with a deadly weapon. Yet another arrest for extortion. And then the worst: On the morning of June 17, 1963, Furlotte picked up an old Japanese rifle, shot his wife to death at their apartment at 2209 Florida, then turned the gun on himself. He survived, but spent months in the hospital. After he recovered, a judge declared him insane and committed him to the Central State Hospital in Nashville. After several years, he was transferred to the state prison, and in 1969, newspapers announced he would be paroled "as soon as a suitable program, including employment, for him is complete."

I don't know what happened after that, but he died in Sumner County, Tennessee, in 1978 at the age of 71. Most of his restaurants are now vacant lots. As I said, not a happy story, is it? **M**

GOT A QUESTION FOR VANCE?
Email: askvance@memphismagazine.com
Mail: Vance Lauderdale, Memphis magazine, 460 Tennessee Street #200, Memphis, TN 38103
Blog: www.memphismagazine.com/askvanceblog

▸ **ASK VANCE**
Our trivia expert solves local mysteries of who, what, when, where, why, and why not.

BIG DAY AT BIG STAR

DEAR VANCE: When I was just a kid, sometime in the early 1960s, I remember that a grocery store on Macon Road buried a time capsule as part of its grand opening. Is that time capsule still there?
— D.J., MEMPHIS

DEAR D.J.: When I was a child, I created my own time capsule from an old mayonnaise jar. I filled it with various coins, some newspaper clippings that I thought interesting, a list of my friends and favorite toys, and all sorts of other things that would tell future generations about my life as a Lauderdale. I carefully sealed the lid with fingernail polish — my mother's, not mine! — and buried it beneath an azalea bush in the back yard.

Time passed, and finally I decided to dig up my time capsule to see how the world had changed around me. After all, it had been a whole *two months* — an eternity for a young child with nothing to do all day long. When I opened it, I discovered to my dismay that everything inside was wet and moldy. The coins were okay, of course, but everything else was ruined.

This taught me a valuable lesson in life, one that I have carried with me to this day. Namely, that fingernail polish is lousy for sealing mayonnaise-jar time capsules. And now I pass that helpful bit of advice on to you, dear readers.

Your query intrigued me, D.J., so my first step was to determine the location of this grocery store. A quick search through 1960s city directories gave me a half-dozen possibilities: Silver Saver #7 at 3394 Macon, Jack's Drive-in at 3425, the Quick Shop Market at 3870, Stepherson's Big Star at 3942, Big D Food Store at 4280, and Handy Pantry #9 at 4497. I narrowed it down to the two larger establishments — Stepherson's and Big D — ones that I figured would actually celebrate a grand opening in an unusual way, and journeyed to the University of Memphis library to look through their old newspaper files.

Pay dirt! Within minutes I uncovered an article and photo (above) that answered your question. The store was indeed Stepherson's Big Star, owned by three brothers: Jack, Wesley, and Kenneth Stepherson. But it wasn't actually a time capsule, D.J. Instead, while members of the Stepherson family watched, the builders of the supermarket inserted a nice concrete cornerstone into the brick façade. Inside, they had stuffed a rather odd collection of things, including six sealed copies of the *Memphis Press-Scimitar* and a zoning petition "signed by 5,000 housewives, so the store could be built." According to the article, the store originally opened one block west of where it stands today. The city's planning commission turned down the application to construct a larger store down the street, "but the housewives got them to change, so the Stephersons call it the 'customers store.'"

It's all very confusing. But including the newspapers was a clever stunt, you see, since it practically guaranteed a nice story in the *Press-Scimitar*.

In case you're curious, the people in the photo — posed in front of some of those housewives — are (left to right) masonry contractor David Estes, Jimmy Stepherson, City Judge Beverly Boushe, Randy Stepherson, Jack Stepherson (holding the newspapers), and brick contractor Brooks Varner. I don't know why co-owners Wesley and Kenneth aren't in the picture. Maybe one of them was holding the camera.

The newspaper article ended with this interesting statement: "Jimmy and Randy will remove the cornerstone at 9 a.m. on March 15, 2000." Why just 40 years later, I wondered? And more to the point: Was this still there, and had anybody remembered to open it?

The answer is: yes. I drove to Stepherson's Big Star, which is still doing a thriving business on Macon, and right by the front door is the stone you see in the picture. The managers inside told me that family members indeed pried the stone out of the wall 10 years ago, pulled out the contents, and replaced the stone. "They didn't put anything back in it, though," said the woman behind the counter. "I don't know why."

MISSING MEMORIAL

DEAR VANCE: Whatever happened to the plans to build a giant obelisk dedicated to Hernando DeSoto in Memphis? I've seen drawings of it somewhere, but never knew where it was to be located.
— T.L., MEMPHIS

DEAR T.L.: I normally like to provide definite answers to questions, but long ago I realized that I get paid the same whether the answer is complete, sort of correct, or even wrong, so here's what I know, and it's not much.

I've seen those drawings too, and found one (shown here) that adorned the cover of a promotional brochure for our city, published in the early 1960s. I also turned up a newspaper article from 1968, which said that plans for the proposed DeSoto Memorial Tower "had seemingly been consigned to oblivion."

Renderings show what seems to be a dangerously thin, 350-foot concrete shaft in the middle of the new Civic Center Plaza downtown. The newspaper said it would be built "in the general vicinity of Front and Washington," accompanied by an equestrian statue of the Spanish explorer, who gets credit for discovering the Mississippi River. Supporters said it would "provide a handsome gateway to our city."

But a few problems arose. First of all, not everyone was convinced that DeSoto deserved such a monument. The chairman of a citizen's committee to construct the obelisk admitted, "A government study was made to fix the point where DeSoto actually discovered the Mississippi River, but I don't think they ever fixed the spot. I think they said it definitely wasn't Memphis." Oops.

Another issue was money. Somebody on the committee told reporters, "The tower would be built by private subscription, but no one ever spearheaded a drive to build it." Another "oops." Not a dime was raised for what looks like a very expensive project.

It sounds like a botched job from the beginning, if you ask me. At any rate, City Hall stands on the proposed site today, and in the 1970s we put DeSoto's name on the I-40 bridge instead. It's too bad the big tower wasn't built, though; it would have made one heckuva sundial.

M

GOT A QUESTION FOR VANCE?
Email: askvance@memphismagazine.com
Mail: Vance Lauderdale, Memphis magazine, 460 Tennessee Street #200, Memphis, TN 38103
Blog: www.memphismagazine.com/askvanceblog

ASK VANCE
Our trivia expert solves local mysteries of who, what, when, where, why, and why not.

HELTER SHELTER

by VANCE LAUDERDALE

DEAR VANCE: They recently tore down the old Colonial Junior High School in East Memphis, built in the 1950s, and I was wondering if they found any relics from the civil defense bomb shelter in the basement.
— A.N., MEMPHIS

DEAR A.N.: I can tell you with certainty that they never found anything from a bomb shelter there, for the simple reason that Colonial — unlike many other schools and public buildings here — didn't *have* a bomb shelter. The Lauderdale Library contains a copy of the *Community Shelter Plan*, published in 1968 by the Memphis and Shelby County Civil Defense Agency, which shows the precise location of every shelter in Memphis, and the closest one to Colonial was actually miles away.

This document is a fascinating relic from one of the strangest periods in our nation's history. You have to remember that America was a nervous place in the 1950s. After Russia and other countries developed nuclear bombs, we became fretful that Memphis would become the next Nagasaki. It wasn't a completely unreasonable fear; then as now, Memphis was a transportation hub, and years ago we had important industries — Firestone and International Harvester, among them — that could be considered strategic targets.

But the bomb shelters — technically, "fallout" shelters since they shielded occupants from radiation, not explosives — came later. First came a much more disturbing plan. In the 1950s, the government printed millions of bright yellow pamphlets called "Be Safe from the H-Bomb" — an ironic title since there is, of course, no way to be "safe" from a hydrogen bomb. Instead, the government's proposal was best summarized by that Monty Python movie, whenever the knights are confronted with danger: "Run away!!" And that was the general plan here. Just not as funny.

The little booklet, inserted in copies of *The Commercial Appeal* and *Memphis Press-Scimitar* (if you weren't a subscriber, tough luck!), basically advised Memphians to get out of the city — fast. "We can be fairly sure of a two-hour warning before the enemy can get here," said the booklet. In case of an impending attack, the air-raid sirens that had been mounted on rooftops around the city would sound a "five-minute steady blast." So — if the bombing was conveniently timed to take place when your family was together at home — you hopped in your car and followed one of the emergency evacuation routes printed in the booklet.

Where were you going, exactly? Well,

that was another problem. You were instructed to drive out of the "Danger Zone," a circle that extended 15 miles from downtown Memphis (authorities apparently felt that a nuclear bomb would be dropped precisely on Mud Island). So you drove and drove until you reached the towns and communities beyond the "Safety Line." There, you were expected to stay a while with friends or relatives. Hmmm, didn't know anybody in, say, Rossville or Grand Junction? In that case, the booklet reassured you, "arrangements will be made to feed, clothe, and shelter the thousands who will need help." Oh, sure . . .

The dog-eared "Be Safe from the H-Bomb" booklet in my possession has some pencil scribblings, indicating where a local family, apparently living on Given Road in East Memphis, highlighted the route they were supposed to follow — south on Graham, then eastward out Summer past the Safety Line. I could just imagine some grim-faced father back in 1958, gathered around the dinner table with his family, showing them the disaster plan, and trying to convince them it was a good idea.

It was a *terrible* idea — trying to move the entire population of Memphis out of town in two hours? Authorities seemed to regard a nuclear attack as a minor inconvenience, and the "H-Bomb" manual — like most Civil Defense materials, always upbeat in the face of doom — never suggested that there might be no home — or city, for that matter — to return *to*. Anyone who has seen photos of Nagasaki or Hiroshima surely realized that a nuclear bomb caused one heckuva mess, and then there would be that pesky problem of invading armies. I mean, I am no military genius, but it seems unlikely that our enemy — whoever it might be — would just drop a couple of bombs and then give up.

Officials grudgingly admitted there would be certain aggravations: "Moving over 400,000 people is a tremendous task," said the booklet. "With everyone evacuating the city at the same time, roads will be clogged and traffic will be slower than normal. Be patient."

Patient? With an H-bomb about to drop on our heads? We're talking about people who freak out when they wait in line at the inspection station!

So the civil defense experts finally came up with an entirely different plan. Instead of running away, take shelter. In 1961, Congress created the National Shelter Program. This incredibly ambitious, outrageously expensive program built hundreds of fallout shelters in every city in America, their locations marked on buildings with the familiar cluster of yellow triangles in a black circle (below). In Memphis, we set up 279 shelters, with 251 of them fully stocked with food and medical supplies. Property owners were persuaded to donate space for these places, usually in basements or other secure areas.

Water was stored in 17-gallon drums. Packets of food (if you can call it that) came in the form of "survival crackers and biscuits" — which by all accounts tasted gosh-awful. Special sanitation kits, housed in heavy cardboard drums, contained toilet paper, drinking cups, and other necessities. Not included were things like beds, chairs, or even cots. Shelter users were supposed to bring their own.

So this was the new plan: In case of an attack, you were instructed to walk — not drive — to your nearest fallout shelter, bed down there for a week or so with all your neighbors, and then, when radiation levels had subsided and the "All Clear" message was sounded, come out into the sunshine and life would just be peachy again.

The locations of all these shelters were clearly marked on a 16-page *Community Shelter Plan*, published in November 1968. Once again, immediate problems are apparent. First of all, there weren't enough shelters to hold even half of our city's population. Second, they weren't scattered very evenly over the area. With nuclear missiles providing the worst threat, forget about that two-hour warning in the 1950s; the best you could hope for now was 45 minutes. I don't know how well you can see this detail from Map 8, but it includes a good portion of East Memphis, and almost all the shelters (indicated by numbered circles) are clustered up and down Poplar Avenue. If you happened to live miles away on, say, Willow, in southeast Memphis, there was simply no way your family was going to gather their belongings — don't forget the chairs! — and trudge to a shelter on Poplar in 45 minutes.

And even if you did, you can imagine the chaos if the shelters were already full, and they tried to turn you away.

The lucky ones who made it to the shelters didn't exactly enjoy a holiday. The woman shown here is perched happily on one of the supply drums, pretending to munch on one of those tooth-breaking crackers. Well, she looks pretty spiffy now, but give her a few days. Because after you emptied that drum, you slapped a plastic seat on the top, and that single container became the public toilet for the entire shelter. Do I really need to go into the details? Tucked away in unventilated basements, with no bathtubs or even sinks, it wouldn't take long for conditions inside the shelters to become unbearable.

The "community shelter program" just faded away. Most of the shelters were closed down and eventually emptied, but people still stumble on them from time to time. Years ago, Tommy Bronson Sporting Goods moved from Union Avenue to a new location in Poplar Plaza. When employees ventured into the basement, they discovered a still-unopened cache of civil defense supplies. In case you were wondering, they were quickly retrieved by the current Emergency Management Agency.

Many people, seeing the flaws in these disaster plans, just decided to stay home during a crisis, and magazines like *Popular Mechanics* showed readers how to build their own bomb shelters. In case of a disaster, I plan to retreat to the fortified basement of the Lauderdale Mansion. Because of the constant threat from kidnappers and assassins, it's pretty much where I live these days anyway. M

GOT A QUESTION FOR VANCE?
Email: askvance@memphismagazine.com
Mail: Vance Lauderdale, *Memphis magazine*, 460 Tennessee Street #200, Memphis, TN 38103
Blog: www.memphismagazine.com/askvanceblog

ASK VANCE
Our trivia expert solves local mysteries of who, what, when, where, why, and why not.

ROUGH RIDE

by VANCE LAUDERDALE

DEAR VANCE: My parents told me about an old amusement park in East Memphis that had cable cars. One day, the ride somehow got stuck, and many of the riders were stranded overnight. True story?
— G.T., MEMPHIS

DEAR G.T.: That old park was called Lakeland, and I was halfway tempted to put your query off for exactly one year, because June 2011 would mark the 50th anniversary of its opening. However, my team of highly paid veterinarians say I have picked up a severe case of kennel cough. They offer little hope of a full recovery, though they've given me shots and dog biscuits and a warm blanket and told me to "hope for the best," so I'd better not wait any longer.

I'm sure your parents meant well, but most of the tales about Lakeland are always just a bit off. First of all, it wasn't located in East Memphis; it was several miles to the northeast, around the intersection of I-40 and Canada Road. It was definitely an unusual place, developed in the early 1960s by an enterprising fellow named Louis Garner, who visited Ruby Falls near Chattanooga and came back to Memphis convinced that he could build "The Disneyland of the Mid-South."

So Garner bought 1,200 acres along Canada Road, built a massive dam, dug artesian wells, and soon had the largest lake in Shelby County, which he named Garner Lake, in his modest way. I admire that. He then proceeded to piece together what he would describe as "The World's Largest Playground."

A mile-long skyride (above) scavenged from the 1958 Brussels Worlds Fair carried visitors through the woods and high across the wide lake (more about that later). Down below, folks enjoyed a full-scale amusement park, trampoline pits, the largest swimming pool in Shelby County, and an outdoor dance pavilion. A paddlewheeler called the *Roberta E. Lee* ferried passengers around the lake.

A major attraction was the Huff-n-Puff Railroad, an old-timey steam locomotive that circled the lake. A racetrack called the Lakeland Speed Bowl opened on Canada Road, and an even larger facility, complete with dragstrip and road course, opened a few miles to the south, called the Shelby

102 • ASK VANCE II

County International Raceway.

Still to come, Garner promised, would be a 300-foot-tall observation tower with a Coletta's restaurant perched at the top, a horse-racing track, gardens "as outstanding as the ones at Bellingrath," a 10,000-seat amphitheatre, hundreds of rental cottages, an animated jungle ride, glass-bottom boats, a lighted 18-hole golf course — why, even submarine rides.

Lakeland opened on June 2, 1961, but the place he built was a far cry from his original plans. Disneyland offered visitors gleaming monorails, soaring castles, and even a replica of the Matterhorn. Lakeland was decidedly more humble, with its slides and swings and dunking tanks and a rickety fishing pier.

"We had the ideas Disney had for Disneyland," Garner told reporters, "but we didn't have the resources to put it together."

The skyride was definitely a unique attraction, and a newspaper reporter who climbed aboard when Lakeland opened said, "The sensation is one of floating in complete silence, like movement in space." Riders a few years later had an entirely different experience. The four-passenger cars dangled from a half-inch cable riding through grooved pulleys mounted on a series of 90-foot pylons. On the afternoon of May 27, 1968, a mighty gust of wind caused the cable to jump its track, jamming it and stranding 55 passengers high over the lake. The 20-minute ride became a nine-hour ordeal.

They weren't there overnight, but it surely seemed that way to the unfortunate passengers — most of them children. The ride broke down at 4 p.m., and rescue crews struggled for hours to end what newspapers called "a chilling adventure." In addition to fire departments from Memphis, Raleigh, Bartlett, and Germantown, the effort involved Memphis Light, Gas and Water crews and even something called the Marine Rescue Squad. No one had anticipated such an event, and there was simply no way to position a rocking boat under some of the gondolas and extend a ladder almost 100 feet during a windstorm. Fire department ladder trucks initially couldn't get close enough because they got mired in the soft soil, but everybody was finally pulled from the cars.

After swaying in the wind for that long, many passengers were so dizzy they were unable to walk once they got down, and they were taken to hospitals for observation. Newspapers reported, "As the skyriders were rescued, the Red Cross was on hand to dispense food and warm blankets, while some of the children were walked around in a roped-off area until circulation was restored. They received arm and leg massages."

Garner and his crews used loudspeakers to keep everyone apprised of the rescue efforts: "They knew what we were doing all the time and remained calm. The parents showed more apprehension on the ground than the children in the gondolas."

As far as I know, everyone recovered, though I bet none of them ever ventured aboard *that* thing again.

Lakeland officials quickly announced they would install special rescue baskets, similar to those used at ski resorts, just in case such a freak accident happened again (it didn't). And Garner took pains to point out that more than five million passengers — that number seems impossibly high, if you ask me — had ridden the skyride since it opened six years before, "and this was the first mishap." Despite the inconvenience, he said, "There was never any danger of the gondolas falling, because each tower has a safety mechanism."

It's hard to imagine that much-smaller Libertyland could put anybody out of business, but when it opened in 1976, Lakeland couldn't compete. The new park was a lot closer for most Memphians. "We tried everything in the book — and a lot that's not in the book — to stay alive," Garner admitted to reporters.

The park finally closed in 1978, though the racetrack stayed busy for several more years. The skyride was dismantled and sold, but I can't remember who bought it. For years, one of the gondolas gathered dust in a barn off Canada Road, and the ruins of the dragstrip have survived in the woods south of I-40. The "Disneyland of the Mid-South" gradually evolved into the town of Lakeland, a nice town of some 8,000. I wonder how many of them drive past "Huff-n-Puff Road" and think about how it got such an unusual name?

DESCENT OF THE BLUES

DEAR VANCE: Whatever happened to that weird music-related sculpture that was erected in the park next to the Morgan Keegan Tower?
— C.D., MEMPHIS

DEAR C.D.: *The Ascent of the Blues*, as it was called, made a sudden and unexpected descent to the ground on May 30, 1990. The $250,000 sculpture was an odd-looking and, in my humble opinion, decidedly top-heavy assemblage of bronze castings of musical instruments — horns, guitars, keyboards, and more. It had been created by a French artist named Arman — yes, just Arman — and erected in the open space originally set aside for a second Morgan Keegan Tower.

When those plans fell through, the land was sold to make way for the Sleep Inn, and the 30-foot structure had to be moved. An engineering professor from Christian Brothers University had already warned that the heavy sculpture was dangerous. "It had no spine, no backbone, nothing to carry the load," Dr. Tom Morrison told reporters shortly after *Ascent* was unveiled in 1987.

Apparently he was right. Just three years later, crews from the National Ornamental Metal Museum began to carefully dismantle the piece, one instrument at a time, when it snapped in half, tumbling to the ground and slightly injuring one of the workers. They were lucky no one was killed. All the pieces were eventually scooped up and stored in a warehouse somewhere, but Metal Museum experts said it would cost almost $100,000 to repair it, so *Ascent of the Blues* just gathered dust.

I asked Carissa Hussong, museum director, if she knew where the piece was today.

"If I did, the piece would already have been repaired and installed somewhere in Memphis," she said. "I tried to find it when I was the director of the UrbanArt Commission. My guess is that the piece was scrapped by someone who had no idea what it was or why it was in storage. So perhaps your article will trigger someone's memory and it will finally come out of hiding." **M**

GOT A QUESTION FOR VANCE?
Email: askvance@memphismagazine.com
Mail: Vance Lauderdale, Memphis magazine, 460 Tennessee Street #200, Memphis, TN 38103
Blog: www.memphismagazine.com/askvanceblog

ASK VANCE

Our trivia expert solves local mysteries of who, what, when, where, why, and why not.

FAIRVIEW HOSPITAL?

by VANCE LAUDERDALE

DEAR VANCE: I went to Fairview Junior High School and was always told it used to be an old hospital. Is that true?
— V.W., MEMPHIS

DEAR V.W.: I'm surprised nobody has asked me about this fascinating establishment before. Constructed sometime in the mid-1800s on a hill overlooking East Parkway, Fair-View (as it was then called) served as a place of refuge and recovery for victims of the battle of Shiloh during the Civil War. Years later, the building that now serves as the school gymnasium operated as a makeshift morgue for hundreds of Memphians who died during the yellow fever epidemics. And on that awful day of June 2, 1928, doctors here treated the unfortunate children crippled during the Great Zippin Pippin Disaster, when . . .

Oh, none of that's true. I was just seeing if you were paying attention. For one thing, East Parkway wasn't even laid out until 1904. And anyone who walked through the front doors of Fairview passed right by a six-foot-tall stone plaque that clearly shows the Memphis Board of Education erected the building in 1930.

The inscription gives the exact dates of construction: FAIRVIEW JUNIOR HIGH SCHOOL — Erected from April the First to September the First 1930." It then lists the members of the Board of Education responsible for approving construction of the new school: W.J. Prescott, president; H.H. Honnol, vice president; and three others without titles: J.C. Carruthers, Mrs. Mamie Cain Browne, and Mrs. Eldren Rogers.

Even so, I can understand some people might think Fairview wasn't originally a school building, because it doesn't resemble any other educational facility in our city. With its distinctive buff-colored brick, its stunning art deco design, and — most of all — its tons of brightly colored terra-cotta detailing, this is not your typical red-brick schoolhouse. In fact, Eugene Johnson and Robert Russell Jr., the authors of *Memphis: An Architectural Guide*, consider it "the architectural gem of the school system and one of the finest buildings in the whole city."

That plaque by the front door says the school was erected by S&W Construction Company, and the architectural firm was E.L. Harrison. Most of the work on this building was done by one of Harrison's young associates. "The real mind behind

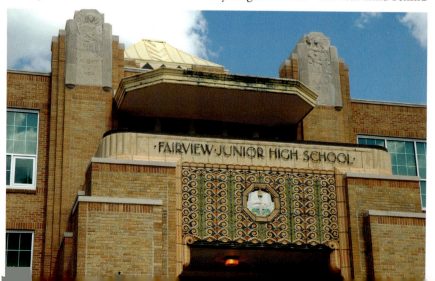

Fairview was Noland Van Powell," say Russell and Johnson, "and it is fair to say that this is his surviving masterpiece."

Powell (1904-1977) was an accomplished painter and architect, and his work lives on in the classical elegance of The Peabody's Plantation Room and the colonial charm of Chickasaw Oaks Mall. Other notable projects — done alone or in conjunction with other architects — include the Memphis Steam Laundry Building, the old Three Sisters Building downtown, Greyhound bus stations and Toddle House diners throughout the Mid-South, and dozens of fine Memphis homes.

Without any formal architectural training, Powell served as an apprentice for the Harrison firm before eventually branching out on his own. But if he designed Fairview as an apprentice, then that makes the finished building even more remarkable. You can spend quite some time in front of the school admiring all the wonderful details: the elaborate two-story entrance pavilion (shown here), the almost-gaudy mosaic-tile frieze above the doors, the flanking towers with their stylized representations of "Day" and "Night," the stone plaques set into the brickwork along the façade — it just goes on and on.

On a recent visit to photograph the school, I peered through the doors and made the same discovery noted by the authors of *An Architectural Guide*: "Lots of schools put all their architectural power on the outside and leave the inside to the students. At Fairview, however, the outside part of the entrance is just half of the experience of coming into the school."

Inside, you'll find sweeping black-and-tan marble staircases, art deco-designed trophy cases, and even rows of incredibly elaborate light fixtures that have somehow survived more than eight decades of students.

Fairview was never a hospital, but for any admirer of fine architecture, it sure makes you feel good to look at it. "Fairview is a wonderful building," conclude Johnson and Russell. "It takes a difficult architectural problem — the American secondary school — and does great things with it."

ESTATE PLANNING

DEAR VANCE: I heard that a "community of the future" was built in East Memphis in the 1950s. Are they talking about the Williamsburg Colony in Parkway Village?

— D.T., MEMPHIS

DEAR D.T.: Hmmm. I think I can safely say that the residential development on Knight-Arnold, with a dozen or so homes based on

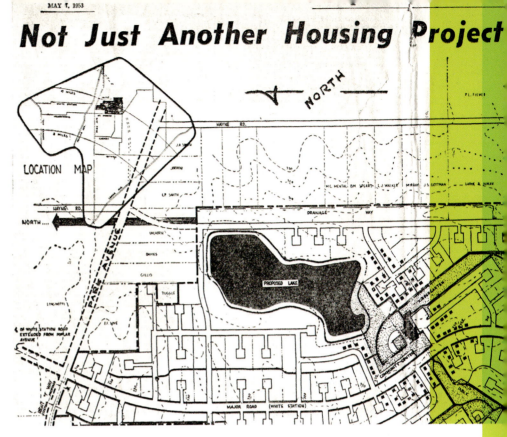

Not Just Another Housing Project

historic properties in Colonial Williamsburg, would actually be a community of the past — not of the future.

No, what you are surely talking about is the innovative Country Club Estates, a "city of the future" to be developed in the area bounded by Park Avenue, White Station, Quince, and Estate. It was patterned after a rather unusual subdivision in Radburn, New Jersey — surely one of the few times that New Jersey has been used as a good model for anything.

I've included a rather fuzzy map that ran in the May 1, 1953, edition of the *Memphis Press-Scimitar* that showed how the Radburn Plan, as it came to be called, would be applied here. It's basically a grid of major thoroughfares, with the residential streets laid out as neat rows of cul-de-sacs (most of us call them "coves"). A centrally located park would include a lake and community center, and a large retail center would be constructed to the south. All the streets would be pedestrian friendly, with the smaller streets actually tunneling beneath the larger ones so nobody would have to battle traffic.

As the newspaper explained, "It winds walkways through the entire development, over grassy areas and beneath trees — with pedestrian underpasses to carry residents from any place in the community to any other place in the community, without having to cross a street."

Country Club Estates would include precisely 1,750 single-family homes, described as "contemporary architecture of the Nth degree" — a precise scientific measurement which, I assume, is much better than homes of "L" or even "M" degrees. Renderings actually showed rather small, plain-looking single-story homes with flat roofs and detached carports. The Lauderdales would never purchase such a thing, let me tell you.

Local developer J.A. Montgomery claimed the development would "serve present-day requirements of good living in a more practical and pleasant way than does the conventional pattern of subdivision living." The newspapers of the day supported the idea in every possible way, with the *Press-Scimitar* printing special editions that touted the Radburn Plan, calling it "a development of the future — not just another housing project, but a design for living."

But it never happened. Country Club Estates never broke ground. The local planning commission objected to the cheap-looking houses on small lots and fretted that "this type of home will be slums in a few years." Memphis eventually built the curiously named Sea Isle School in the land originally set aside for the community center. Other developers opened a bowling alley, Big Star grocery store, and other businesses at Quince and White Station, but the neighborhood today bears no resemblance to the original plan. In fact, the only vestige of this grand scheme is the name of the street that would have served as its eastern boundary: Estate. **M**

GOT A QUESTION FOR VANCE?

Mail: Vance Lauderdale, Memphis magazine, 460 Tennessee Street #200, Memphis, TN 38103
Email: askvance@memphismagazine.com
Blog: www.memphismagazine.com/askvanceblog

▶ # ASK VANCE

Our trivia expert solves local mysteries of who, what, when, where, why, and why not.

by VANCE LAUDERDALE

LIFE AT LEAHY's

DEAR VANCE: Is it true that James Jones wrote his classic novel *From Here to Eternity* while living in Memphis — at Leahy's Trailer Court, of all places?
— J.H., MEMPHIS.

DEAR J.H.: I initially found this claim hard to believe. I mean, Memphis certainly has its share of legitimate literary milestones. Tennessee Williams wrote (and performed) his first play here. William Faulkner based many scenes and characters on people from our city, and *The Reivers* was even set here. And then there is, of course, *Bound for Glory: The History of the Lauderdales in America*, the 37-volume epic I am working on, scheduled for publication just as soon as I can figure out how to handle my various incarcerations in a suitable manner.

So this bit about Jones (1921-1977) made no sense. He wasn't *from* here, and the book wasn't set here, that's for sure, so why would he venture to our city to work on one of the most famous novels of the twentieth century?

But I thought I'd at least devote, oh, five minutes to checking it out, and I certainly made some interesting discoveries. First of all, even the most basic biographies mention that Jones, who served in the U.S. Army's 22nd Infantry Division during World War II, was wounded in action at Guadalcanal in 1943. He was shipped here for seven months of treatment at Kennedy General (later Veterans) Hospital for a serious ankle injury. (He would later recall those days in his final novel, *Whistle*, though changing the name of our city to Luxor.)

But back to Leahy's.

Hot on the trail, I discovered a nice collection of old Memphis postcards compiled on Flickr by a former Memphian named Birch Harms, now working as an attorney in New York City. One of the cards showed Leahy's Tourist Court, the motel and trailer park on Summer

Avenue that has — let's face it — seen better days. A lengthy caption beneath this postcard certainly caught my eye, because Harms had written:

"This still-existing Summer Avenue trailer park was once home to the writer James Jones while he wrote the National Book Award-winning (and famous beach kiss scene in the movie adaptation) *From Here to Eternity*."

Now pay attention, because here it gets a bit confusing. On the Flickr site, Harms then included a long comment from a fellow named Patt Meara, a professional photographer (among many other occupations), who talked about Jones' days at the old trailer park. Meara had this to say, regarding the postcard:

"Fifty years ago Jim and Lowney [Jones' first wife] and their Spartan trailer were my next-door neighbors in Leahy's Trailer Court on Summer Avenue in Memphis, Tennessee. Jim had a crazy routine. He arose, made a pot of 'hobo' coffee, sat down at the typewriter, and stayed there until noon. Sometimes a chapter, occasionally only a few lines, emerged.

"Each week he made seven one-pound jars of beef stew, seven one-pound jars of Jell-o. Each day of the week he consumed one of each for his noon meal.

"I was a G.I. student, in school until 1 p.m. After school we'd pool our resources and split a bottle of beer or go out to the golf course and practice yoga. At 4 o'clock we returned to the trailer park, mixed a large pitcher of martinis, made a large salad, and Jim would read the product of his day's efforts to Lowney and me while the martinis disappeared.

"I took him to the airport for his trip to New York to pick up the check for the first eight chapters [of *From Here to Eternity*]. When the book was published, the picture on the dust cover bore my credit line, as did the pictures in *Life*, *Time*, *Saturday Review*, and *Editor and Publisher*. Although my name is actually spelled with two Ts, no editor was ever prone to accept that fact so the credits are in the name of 'Pat' Meara.

"By the time it hit the book stores, I was the staff photographer for the *Santa Fe New Mexican*. Jim and a gentleman from Scribner's drove out to Santa Fe, spent a few days with me, and presented me with a copy of the presentation edition with the inscription, 'Patt, Memories of Memphis, Shades of Santa Fe — Jim' on the fly leaf.

"I retired from the Department of Communication Arts at the University of Wisconsin at the age of 42, moved to the Caribbean, worked for the *St. Thomas Daily News* for about six months, taught scuba for a year-and-a-half, obtained my captain's papers, and ended 23 years in the islands as captain of the 63-foot schooner, *Victorius*. We took divers and others for one-week (or longer) charters through the Caribbean.

"Jim became the renowned writer," wrote Meara, "while I lived out his dreams."

Now this was a fascinating story, but was it true? Well, Harms put me in touch with Captain Patt Meara, now living in Florida, who confirmed everything he had written about the postcard, and then Meara told me even more about Jones and their life in Memphis back in the early 1950s:

"I must plead 'Guilty as Charged.' I *did* write it," Meara said. "About ten years ago, I [came to Memphis] and checked out the old tourist court. In the time when Jim, Lowney, and I lived there it was entirely different. The place was laid out in neat streets, and if memory serves there were about 350 units there.

"One year during Cotton Carnival, Gypsy Rose Lee and her husband — I believe his name was Julio de Diego — lived in their trailer directly across the street from us. Oh yeah! And one of our neighbors was a contributing editor to *Encyclopedia Britannica*. Leahy's is definitely not the same.

"Jim used to hang out with me at the Plantation Inn in West Memphis. In 2007 the city of West Memphis had a celebration to honor the Plantation Inn. The city gave us, my wife, Carolyn, and me an all-expense trip to West Memphis for the festival and to take part in a symposium on the old days at the PI.

"During my time working there the piano player and vocalist with the band was a kid named Isaac Hayes [photo above]. I ran into Isaac again, in the islands, when he hired my friend Sammy Watts to play lead guitar for his group. I was amazed when, during the symposium in West Memphis, he walked in the door. Isaac was not in good physical condition at the time and we talked for just a few moments. End of story; shortly after, he died.

"While I was working on the newspaper in New Mexico my former wife 'took off' with a freelance writer along with my copy of the presentation edition that Jim had given me. Last year my daughter found a copy of the first edition of *From Here to Eternity* with intact cover [bottom left], on the Internet, bought it and gave it to me for Christmas. I treasure it, for the byline is there and other than memories and a few photos, that's it.

"My apologies for rambling but hey! At 86 what do you expect?"

Based on such personal testimony, I think we can pretty much agree, then, that Jones did indeed write a good portion of *From Here to Eternity* while living at Leahy's Tourist Court on Summer.

The part that confused me, though, was the missing "gap" in the timeline. Jones was hospitalized in 1943, and he finished *From Here to Eternity* in 1950. Where was he during those intervening seven years?

Not in Memphis. According to *James Jones: A Friendship*, a fine biography published in 1978 by his fellow scribe Willie Morris (author of the novel *My Dog Skip* and later editor of *Harper's* magazine), the Army transferred Jones to Kentucky after he recovered, and after the war ended he moved around the country in a travel trailer with his new wife, Lowney, living in North Carolina for several years. He returned to Memphis in 1949 or 1950, taking up residence at Leahy's while he finished the novel that would eventually win the National Book Award for fiction and be ranked #62 on the Modern Library's list of "100 Best Novels." Oh, and the 1953 film was nominated for 13 Academy Awards, winning eight — including Best Picture, Best Director, Best Writing — it just goes on and on.

So when you drive past Leahy's on Summer and look at the battered sign, try to remember that this humble trailer park once played an important role in the life of one of America's greatest writers. **M**

GOT A QUESTION FOR VANCE?
Email: askvance@memphismagazine.com
Mail: Vance Lauderdale, Memphis magazine, 460 Tennessee Street #200, Memphis, TN 38103
Blog: www.memphismagazine.com/askvanceblog

▶ ASK VANCE

Al & Susie Fister

AL'S GOLFDOM

Our trivia expert solves local mysteries of who, what, when, where, why, and why not.
by VANCE LAUDERDALE

Meet Your Friends
And Have Fun At

Al's Golfhaven INC.

MULTI-HOLE MINIATURE GOLF

1884 EAST RAINES
Just east of I-55

332-9481

Also Enjoy Our...

GOLF DRIVING RANGE
OPEN FIELD BASEBALL BATTING RANGE
REFRESHMENT CENTER
PING PONG – GO KART
SOFTBALL RANGE

Dear Vance: What's the story of the big miniature golf complex that opened on South Perkins in the 1950s? I think it was demolished when they built the Mall of Memphis.
— D.N., MEMPHIS.

DEAR D.N.: Anyone who attended athletic events in Memphis surely recalls the Lauderdale family's dominance in these endeavors. We were routinely hailed as champions at bowling, croquet, badminton, ping-pong, and tiddly-winks. At one point even the mayor honored Father for his remarkable accomplishments — in hop-scotch, I believe.

One sport we truly enjoyed was golf, and not a weekend passed that a Lauderdale was not found on the links of Memphis, working on our driving and putting and hooking and slicing. So you can imagine our dismay when, in the late 1950s, we heard the sad news that the Cherokee Driving Range on Lamar, the only golf range in town, was being closed to make way for the new expressway.

But we never suspected that an energetic and enthusiastic out-of-towner named Al Fister would come to our rescue.

Al was born in Illinois, and earned a master's degree in Health, P.E., and Recreation from Indiana University. There he met a lovely woman named Susie, who was working on her MBA. They got married, and after graduation Al took a job coaching high-school basketball and football up in Three Oaks, Michigan.

But Al wanted to try his hand at something new, so in the late 1950s, he wrote to the chambers of commerce in about 20 cities across the South, trying to see if anybody was interested in having him come down and open a golf driving range.

Memphis certainly was, so Al and Susie moved here in 1960. They drove around looking at land all over the county, and then spotted a big cotton field on South Perkins Road, just outside the city limits. Al bought the property, and within just a

few months opened Al's Golfdom, the only driving range in the city.

It was slow-going at first. Susie once told me, "We weren't just operating on a shoestring. More like half a shoestring." But not for long. Within just a few months, it was a huge success, and Al and Susie greatly expanded the place, adding not just one but two 18-hole miniature golf courses, a snack bar offering ice cream cones and hamburgers and hot dogs and pizza, a go-kart track that tested the skills of even the Lauderdale chauffeur, baseball batting cages, picnic tables — oh, it was an entertainment complex that the whole family could enjoy.

That was, in fact, the key to the success of Al's Golfdom — it was a clean place, owned and operated by a decent family, who knew how to keep their customers happy. I turned up an employee manual for Al's, which specified such quaint policies as "Always address customers as 'Ma'am' or 'Sir'" and "Remember — everyone appreciates a smile."

Al was a shrewd businessman. He knew that constant promotions were the key to his success. Hundreds of ads in the local newspapers and magazines offered coupons for go-kart rides or baskets of golf balls or games of miniature golf. They offered two-for-one admission on certain hours of certain days. And they bragged about the prizes given out every night during the ever-popular City Driving Contest. Modesty prevents me from listing all the trophies I brought home from that.

Al's was, quite simply, the place to be. In the 1960s and '70s, anyone searching for pals from high school checked out Shoney's or the Tropical Freeze, and then drove out Perkins to see if they were hanging out at Al's, because everybody was. Celebrities such as Lee Trevino and even Bob Hope showed up at Al's whenever they were in town.

In 1965, Al expanded his operation, buying up 20 acres of farmland on Raines Road out in Whitehaven, and opening Al's Golfhaven. It had pretty much the same attractions as you could find at the original Golfdom, and everything was fancy and state-of-the-art.

Other miniature-golf places around town weren't that elaborate, but Al brought in — and sometimes made his own — concrete and plaster creatures and critters to decorate the course. In rainy weather, the driving range offered covered tees and, in the winter, even heated ones.

He bought a tractor and converted it into a machine that automatically swept up the golf balls, and everyone remembers how fun it was to try to bang a golf ball off the wire cage that protected that poor tractor driver. Golf was fun, all right, but adding a moving target gave it just a bit more thrill. I speak from experience.

Why, Al — ever the stickler for cleanliness — even purchased a machine that automatically scrubbed the golf balls. It sure beat washing them by hand. After all, when the Golfdom and Golfhaven were at their peak, Al once estimated that golfers drove over 15,000 balls a year at his two ranges.

The places were so successful that they stayed open 24 hours a day, to accommodate all the late-night workers who wanted to have some fun when they got off work. With its bright colors and lights and music playing from speakers, Al's was truly a sight to behold. After Interstate 240 cut just north of Al's — bringing them even more business, I might add — Susie told me how exciting it was to come over that expressway bridge at night and see Al's Golfdom, brilliantly illuminated. "It was like a dream come true," she said.

Now you'd think a place like Al's wouldn't be so popular when the weather turned cold, but you'd be wrong. Al's devoted following kept the place hopping year-round, and in the winter Al added a sideline operation — he sold Christmas trees from his parking lots. He called it "Al's Christmas Forest."

Al poses with his golf ball picker-upper.

But all good things seem to come to an end, and Al's was no exception. Al's Golfdom closed in 1973. The land was sold to developers who put American Way through there, and the driving range eventually became the site of the Mall of Memphis. And we all know how *that* turned out. Last time I looked, it was a sad-looking field.

Al's Golfhaven lasted for more than 30 years. It finally closed in 1995, and A. Maceo Walker Middle School now stands on the site, right by I-55.

Both the Golfdom and Golfhaven were remarkable places — built, owned, and operated by the same family for their entire existence. How many companies can say that? They created a lot of fond memories for many Memphians of all ages. And for all those good times, we owe a debt of thanks to Al and Susie Fister, who began searching for a new life 60 years ago, and found it in Memphis. **M**

GOT A QUESTION FOR VANCE?
Email: askvance@memphismagazine.com
Mail: Vance Lauderdale, Memphis magazine,
460 Tennessee Street #200, Memphis, TN 38103
Blog: www.memphismagazine.com/askvanceblog

ASK VANCE

TODDLE HOUSE

Our trivia expert solves local mysteries of who, what, when, where, why, and why not.

by VANCE LAUDERDALE

Dear Vance: Is it true that Toddle Houses actually got their start in Memphis?
— K.D., MEMPHIS.

DEAR K.D.: I guess you'd have to define "got their start." The company was actually founded by a fellow in Texas, but it didn't — and wouldn't have — become such a success if it weren't for a rather famous Memphian.

It seems folks in Tennessee are always helping out people in Texas. Why, if it weren't for sharp-shooting, hard-fighting pioneers like Davy Crockett, we wouldn't have won the Battle of the Alamo.

What's that? We *lost*? Oh. Bad example.

Back to Toddle House then. One of the largest restaurant chains in the country

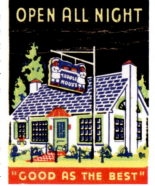

actually started by accident. In the late 1920s, a lumberman in Houston, Texas, by the name of J.C. Stedman found himself with leftover supplies. So he went around to little neighborhood groceries and laundries and arranged to construct nice little cottages for their branch offices.

One day, somebody asked Stedman why he didn't turn one of his buildings into a cozy diner, and that's how it all began.

But Stedman didn't stay in Houston. He came to Memphis and persuaded the owners of Britling Cafeteria, which had started up here a few years earlier, to build his restaurants in our city. So for a while, Britling owned Toddle House.

But not for long. Because then he met Fred Smith.

No, not the Fred Smith of FedEx fame. But his *father*, who had started the Dixie Greyhound Lines, part of the national Greyhound bus fleet. Smith met Stedman and said, "I want in." Or words to that effect. I wasn't invited to that meeting, you see. Well, Smith took over the entire operation, moving the company's headquarters to Memphis and making himself president of the Toddle House Corporation.

"Toddle" House? Why on earth would anyone give such an odd name to a diner? Well, the story goes that Stedman's little buildings were meant to be transportable, and some bratty kid — I believe it was one of the Lauderdale cousins — was watching one of them loaded onto a truck. It wobbled back and forth, and the kid said, "Look, Ma, how that little house toddles!" Stedman was standing nearby and realized he had a distinctive name for his restaurants.

All Toddle Houses were exactly the same — a tiny brick cottage, painted white with a blue roof. Inside, diners found no tables — just a row of 10 stools at a stainless-steel counter. Everything was gleaming steel or white tile, and crammed into the tiny space were fryers and ovens and broilers and toasters and — well, just about everything needed to prepare anything from a cup of coffee to a steak dinner.

Toddle House was quite proud of its hamburger, even calling it "World Famous." Their scrambled eggs were mighty tasty, I recall, but Toddle House merely noted that they were "well-known." Not exactly the highest praise, was it? And as for their pecan waffle? Well, they were "so waffly good."

One thing missing from a Toddle House was a cash

register. Instead, the business operated on the honor system. Standing by the front door was a steel and glass box called the "Auto Cashier" and customers simply paid their bill by dropping in their money as they left. And signs made it clear: "No Tipping Allowed."

The first Toddle House in Memphis opened at Cleveland and Union in the 1930s. It was actually called Stevens Sandwich Service because, in the beginning, the owners of the franchises kept their names on their signs. Other Toddle Houses quickly opened all over town — on Poplar and Union and Madison and Lamar.

Business boomed, and in 1947 the owners announced plans for a Master Toddle House, to open downtown across the street from the Sterick Building. This one had 40 seats — four times the size of the original diners — and the interior featured the latest innovations: automatic doors, air conditioning, fluorescent lighting, and something called "Conduction Cookers," which could fry bacon in 30 seconds and ham in a minute.

By the 1950s, Toddle House had more than 200 locations in almost 90 cities. But then came changes. In 1961 Dobbs House, the Memphis company that had its own nationwide chain of diners and handled catering for most of this country's airlines, bought Toddle House. The purchase price of $18 million was, at the time, the largest transaction between Memphis businesses in our city's history.

It was too confusing to have Dobbs Houses *and* Toddle Houses, so all the Toddle Houses were shut down, or changed to Dobbs Houses, or converted to Steak & Egg Kitchens. Most of the cute little buildings were demolished, though rumor has it that at least one Toddle House found its way to the grounds of the Lauderdale Mansion, where — they say — it served for years as a ticket booth and souvenir stand.

But that's simply not true. People are confusing our mansion with Graceland. It happens all the time.

DEATH AT COLUMBIA

DEAR VANCE: What is the story behind the curious gravestone at Elmwood (right), blaming a young man's death on the "carelessness" of his fellow students?
— A.N., MEMPHIS.

DEAR A.N.: It's not very often that a gravestone mentions the cause of death, much less blames others for their demise. But the nice tombstone for William Eastman Spandow (1897-1922) is inscribed, "Killed in Chemical Laboratory of Columbia University by an Explosion Due to the Carelessness of Others."

Thanks to the wonders of the Internet, I was actually able to find an old *New York Times* article on this tragedy. It seems Spandow was a Memphian who had earned his bachelor's and master's degrees from the University of Denver. In the early 1920s, he was working on a Ph.D. in chemistry at Columbia University in New York City.

On the afternoon of November 17, 1922, Spandow and another student, Reginald Sloane, were working with a gas-fired device called an autoclave, "experimenting in the manufacture of intermediate compounds for aniline dyes." The machinery works under intense pressure, and Spandow bent down to read a gauge. "Suddenly the needle started darting around, showing a sudden activity of the gases, and Spandow instructed Sloane to turn off the supply of gas."

Before Sloane could reach the valve, some 15 feet away, "Spandow opened the valve on the side of the vessel, which the students had been warned not to do as long as there was any danger of flame in the heater."

The autoclave exploded with a blast that hurled shards of metal throughout the lab. Spandow was killed instantly. Sloane was seriously injured, and "the lives of other graduate students in the laboratory were imperiled by flying steel missiles." The explosion blew out every window in the room and rattled buildings hundreds of feet away.

Despite the wording on the grave, the death was not due to the "carelessness of others." In fact, an investigation revealed that "Spandow, who was in charge of the apparatus for the day, in part had at least disregarded instructions given by the professors. He opened a valve on the side of the heavy steel apparatus before a gas flame had died out underneath. A tongue of flame darted into the chamber and detonated the imprisoned gas."

Spandow's body was returned to Memphis and buried in Elmwood. Years later, his mother, Florence Gage Spandow, was laid to rest in an adjacent plot, and her name was added to

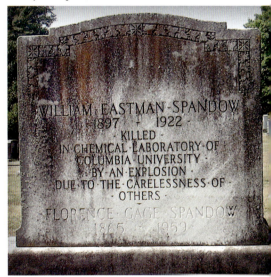

her son's tombstone. I can understand a distraught mother's desire to blame others for the death of her only son, but that doesn't seem to be what actually happened here.

The young man is remembered, however, by more than just an unusual gravestone at Elmwood. Since the 1930s, thanks to a grant from his family, Rhodes College has offered the William Spandow Scholarship in Chemistry to a deserving student. **M**

GOT A QUESTION FOR VANCE?
Email: askvance@memphismagazine.com
Mail: Vance Lauderdale, Memphis magazine, 460 Tennessee Street #200, Memphis, TN 38103
Blog: www.memphismagazine.com/askvanceblog

▶ ASK VANCE

HOME OF THE ELKS

Our trivia expert solves local mysteries of who, what, when, where, why, and why not.

by VANCE LAUDERDALE

DEAR VANCE: I recently bought an old photograph that purports to show the Elks Club in Memphis (above). Where was this building, pray tell, and what happened to it?
— D.G., MEMPHIS.

DEAR D.G.: I'm sorry, but I normally don't answer any question that uses the word "purports" or the phrase "pray tell." You'd have to be a Lauderdale to understand. But then I glanced at the photo and decided it wasn't even taken in Memphis, and you had wasted your money and had suffered enough, so thought I'd at least investigate just where this particular Elks Lodge might have been located.

And what do you know. Everything *purports* to indicate it was indeed one of the first — if not *the* first — Elks Clubs in our city. The real clue was the building at the far right in the photo, bearing the humble sign "Hopkins House." I journeyed to the University of Memphis Special Collections, where they have a nice set of old city directories, and in 1903, a hotel/tavern called the Hopkins House stood downtown at 67 Jefferson. Sure enough, those same books show the Elks Club next door, at 69-71 Jefferson.

It's a fine-looking structure, a two-story brick building with a matching pair of gently curving bay windows. Look closely, and high above the entrance is the figure of an elk's head, and "ELKS" is even etched into the glass of the lantern. I don't know when the club was built, but you didn't ask that, D.G., so I don't feel so bad about glossing over such a pesky detail.

Back in the early 1900s, the Benevolent and Protective Order of the Elks couldn't have found a better place to erect a festive clubhouse. That block of Jefferson, between Main and Front, held a variety of interesting businesses that would have appealed to their all-male membership: Ralph Mitchell's Grocery, Matt Monaghan's Produce, Fisher & Co. Meats, Lewis Hat Company, Sambucetti Cigars & Tobacco, Louis Aehle's Soft Drinks, Samuel Lebovitz Clothing, and more. And it was also home to three saloons. In addition to the Hopkins House, you could heft a mug of beer at a joint called Nixon & Alston's or the Equitable Saloon.

The Elks called this nice building home until 1926. Then they tore it down, along with everything else on the block, and embarked on one of the most impressive structures ever erected in our city — the 12-story tower they would call, quite simply and logically, the Elks Club Building.

Crafted by the Memphis firm of Mahan and Broadwell, this was a combination lodge and hotel at the southeast corner of Jefferson and Front that was, according to a promotional brochure, "attractive

From top: the Bowling Alley, the Ladies Writing Room, the Lounge in the new Elks Club Building.

ming pool with "crystal clear waters"; a "spacious, airy, and inviting" six-lane bowling alley; a handball court "pulsing with life and action"; and "one of the most attractive ballrooms in the city." All that was in addition to the Club Grille, the coffee shop, the library, the lounge, and the Turkish baths, where Elks members "may receive the expert attention of trained masseurs, and sally forth thence refreshed and invigorated."

Unfortunately for half of this city's population, all these wonders were reserved for the *men*. But the new Elk's Club did have one feature designed with the women in mind. On the top floor was the Ladies Writing Room, complete with fancy desks and comfy chairs, "an ideal retreat, where feminine correspondence may receive its proper attention."

This stunning structure — all brightly colored terra cotta and spires, with four stone griffins perched at the top — was called the Elks Club Building for only a few years. When Clarence DeVoy, the Elk's Exalted Ruler, died in 1931, the name of the building was changed to the Hotel DeVoy — a very classy name indeed. In 1945, however, the name was changed again, to the one most Memphians remember today — the Hotel King Cotton.

That's right. One of downtown's most memorable hotels actually began life as an Elks Club.

But the grand building turned out to be a burden. Over the years, the tremendous cost of construction and upkeep became too much for the members to handle. In 1937, Memphis Elks Lodge #27, one of the oldest and largest in the country, actually surrendered its charter and moved out of its fancy headquarters. The million-dollar-plus building was sold at a foreclosure auction for just $200,000. The Elks, determined to survive, began to hold meetings in a cramped space above a Pantaze Drugstore on Main Street. In the late 1940s, they moved again — this time into a nice-looking former apartment building on Adams called the Cannon Flats.

The Elks Club Building, Front Street and Jefferson, overlooking Confederate Park and the Mississippi River.

in design, mammoth in size, and furnished luxuriously and in excellent taste — simple dignity without in any way losing the informal, homelike air of a true club." Erected at a cost of some $1.3 million (an enormous sum in the 1920s), the new Elks Club featured "150 delightful rooms with bath and outside exposure, circulating ice water, free electrical fan service, and a new and sanitary coffee shop." That was just the hotel portion of the building, which was available to the public.

The Elks themselves enjoyed considerably fancier amenities (above). The building included a complete gymnasium that would allow members to "enter the day's work with new zest, boyish vim, and vigor"; a billiards room with "first-quality tables, balls, cues, and scoring equipment"; a huge indoor swim-

For reasons I don't really understand (as a Lauderdale I was never an Elk, or a Moose, or a Lion, or anything, really — we were above all that), that building wasn't suitable either and was eventually demolished. I suspect they didn't really need their own building anymore. At one time, the Elks here claimed 4,000 members; by 1976 enrollment had dropped to just 300. I can't say what happened to the club over the years, but in the mid-1970s, the Elks actually returned to their former home, this time renting out meeting space in the Hotel King Cotton. It must have been a bittersweet experience, looking around and thinking, "At one time, all this was ours."

Well, they didn't have to feel sad for very long. On the morning of April 29, 1984, the King Cotton came tumbling down with a blast of dynamite to make way for the Morgan Keegan Tower. The magnificent stone griffins that once guarded the top four corners of the old hotel grace the lobby of the new tower. For awhile, the Elks met in the former Starlight Supper Club, a little place on Highway 51 North. Nowadays, they convene once a month in a somewhat industrial section of Atoka, Tennessee.

It's a sad story, really. When the Elks Club Building first opened, a promotional booklet gushed, "The new building will be a monument to the finest American ideals of physical expression and the fullest expression of true Elk fellowship." The Elks are still quite active in this area, as are the Moose lodges and other fraternal organizations, but they don't occupy a stunning tower that was a true Memphis landmark for more than half a century. **M**

GOT A QUESTION FOR VANCE?
Email: askvance@memphismagazine.com
Mail: Vance Lauderdale, Memphis magazine, 460 Tennessee Street #200, Memphis, TN 38103
Blog: www.memphismagazine.com/askvanceblog

ASK VANCE

OLLIE'S TROLLEY

Our trivia expert solves local mysteries of who, what, when, where, why, and why not.

by VANCE LAUDERDALE

DEAR VANCE: What was the name of that little trolley-shaped diner they built on Main Street Mall, and what happened to it?
— K.T., Memphis.

DEAR K.T.: Although the Lauderdales acquired vast wealth because of savvy business decisions, sometimes we struck out. One time our pal Kemmons Wilson approached Father about investing in his new chain of hostelries. With so many thriving tourist courts on every highway in America, we considered it a foolish undertaking, and so lost out on a chance to own a 99 percent stake in Holiday Inn. Years later, another family friend, Fred Smith, invited us to join his overnight delivery service. Why anyone would send their letters and packages on those newfangled jets, when they could transport them on the majestic Lauderdale Line of dirigibles, baffled us, so once again we said no. I think about that decision every time a gleaming FedEx jet flies over our mansion.

But on one occasion, we made the right decision. Back in the mid-1970s, a Kentucky businessman named John Brown came to the Lauderdales, urging us to purchase a franchise in a fast-food outlet that he called Ollie's Trolley. We declined, and we've never regretted it.

Brown was, and still is, an impressive figure in these parts. Among other accomplishments, he served as the governor of Kentucky, purchased Kentucky Fried Chicken from Colonel Harlan Sanders and turned it into a jillion-dollar empire, started the successful Lum's chain of restaurants, and ended up marrying a Miss America (Phyllis George). At one point, he was even the owner of the Boston Celtics basketball team.

In so many ways, his life has paralleled my own.

In the 1970s, he came up with the notion of building fast-food outlets in replicas of old-fashioned streetcars. Each Ollie's Trolley was a tiny place, with just a counter inside. They bragged that they cooked "the world's best hamburger" with 23 special herbs and spices, which they called "Ollieburgers," and also offered typical diner fare like hotdogs, chicken sandwiches, Ollie's fries, and milkshakes.

The first Ollie's Trolley opened in Louisville in the mid-1970s, and the company quickly built more than a hundred, most of them east of the Mississippi. Two made their stop in Memphis – one on Mendenhall north of Poplar, and this one, shown here under construction in 1976 on Main Street Mall, just across from City Hall. I barely remember the bright red-and-yellow structure, so can't say for certain whether the Ollieburger was indeed "the world's best."

Ollie's Trolley was a rare business failure for Brown, and the Memphis location, along with most others, closed after just a few years. Drive-through eateries like McDonald's and Wendy's were more convenient, it seems, since Ollie's only offered walk up service, and even if you wanted to eat inside a little streetcar, you couldn't. All they had were some tables and benches outside. In fact, I don't think the place even had a bathroom for customers. A few Ollie's have survived in other cities — Louisville, Cincinnati, and Washington, D.C. — but there's no trace of the one here.

Oh, and who was Ollie, anyway? The little trolleys were named after Ollie Gleichenhaus, a Miami restaurant owner Brown hired to oversee the Lum's chain. "Gleichenhaus' Trollies" just didn't have the right ring to it, I guess.

MAKING TRACKS

DEAR VANCE: Is it true that the old Frisco Bridge was, at one time, the longest bridge in North America? That's hard to believe.
— D.F., MEMPHIS

DEAR D.F.: Well, I haven't actually measured it and compared it to other structures built at the time. But in its day — and we're talking 1892 here — the half-mile span of the Great Memphis Bridge (as it was then called) was indeed promoted as not only the longest in North America, but the third longest in the world. And I'll take their word for it.

Since it's not a highway bridge, most Memphians probably never notice the Frisco Bridge, as we call it today. But as an engineering achievement, it certainly ranks as one of our city's greatest accomplishments, right up there with The Pyramid and the Zippin Pippin. Okay, maybe those are bad examples.

St. Louis had spanned the Mississippi River with its famous Eads Bridge in 1874, but no other bridges crossed the lower river in the 1800s. To reach the Arkansas side, everyone in Memphis boarded ferries — even the railroads. Trains would stop in Memphis, unhook their cars and locomotives, roll them onto ferryboats, cross the river, and hook everything back up again — an incredibly tedious and time-consuming undertaking. It wears me out just to type about it.

So the Kansas City, Fort Scott, and Memphis Railroads began to search for a solution. They eventually hired George Morrison of Chicago, who had constructed other bridges across the Missouri and Mississippi Rivers, but much farther north, where the river wasn't so wide. The Memphis bridge would be his greatest challenge.

Construction began on November 7, 1888, and newspapers said the new bridge involved "a unique scheme of such intricacy as to baffle description." It really wasn't that fancy: A series of mighty stone piers would support a cantilevered steel bridge. The immense size of it was the problem, especially when you were working with the shifting, unstable bottom of Old Man River.

Morrison's crews built box-like caissons that were lowered into the Mississippi. The water was then pumped out, allowing workers to actually stand on the dry river bottom while they built, stone by stone, the support piers. After that came a steel superstructure that weighed 9,500 tons and used some 100,000 rivets. Still not impressed? Then consider that the steel frame that linked the first two piers was the largest steel plate ever fabricated in the United States.

It was incredibly hard and dangerous work, and before the bridge was finished, four workers died in accidents.

All the sections were linked into a single span on April 6, 1892. And what a bridge it was: five steel spans soaring 2,597 feet across the river, linked to a 2,500-foot concrete viaduct that stretched over the low-lying fields of Arkansas.

The Great Bridge Celebration kicked off on May 12, 1892. Volunteers from 18 different railroads boarded locomotives lined up at the Memphis approach to the bridge, and more than 50,000 people jammed the riverbanks to watch the first crossing. Many of those apparently expected the worst. One newspaper reported, "Weeping women kissed their husbands and sweethearts goodbye, all positive the bridge would collapse with their loved ones who had volunteered for the test."

The train slowly made its way across, and — just as Morrison promised — the bridge stood. The engines roared back at full speed (I assume in reverse), and an eyewitness said, "Everyone in the boats below or along the riverbanks either shot off a gun or a firecracker. It was the most deafening and most glorious din I have ever heard."

The celebration ran into the evening and included long speeches from the governors of Tennessee and Arkansas. The keynote speaker was Indiana Senator Daniel Voorhies, known as "The Tall Sycamore of the Wabash," though I have no idea what he — or Indiana — had to do with our bridge. After that came parades ("with beautifully deco-

An old postcard shows the Great Memphis Bridge (as it was then called) shortly after it opened. The view is looking west, towards Arkansas, before any other bridges were built here.

rated fire engines") and a fireworks show that culminated with "an exact facsimile of the new bridge, accurately and artistically depicted in jets of fire covering a space of 1,500 feet." To help commemorate the event, the Woman's Exchange sold medallions coined from aluminum, "the beautiful new metal," and the Lauderdale Library owns one of these rare medals (shown here, complete with its original ribbon).

More than a century later, the Frisco Bridge is still standing, but I'm afraid it is no longer ranked among the world's great bridges. Not even close. Its mighty span can't compare, for example, with the Danyang-Kunshan Bridge, scheduled to open later this year in China, which has a total length of — get ready for it — 540,700 feet. That's right: a bridge more than 100 miles long. In fact, in a list of the world's 100 longest bridges, the Frisco Bridge doesn't even show up.

Well, let's just see how many of those are still standing — and carrying heavy railroad traffic at that — a hundred years from now. **M**

GOT A QUESTION FOR VANCE?
Email: askvance@memphismagazine.com
Mail: Vance Lauderdale, Memphis *magazine,*
460 Tennessee Street #200, Memphis, TN 38103
Blog: www.memphismagazine.com/askvanceblog

ASK VANCE
VERY CURIOUS

Our trivia expert solves local mysteries of who, what, when, where, why, and why not.

by VANCE LAUDERDALE

DEAR VANCE: Can you tell me anything about a massive folk-art structure that was built in the 1950s somewhere south of Memphis? I think it was called "Curiosity" but I never knew much else about it
— R.W., MEMPHIS.

DEAR R.W.: My half-dozen readers may remember that back in the 1940s and 1950s, before the interstate highway system spread its concrete tentacles across America, Memphians journeyed to the Gulf Coast along the regular state highways and byways of Mississippi and Alabama. Over the years, quite a few of those travel-

ers returned to Memphis with tales of an extraordinary structure they had seen alongside the road. Descriptions varied. Some said it was apparently a form of art — a huge sculpture, assembled from telephone poles and chunks of wood and scraps of iron. Others insisted it was actually a residence of some kind, adorned with old signs and slabs of plywood. But whatever it was, everyone agreed that it seemed to grow larger and larger every year.

And it went, so they said, by the entirely appropriate name of "Curiosity."

I have been asked about this oddity many times over the years, but was unable to learn just what the place was, where it was located, and who built it.

Until now. A Memphis family, whose name shall not be mentioned here, was scrolling through their old home movies recently, and discovered they had filmed "Curiosity" on their way to Florida in the late 1950s. Some of those tiny, grainy scenes, taken from the original 8mm footage, are shown here, and I think they give you a good idea why people had so much trouble describing the place.

It is indeed a residence, but few homes in America have ever looked like this.

By carefully scrutinizing some of the movie images, I was able to make out the name of the owner — "Stephen Sykes" — hand-painted on a slab of wood over the entrance. Thanks to the wonders of the Internet, that clue led me to an April 1963 copy of *Ebony* magazine, with a feature story called "Do It Yourself Skyscraper," which told the whole remarkable saga of this African-American gentleman and his amazing creation.

For one thing, the actual name of the structure was "In-Curiosity" and yes, it served as Sykes' residence for many years. The *Ebony* article called Sykes "a 69-year-old bachelor with a driving ambition to rise above his fellow man," and he did that literally, by erecting a six-level, 65-foot-high dwelling from junk, poles, signs, hubcaps — whatever he could find. *Ebony* called it "an architectural maze of grotesquely joined wooden poles interspersed with a conglomeration of odds and ends." The whole thing was erected right alongside Highway 45, just a mile or so north of the little town of Aberdeen, Mississippi.

"When viewed from the ground, In-Curiosity inspires immediate concern about its ability to survive the next gentle breeze," said *Ebony*. "But once inside, the visitor's apprehensions are dispelled by its sound construction." The article explained that the home actually contained "numerous functional items, including a four-burner wood stove, sink, antiquated ice box, rainwater shower bath, and an intercom telephone made from a rubber hose." That last feature allowed visitors to contact Sykes, who lived on the very top level of the structure, his bedroom ventilated by an old smokestack converted to catch the breeze.

"I'm not a fresh-air fiend," Sykes told the magazine, "but I believe it's healthful to sleep and live in fresh air, and I haven't had a cold since I began staying in this room year-round."

In the days before "folk art" became trendy, Sykes adorned his home with wonderful handmade signs and posters. One advised visitors, "Don't talk so much. Keep your mouth closed and your bowels open and believe in Jesus."

So who was Stephen Sykes? That's hard to say. Biographical information is rather skimpy, and I was unable to locate a decent photo of him. The *Ebony* article described him as a World War I veteran who had "followed the sun and moved west. Inspired by the oil rigs he saw, he dreamed of going back to Mississippi to build something great out of common materials." In the early 1950s, he settled down on 20 acres of land owned by his sisters outside Aberdeen and began work on In-Curiosity. "The longer he worked, the more friends he made, and soon all types of objects were hauled or mailed to him from every part of the U.S., donated by motorists for inclusion in his project."

Sykes gave tours of his home to anyone who stopped by, and was obviously proud of his creation. "It takes a lot of nerve and good thinking to keep a project like this going," he told reporters.

So what happened to Sykes and his In-Curiosity house? I can't say for sure. I had heard stories that he died in the 1960s, and the house remained a picturesque ruin for some years afterwards. It blew down

> **Sykes and his amazing creation** live on in the memories of hundreds, perhaps thousands, of travelers in this area, and in grainy home movies and snapshots tucked away in boxes and scrapbooks.

one day in a storm, somebody said. Others told me it burned. Since Highway 45 is now a wide double-lane highway linking Aberdeen to points north and south, it's almost certain that In-Curiosity would have been demolished to make way for the new road. But Sykes and his amazing creation live on in the memories of hundreds, perhaps thousands, of travelers in this area, and in grainy home movies and snapshots tucked away in boxes and scrapbooks.

MEMPHIS FLYERS

DEAR VANCE: A while back, you wrote about Wilson Field, an old airport off Winchester Road. But wasn't there another airport also on Winchester, but a few miles farther west?
— T.J., MEMPHIS.

DEAR T.J.: Someday when time permits, I guess I should do a story about all the little airfields and landing strips that dotted the countryside around Memphis. There were a surprising number of them, and the one you remember, T.J., was Memphis Flying Service. As shown on this old Esso map (below), it was located on the north side of Winchester, between Perkins and Mendenhall.

Memphis Flying Service was like the other airfields around the county — a grass landing strip, a couple of hangars, and some basic maintenance facilities. It had no tower, and probably not any navigation lights. A wind sock told flyers which way the wind was blowing, and that was it.

But what made this particular base unusual was the person who ran it. According to an old *Memphis Press-Scimitar* article, "For the first time in the history of Memphis aviation, a woman has been named general manager of one of the city's largest privately owned aviation enterprises." In fact, at the time — we're talking late 1940s here — LaVelle Walsh was the only female airport operator in the United States.

Not for long. Walsh stepped down the following year, for reasons not made clear in the newspaper articles. Even so, "she injected new life into the local flying game, and made Mid-South operators sit up and take notice." Among other accomplishments, she made Memphis Flying Service the largest veterans flight-training school in this region.

The little airfield, and most others around the county, closed sometime in the late 1960s. The area is now filled with houses and apartments. **M**

GOT A QUESTION FOR VANCE?
Email: askvance@memphismagazine.com
Mail: Vance Lauderdale, Memphis *magazine, 460 Tennessee Street #200, Memphis, TN 38103*
Blog: www.memphismagazine.com/askvanceblog

LaVelle Walsh

▶ ASK VANCE

STILL STANDING

Our trivia expert solves local mysteries of who, what, when, where, why, and why not.

by VANCE LAUDERDALE

DEAR VANCE: While looking through some 1925 copies of *The Architectural Record*, I found a fascinating old advertisement for a mansion in Memphis owned by a Judge Julian Wilson. Has this nice house survived?
— R.B., MEMPHIS.

DEAR R.B.: Sometimes I think my humdrum life lacks the thrill of my younger days, especially when I spend the entire weekend poring over yellowed copies of *True Detective Mysteries* (often featuring crimes committed by my family) or idly perusing my first editions of Edgar Allan Poe.

Then *you* show up, telling me that you actually read back issues of something called *The Architectural Record* — apparently paying special attention to exciting ads from the American Hardwood Manufacturers Association — and I feel much better about myself.

Still, I have to admit that your query actually interested me, so I carefully conceived a two-phase approach to solving this puzzle. First, I looked up Julian Wilson's address in old telephone books archived in the Lauderdale Library. After a few days' rest from that ordeal, I began phase two: I actually drove to that address — 170 East Parkway South — to see if the house was still standing.

And it is, as you can see from the fine photograph here.

118 • ASK VANCE II

But it's no longer a residence. Nowadays, renamed Cumberland Hall, it's part of the campus of Memphis Theological Seminary. And except for a few minor details, it looks as if it hasn't aged in the 70-plus years since it was featured in *The Architectural Record*.

John Vaughn, the seminary's director of facilities, was kind enough to give me a tour of the former home, which has been converted into classrooms and offices. In their ad, the hardwood association folks chided anyone who might try to improve their product, saying, "Red gum should be finished as to bring out its own charm of color. It is absurd to destroy this in an attempt to imitate other wood less worthy." Well, as Vaughn proudly pointed out, the red gum moldings, banisters, bookcases, and doors throughout the former home still glow with a golden-brown patina — untouched by new paint or varnish. I guess the hardwood association was right, after all.

Naturally I was curious about the home's original owner, but I wasn't able to find out very much. Not by my nitpicky standards, anyway. Julian Wilson was born in 1872 in Brookhaven, Mississippi. His name first shows up here in old city directories, where he is identified as a lawyer, living at 1137 Eastmoreland and maintaining offices in the Tennessee Trust Building.

In 1920, he moved up in the world, it seems, because he became a partner in the law firm of Wilson and Armstrong, one of our city's largest. About this time he moved into the grand home on East Parkway, with his wife, Mary. He was in good company there. Neighbors along that stretch of East Parkway at the time were wealthy owners or presidents of local cotton and lumber companies.

Though the ad shown here clearly calls him a judge, throughout his career the telephone books identify him as an attorney. Wilson died in 1944 at the age of 71, and even his death certificate calls him an attorney, not a judge. He was laid to rest back home in Brookhaven. When his wife passed away a few years later, the home went through just a few owners before 1986, when it was acquired — and in fact, physically linked to — Memphis Theological Seminary. It's a fine-looking building; I'm glad they were able to save it and put it to such good use.

SEARCHING FOR CIBO

DEAR VANCE: What do you remember about a snazzy chain of pizza restaurants call Cibo Houses?
— T.J., MEMPHIS.

DEAR T.J.: I remember nothing, but that shouldn't surprise you. My family rarely ventured outside the Mansion to dine, and on those rare occasions when we did — birthdays, anniversaries, and Lauderdale Day — we didn't journey to cheap little takeout places, no matter how "snazzy" they appeared. It just wasn't done, you see.

> I have to admit that **your query actually interested me**, so I carefully conceived a two-phase approach to solving this puzzle.

But then I turned up this wonderful old postcard for a Cibo House, and realized that perhaps my family had passed up a real dining adventure, because just *look* at the place. It's like a pop art wonderland — a bright red-and-white building, with glass walls, rows of arches, and diners perched on stools beneath a colorful awning inside. The back of the postcard casually mentions the "distinctively different exterior, and the smart, efficient, colorful interior." Who cares if the pizza was good or bad, when you got to munch on it in such a festive environment?

Ah, but wait. This card (below) is obviously just an illustration; it's not an actual photograph of a Cibo House, so I began to wonder if they really existed, and if they actually looked like this.

Well, I can say "yes" to the first part. In 1962, a fellow named J. Douglas Woods formed the National Cibo House Corporation, and opened three of the little pizza parlors in Memphis: at 1142 Jackson, 3755 Southern, and 4495 Summer. A year later, it seems he opened a couple more, at 3180 Thomas and 706 Waring.

The phone books told me that the Cibo House company had gone out of business years ago. But I spent the day driving to all these locations, hoping that the rather fantastic architecture depicted on the postcard had survived. I'm sorry to say that my travels were in vain. Most of the original Cibo locations are now vacant lots; the one on Jackson was demolished to make way for the I-240 entrance ramp. As far as I can tell, 4495 Summer wasn't even a freestanding building, but was tucked into a row of humble brick structures, so it's safe to say that particular Cibo never looked like the one depicted on the postcard.

Woods' pizza venture didn't last 10 years, and despite the "national" part of the company's name, I just don't know if other Cibo Houses were erected in other cities. Perhaps the firm's demise had something to do with the name. "Cibo" is Italian for "food," and it's not easy to persuade the family to hop in the car and drive across town for a big slice of "food pizza." Not a family like the Lauderdales, anyway. **M**

GOT A QUESTION FOR VANCE?
Email: askvance@memphismagazine.com
Mail: Vance Lauderdale, Memphis *magazine*,
460 Tennessee Street, Memphis, TN 38103
Blog: www.memphismagazine.com/askvanceblog

Ask Vance

The Lyceum

Our trivia expert solves local mysteries of who, what, when, where, why, and why not.

by VANCE LAUDERDALE

This building at Second and Jefferson was once the gathering place for Memphis society.

DEAR VANCE: What can you tell me about our city's old Lyceum Theater? I've heard of the Orpheum, Warner, Loew's State, and Loew's Palace, but I've never read much at all about the Lyceum.
— *T.Y., Memphis.*

DEAR T.Y.: An architectural masterpiece. A gleaming symbol of a progressive, educated city. A glittering entertainment palace that was a magnet for the finest families of Memphis. And, in its last days, an eyesore and an embarrassment.

I'm talking, of course, about the Lauderdale Mansion.

But all these phrases could, and have been, applied to both the *old* and the *new* Lyceum Theaters, for there were actually two of them, you see. And since I've got two pages here, I'll tell you about both. And I'm able to do that because I ventured to the main library, hoping to find at least a few yellowed newspaper clippings on this equally faded establishment, which I could stretch into a halfway-decent column. Imagine my surprise, then, when the librarian brought out not one, not two, but *three* whopping books devoted to the Lyceum — each one a master's thesis composed of some 200 pages devoted to a particular phase of both theaters' creation, growth, and destruction.

So let me offer my thanks right now to the amazing work compiled by: Carolyn Powell, 1951 author of *The Lyceum Theater of Memphis: 1890-1900*; James Wesley Ouzts, 1963 author of *The History of the Lyceum Theater, Memphis, Tennessee, 1900-1910*; and Gordon Batson, 1971 author of *The Theatrical History of the Lyceum Theater of Memphis, 1910-1935*. I hope they were awarded their degrees, because these three scholars pretty much covered everything you could possibly want to know about this old place, T.Y., during its 47-year history.

The Lyceum got its start way back in 1888, when the Memphis Athletic Association erected a stunning new clubhouse at the northwest corner of Third and Union. Newspapers described it as "a handsome structure of pressed brick and iron, with stone trimming." The five-story building mainly served as a gymnasium and offices for the club members, but the first floor was devoted to a 1,200-seat theater. Not for movies, of course — it was way too early for that — but for plays.

The first Lyceum wasn't as ostentatious as later theaters like the Warner or Orpheum. In fact, Powell writes that it was "decorated in quiet, restful shades. The woodwork was very plain and highly polished, with here and there bits of finely wrought carving." The chairs, of all things, were apparently unique, though I'm not sure why, exactly. Powell notes that a Chicago company made them "especially for this house, and they were known as the Lyceum chair and were copied all over the country."

The first Lyceum was a nice enough building, I suppose, but Memphians didn't get to enjoy it for very long. On the night of November 7, 1893, all that polished woodwork and those Lyceum chairs somehow caught fire, and the two-year-old building burned to the ground.

From the ashes, however, came a much grander Lyceum, the fine building shown on this old postcard. Civic leaders, led by local businessman Hugh Brinkley, purchased a lot at the southwest corner of Second and Jefferson and erected a new Lyceum. I've often wondered why they didn't use the old site on Union, but they didn't consult with me about that.

The "new" Lyceum was considerably more fancy. It was constructed of "buff Roman brick and Bowling Green limestone, with Ionic columns of blue Ryegate granite." A two-story arched entrance beckoned visitors, and *The Commercial Appeal* wrote, "If architecture be frozen music, the new Lyceum Theater was an example of the floritude of Orpheus."

I really have no idea what that means. Floritude?

At any rate, as with the other building, the theater occupied the ground floor. Other sections housed the Theater Club, the Nineteenth Century Club, and — as you can see if you squint at the old postcard — even such mundane businesses as dentists' offices. In the basement was a barbershop, Turkish bath, and — so the story goes — a private swimming pool for Brinkley.

> **The Lyceum got its start way back in 1888, when the Memphis Athletic Association erected a stunning new clubhouse at the northwest corner of Third and Union.**

The interior was lavish, decorated in an overblown Spanish motif, with everything painted "imperial green, rich yellow, and gold." Four huge murals painted by Victor Torghetti, "the celebrated figure artist of this country," depicted music, comedy, drama, and dance. The whole effect, according to the newspaper, was "refreshing and exhilarating."

Theater-goers obviously thought so. The curtain rose on December 4, 1894, for a performance of *The Count de Grammot*, and the actors faced a packed house. So it was, night after night. In fact, the Lyceum almost immediately became *the* place to go in Memphis. The

Commercial Appeal observed that it "was always a place for style and dress. Night after night victories and barouches [those are forms of carriages, you understand] pulled up before the dazzling theatre and the well-dressed passengers stepped forth to the chief enjoyment that the day afforded."

It was the gathering place for the Lauderdales and other elite members of society. Though she doesn't mention my family by name (surely an oversight), Powell says, "The select of the town were to be seen in the rows of glittering boxes in the balcony known as 'The Golden Horseshoe.' Men, decked out in full tails — none of your compromise tuxedos or monkey-jackets in those days — were most conscious of their habit. The Lyceum saw the American gentleman at his dashing best."

Part of the dazzle came from the theater's new electric lights — supposedly the first playhouse in Memphis to have them — and so powerful that the Lyceum had its own generating station in the basement because "the city plant was unable to handle such a tremendous demand."

Within months of opening, the Lyceum developed a reputation as one of the finest theaters in the entire South, attracting the most popular plays of the day. A thrilling production of *Ben Hur*, complete with rumbling chariot races, was somehow presented on the huge stage there. The most famous actors of our time took a bow at the Lyceum: Maud Adams, Lillie Langtry, Anna Held, William S. Hart, George M. Cohan, and Billie Burke — perhaps best known in later years as "the good witch" from *The Wizard of Oz*.

By today's standards, admission seems a bargain. According to the old programs, a box seat was $1.10, floor seats were 50 cents, and a perch in the balcony cost you a quarter. (Those same programs asked ticket holders, "As a special favor, will you please be in your seats on time?")

And it wasn't just a place for plays. Singers and musicians performed before sold-out houses. "An enumeration of those who played or sung at the Lyceum would be like assembling a 'Who's Who' of the drama, operatic, concert, and lecture stage," wrote *The Commercial Appeal*. Among them were such prestigious groups as the French Opera Company and the Imperial Russian Ballet. In the 1920s, according to a nice collection of playbills archived in the Lauderdale Library (such as the one shown here), the Lyceum hosted rather elaborate productions of the Laskin Players and other stock companies.

One of those performances, a 1926 comedy called *The Four Flusher*, was described as "an almost excruciatingly jovial affair." Next came *Secrets*, "a play that has swept across two continents, depicting the life of the English aristocracy and life on the American frontier. Lyceum patrons have a real treat in store for them." Then there was *Under Southern Skies* ("with everything in it that makes up a wonderful entertainment — romance, love, hate, and revenge") and *The Organ Revue* ("with 24 dramatic scenes, the most pretentious production ever attempted in the South").

Okay, if it was such a grand place, what happened?

An old Lyceum program for "The Organ Revue" promises patrons that the show will be "glittering, glorious, and gorgeous."

Well, Memphians can be a fickle bunch. The newly opened East End Park offered rides and thrills and — yes — alcohol. Other theaters opened downtown. But the nail in the coffin, so to speak, was a new form of entertainment entirely. In his thesis, Batson says, "Competition from the ever-improving moving pictures contributed to the degradation of this theatre."

Desperate to fill the house, the Lyceum management resorted to vaudeville acts — magicians, ventriloquists, performing dogs, and more. Nowadays we might find many of these acts enchanting, but it was considered cheap entertainment, and not for "the right people." In 1920, the owners finally converted it to a movie house, but by then the crowds had already discovered the much fancier and larger Lyric Theatre on Madison, and the stunning new Municipal Auditorium on Main Street. When the Loew's State, Loew's Palace, and The Orpheum opened, the Lyceum was doomed.

"The movies sustained the life of the Lyceum until her outdated facilities lost the battle of survival to the newer movie houses," says Batson. "The Lyceum became a theatrical bedlam, falling on progressively evil times. Movies, stock companies, and bits of vaudeville kept the life flowing in her veins."

But not for much longer. Those dapper gentlemen who once arrived in their carriages stopped coming to the Lyceum, and by the late 1920s the *Memphis Press-Scimitar* declared the place "obsolete and outmoded." Owners began to use it for political debates, dance marathons, and even wrestling matches. Perhaps the final blow was a burlesque production called "Scanties of 1934," which featured "a chorus of 40 girls" who were apparently so scantily clad that the police closed the show.

In 1935, the newspapers announced a "one-act tragedy" would take place at the old theater, to be called "The Wrecking of the Lyceum." They meant that literally. What had been one of the premier theaters in the South fell to the wrecking ball in just three weeks. There's no trace of the building today; a parking lot fills the former location. A newspaper story noted that many of the architectural features "had been scattered everywhere" and "bought for further use" but the reporter wasn't more specific. I wonder what pieces of the old Lyceum have survived in Memphis? I could certainly have used those nice columns to prop up the termite-gnawed back porch of the Mansion. M

Got a question for Vance?
EMAIL: askvance@memphismagazine.com
MAIL: Vance Lauderdale, Memphis magazine, 460 Tennessee Street #200, Memphis, TN 38103
BLOG: www.memphismagazine.com/askvanceblog

Ask Vance

Helen of Memphis as it looked in the late 1950s

Helen of Memphis
The Southland's Loveliest Specialty Store

FAMED FOR QUALITY WEARING APPAREL AND ACCESSORIES

Helen of Memphis

Our trivia expert solves local mysteries of who, what, when, where, why, and why not.

by VANCE LAUDERDALE

DEAR VANCE: Who was the "Helen" of Helen of Memphis? — *R.W.*

DEAR R.W.: When I mentioned to my cellmates — uh, I mean colleagues — that I wondered why this question hadn't come up long ago (after all, in the past I've chatted about Admiral Benbow and even Captain D), I was troubled to find so many who asked me, "What was Helen of Memphis?"

Are memories so short in our city that we no longer recall what was considered the finest women's clothing store in the city — a landmark on Union Avenue for more than half a century?

To prove just how fancy this place was, I encourage you to turn to the August 28, 1941, edition of *The Commercial Appeal*, which featured an article headlined "Helen Shop Gala Opening Attracts Many to See Rare Objects of Art." I'll wait right here and "friend" random people on Facebook while you get that volume from your library.

Got it? Now just skip down to the paragraph that talks about the women's clothing department, and the *glove counter*, "where an artisan who learned her trade in Europe hand-tailors gloves to order from leather."

That's right. Helen of Memphis was the kind of place where shoppers didn't buy clothes that could fit just anybody. Not even gloves. No, you went there and had them custom-tailored just for you. Mother Lauderdale bought her bonnets there every year. Oh, how happy it made her.

But I'm skipping ahead a bit. I should start at the beginning, or close to it, when a young Memphis woman, Helen Reinault Ingram, married a local physician named Arthur Quinn. This was on June 18, 1927. Dr. Quinn was a pediatrician, who owned The Babies and Children's Clinic at 1193 Madison. His practice must have been quite successful, because old telephone directories show the Quinns moving to bigger and better residences almost every year throughout the 1930s, eventually making their home at 698 Charles Place.

Meanwhile, across town, an interesting assortment of businesses had moved into a wonderful old Gothic Revival building at the corner of Union and Idlewild that had been constructed in the early 1900s as St. Luke's Church and later First Unitarian Church. For some reason, the church moved out of 1808 Union in the 1930s, and Mary Catherine's Beauty Salon, Holman-Wade Florists, Myrtle Shellenberger's Art Studio, and the Rothschild Sisters Dance Studio moved in.

Back to the Quinns. In 1931, Helen became the shop manager for Phil A. Halle men's clothing store, then located on the ground floor of the old Exchange Building downtown. She worked there three years, and then apparently decided she had what it took to open her own place.

And so in 1934 she opened The Helen Shop at 1648 Union Avenue, in a building that formerly housed Heirloom Antique Shop. The first Helen Shop was also an antique shop, but within a year or so the city directories described the business as "women's furnishings."

Finally, on February 7, 1937, the big move took place. I don't know what happened to the beauty salon, florist, and dance studio that formerly occupied 1808 Union, but Helen moved in. She paid just $12,500 for the two-story building, with its nice turret and rows of big windows.

Could these chic models really be I.C.'s own seniors Carol Moody, Joan Fulenwider, and Hollie Brooks? We think so!

Within a few years, Helen expanded, buying the building next door that had once housed a photography studio. That's when *The Commercial Appeal* published the story I mentioned earlier. The reporter noted that The Helen Shop "played host to the fashionable women of Memphis." In those days, the shop offered all sorts of things for "the city's smart set" (such as these Immaculate Conception High School girls, left) and "debutantes of the past season mixed with many of former seasons, and with the

122 • ASK VANCE II

city's socially prominent matrons." In addition to fine clothing, the Helen Shop offered "a unique gallery of rare and individual gifts in stationery, glass, furniture, and objets d'art."

How rare? Well, the store offered a Chippendale cabinet more than 150 years old, a "Venetian agate floor vase shot through with gold," fine oriental rugs, a French game table inlaid with satinwood, and "a Hungarian fischer jardinière of the seventeenth-century period, when they were last made," among other treasures.

In addition to all the antiques and custom-made clothing, the shop offered a complete infant's department, jewelry of all kinds, shoes, hats, and hosiery "in all the new fall colors."

What's strange to me, however, is that Helen really didn't stay involved with the business for very long. By 1945, the city directories show that a fellow named Richard Busch was now the manager of the establishment. Helen and Arthur Quinn were still living in Memphis, but the phone books no longer indicate any connection with the Helen Shop. And in fact, after 1953, there was no mention of them whatsoever, and despite a solid half-hour of searching the library files, I was never able to find a photograph of Helen herself.

A reporter noted that in those days, the shop offered all sorts of things for "the city's smart set" and debutantes of the past season mixed with many of former seasons, and with the city's socially prominent matrons.

The store on Union survived and even thrived, at some point changing its name to Helen of Memphis. The old buildings went through several transformations, the most dramatic in 1958 when noted Memphis architect Nowland Van Powell was commissioned to give the place a new look. According to the authors of *Memphis: An Architectural Guide*, "Powell gave the ensemble an almost impossible-to-achieve coherence. His solution was to encase all the disparate elements in a sheer wall brought right out to the sidewalk." This gleaming white building is the one that Memphians remember — well, perhaps I should say those who remember it at all.

The business went through several owners over the years — first sold to an out-of-towner, Sidney Berman of New York City, then to Maurice Herman of Dallas, and then to a local businessman, Zachary Levine. A branch store opened in Germantown, plans were announced for another one in Clarksdale, Mississippi, and the flagship store on Union eventually grew to 30,000 square feet.

But you know the old saying: All good things must come to an end. In July 1988, the owners of Helen of Memphis closed the Germantown store "for renovations" but never reopened it. And in late October, shoppers at the Union Avenue store found the doors locked, the windows empty. Finally contacted by reporters, the owners said they were going to turn the site into an "upscale retail" development.

Instead, the old buildings were bulldozed, and a Rite-Aid pharmacy was erected on the site. I'll let readers judge for themselves how "upscale" that is, but I have a feeling you can't purchase custom-fitted leather gloves there.

One more memory: During the demolition of the Union Avenue store, I wandered into the rubble and pulled out a fat roll of embroidered "Helen of Memphis" clothing labels. That night, I sewed them over all the Kent's Dollar Store labels in my shirts and pants. Nothing wrong with Kent's, but hey, no place in Memphis had more class, for so many years, as Helen of Memphis.

Searching for the Sombrero

DEAR VANCE: Please settle a bet for me. I think the first Mexican restaurant in Memphis wasn't Pancho's, but a little place on Lamar called the Sombrero. — H.T., MEMPHIS.

Dear H.T.: Oh, I hate questions like this. Whenever I pronounce something is the first, or oldest, or last, or newest, or anything really, then somebody usually shows up with their pesky *facts* and makes me look foolish. And you know what happens when you insult a Lauderdale? Pistols at dawn. Or at least a sound thrashing from my butler.

The hard thing about this debate is defining Mexican "restaurant." As far back as the 1920s, Memphians could stop at tamale stands all over the city, and in fact, out in Germantown, I believe Dogwood Road was known informally as "Hot Tamale Road" because of a tamale stand located there. Or maybe I dreamed that. But these couldn't be considered restaurants because you couldn't dine inside, and most of them rarely lasted more than a year or so.

But there's no question that the Sombrero came along almost 20 years before Pancho's. Looking through old city directories, as I like to do, night after lonely night in the Mansion, I discovered that Frank and Maude Linche opened the Sombrero Cafe way back in 1936. The little building at 2693 Lamar, in case you were wondering, had originally housed Frazier's Restaurant. Pancho's didn't open in West Memphis until 1956, and there's no listing for a Pancho's in our city until 1959, when the first one opened on South Bellevue.

The Sombrero, as so many restaurants do, had several owners over the years. In 1959, it moved to a larger building at 4003 Lamar, just outside the city limits. The last owner was Eugene Lawson, and he finally closed the place in 1973. As restaurants go, it had a good run — almost 40 years.

While I was searching through the restaurant listings in the 1930s city directories, I came across some eateries with especially intriguing names. Someday, when I get a chance, I think I'll look into such establishments as the Okey Doke Lunchroom on Front Street, the Zero Inn on Walker, the North Pole Sandwich Shop on Beale Street, the Dipsey Doodle on Rozelle, and — my personal favorite for obvious reasons — the Ding Dong Diner on Vance. **M**

GOT A QUESTION FOR VANCE?
EMAIL: *askvance@memphismagazine.com*
MAIL: Vance Lauderdale, Memphis magazine, 460 Tennessee Street #200, Memphis, TN 38103
BLOG: www.memphismagazine.com/Blogs/Ask-Vance

For Further Reading

Interested in Memphis history? If you've already purchased my first book, then it's okay to buy these.
This is by no means a complete list, but it's a good start:

Atkins, Ace. *Infamous.* Putnam, 2010.

Bearden, Willie. *Images of America: Overton Park.* Arcadia Press, 2004.

Branston, John. *Rowdy Memphis.* Cold Tree Press, 2004.

Coppock, Paul R. *Memphis Sketches.* Friends of Memphis and Shelby County Public Libraries, 1976.

Coppock, Paul R. *Mid-South Memories.* Memphis State University Press, 1980.

Coppock, Paul R. *Paul R. Coppock's Mid-South,* Volumes 1-4. West Tennessee Historical Society, 1985, 1992, 1993, 1994.

Crawford, Charles. *Yesterday's Memphis.* E.A. Seemann Publishing, 1976.

Cunningham, Laura. *Haunted Memphis.* History Press, 2009.

Dougan, John. *Images of America: Memphis.* Arcadia Press, 1998.

Dowdy, G. Wayne. *Mr. Crump Don't Like It: Machine Politics In Memphis.* University Press of Mississippi, 2008.

Dye, Robert W. *Memphis: Then & Now.* Arcadia Press, 2005.

Freeman, Mike and Cindy Hazen. *Memphis: Elvis-Style.* John F. Blair, 1997.

Freeman, Mike. *Clarence Saunders & the Founding of Piggly Wiggly.* History Press, 2011.

Guralnick, Peter. *Careless Love.* Little Brown & Co., 1999.

Guralnick, Peter. *Last Train to Memphis.* Little Brown & Co., 1994.

Hall, Ron. *Playing for a Piece of the Door: A History of Garage and Frat Bands in Memphis, 1960-1975.* Shangri-La Projects, 2001.

Hall, Ron. *The Memphis Garage Rock Yearbook, 1960-1975.* Shangri-La Projects, 2003.

Hall, Russell S. *Images of America: Germantown.* Arcadia Press, 2003.

Halloran, Pat. *The Orpheum: Where Broadway Meets Beale.* Lithograph Publishing, 1997.

Harkins, John. *Metropolis of the American Nile.* Guild Bindery Press, 1982.

Herrington, Chris. *The Music That Made Memphis.* Bluff City Books, 2004.

Johnson, Eugene and Robert D. Russell. *Memphis: An Architectural Guide.* University of Tennessee Press, 1990.

Johnson, Russell. *Memphis: Then and Now.* Thunder Bay Press, 2008.

LaPointe, Patricia and Mary Ellen Pitts. *Memphis Medicine: A History of Science and Service.* Legacy Publishing, 2011.

Lauterbach, Preston. *The Chitlin' Circuit and the Road to Rock 'n' Roll.* W.W. Norton and Company, 2011.

Magness, Perre. *Elmwood 2002: In the Shadows of the Elms.* Historic Elmwood Cemetery, 2001.

Magness, Perre. *Good Abode: Nineteenth Century Architecture in Memphis and Shelby County.* The Junior League of Memphis, 1983.

Magness, Perre. *Past Times: Stories of Early Memphis.* Parkway Press, 1994.

Parfitt, Ginny and Mary L. Martin. *Memories of Memphis: A History in Postcards.* Schiffer, 2005.

The Peabody: A History of the South's Grand Hotel. Peabody Management, 2007.

Plunkett, Kitty. *Memphis: A Pictorial History.* Donning Publishers, 1976.

Raymond, Barbara B. *The Baby Thief: The Untold Story of Georgia Tann, the Baby Seller Who Corrupted Adoption.* Carroll & Graf, 2007.

Sharp, Tim. *Images of America: Memphis Music Before the Blues.* Arcadia Press, 2007.

Sides, Hampton. *Hellhound on His Trail: The Stalking of Martin Luther King Jr. and the International Hunt for His Assassin.* Doubleday, 2010.

Simpson, Teresa A. *Memphis Murder & Mayhem.* History Press, 2008.

INDEX

— A —

Aberdeen, MS — 116
Abraham, Jane — 77
Abraham's Oak — 36
Abt, Mike — 66
Adams and Albin, Architects — 8
Al Chymia Shrine Temple — 71
Al's Golfdom — 108-109
Al's Golfhaven — 109
Alamo Plaza — 12
Alexander Plastering Company — 23
Alexander, Kathie — 28
Allied Electrical Contractors — 15
All-Right Parking — 65
Amazing Mr. Baker, The — 11
Ambassador Hotel — 97
American Federation of Labor — 17
American Snuff Company — 58
Anderton, Herb — 31
Anderton's Restaurants — 31
Andrews Grocery — 25
Andrews, Caleb L. — 25
Annaratone, Joseph and Petronella — 63
Annaratone, Theresa — 63
Annie Laurie's Wishing Chair — 36
Apothecary Building — 83
Arrow Food Store — 15
Arrow Glass Boats — 63
Ascent of the Blues (sculpture) — 103
Atomic Pest Control — 10-11
Audubon Park — 15, 61, 85

— B —

Babies and Children's Clinic, The — 122
Baeder, John — 24
Baker Brothers Grocery — 15
Baker, Father C.B. — 15
Baker, Harmon and Ruth — 11
Baptist Service Center — 13
Bass, Ben — 93
Beale Street — 65
Bean Alley — 45
Beaty, Jan — 17
Belt, Charles "Pink" — 69
Bennett's Club Rosewood — 93
Bethany Cemetery — 69
Biagi's Restaurant — 47
Big Star grocery — 105
Bitter Lemon — 76
Bittman, Herbert — 79
Bittman's Appliances — 79
Blake, "Blind Arthur" — 24
Bluff City Photo Service — 27
Bomb Shelters — 43, 100
Bon Air Nightclub — 47
Bonanza Sirloin Pit — 45
Boushe, Judge Beverly — 98

Boyle Investment Company — 18
Boyle, Bayard — 95
Brinkley, Hugh — 120
Britling Cafeteria — 32-33, 110
Brussels World's Fair Skyride — 102-103
Bry's Department Store — 15
Bryonis, James — 66
Buckingham Dry Goods — 29
Burk, Bill — 81
Burke, Billie — 121
Butler, Lori — 77
By-Ryt Food Store — 39

— C —

Café Olé — 35
Callicott, Burton — 33, 66
Calvary Cemetery — 63
Calvary Episcopal Church — 75
Cannon Flats — 113
Caruthers, A.B. — 71
Cassatta, Tony "Monk" — 46-47
Catholic Club — 67
Centennial Exposition — 40
Central Avenue Pharmacy — 25
Central Gardens — 44
Central High School — 64, 80
Chandler, Walter — 82
Chenault, Reginald "Rex" — 35
Chenault's Drive-In — 35
Cherokee Driving Range — 108
Chicago & Southern Airlines — 73
Chicago Park School — 45
Chickasaw Bureau of Publicity — 71
Chickasaw Indians — 97
Chickasaw Oaks Mall — 105
Chickasaw Tourist Court — 12
Cibo Pizza House — 119
City Beautiful Commission — 84
City Stores Co. — 85
Civic Center Plaza — 99
Civil Defense Agency — 100
Clyde Collins Company — 75
Cobb, Norman, Naomi, and Garlene — 68-69
Cohan, George M. — 121
Coleman, David — 53
Collins, Clyde — 75
Colonial Jr. High School — 100
Commercial Restaurant — 83
Community Shelter Plan — 101
Confederate Park — 39, 84
Continental Baking Company — 20
Conwood Corporation — 59
Coppock, Paul — 29, 37, 43, 62, 71, 82, 84
Corncob Fire — 78
Country Club Estates — 105
Court Square — 38, 50, 83
Crone Monument Company — 85
Crosstown Theater — 10

Crump, E.H. — 51, 84, 95
Crump, Metcalf — 95
Crystal Shrine Grotto — 36-37
"Curiosity" House — 116-117
Cypress Creek — 45

— D —

Dairy Dip Dairy Bar — 12
Danvers — 15
Dardano, Ernest and Joseph — 25
Dardano Grocery — 25
David Lipscomb College — 41
Davis, Jefferson — 84-85
Davis, Watson — 48-49
Day, Clarence — 63
Delta Air Lines — 73
Dental Snuff — 58
DeShazo, Verna — 66
DeSoto, Hernando — 97, 99
DeSoto Memorial Tower — 99
DeSoto Park — 38
Dial 'n' Smile — 60-61
Dimond, Maysie — 96-97
Ding Dong Diner — 123
Dipsey Doodle — 123
Dirmeyer, William C. — 27
Dirmeyer's Drugstore — 15, 27
Ditto's Beauty and Barber Salon — 27
Ditty Wah Ditty Motel — 24
Dixie Greyhound Lines — 110
Dobbs House — 67, 111
DonRuss Company — 57
Doughboy Statue — 38
Douglass High School — 79
Dreamland Gardens — 80
Dreifuss Jewelers — 29
Duckett, Marjorie and Doris — 44
Dyess Colony (AR) — 96-97

— E —

Eads Bridge — 115
East End Park — 53, 121
East High School — 14, 95
East Parkway — 31, 47, 55, 104-105, 119
East Parkway Petunia Club — 34
Edwards, Gilbert and Maude — 25
Edwards Pharmacy — 25
Elbaroda (Hoyt Wooten's yacht) — 43
Elks Club and Hotel — 112-113
Ellis Auditorium — 81, 96-97, 121
Ellis, Wm. C. and Sons — 9
Elmwood Cemetery — 28, 85
Elvis Presley Enterprises — 31
Embury, Eileen — 19
Embury, John — 19
Emma Wilburn Funeral Home — 6
Equitable Saloon — 112
Estes & Weeks Custom Metal Works — 15
Evergreen Presbyterian Church — 87
Exchange Building — 122

— F —

Fairgrounds Casino — 55
Fairview Jr. High School — 61, 104-105
Fallout Shelters — 100-101
Fantastic Features — 48-49
Faulkner, William — 106
Fire Museum of Memphis — 78
Firestone Tire & Rubber Company — 45, 63
First Church of Christ Scientist — 85
First National Bank — 43
First Tennessee Bank — 33, 43

ASK VANCE II • 125

First Unitarian Church — 122
Fister, Al and Susie — 108-109
Fleece Station School — 6
Floied Fire Extinguishers — 7
Flying Saucer Café — 97
Folk, Humphrey — 95
Ford Local Building — 15
Forest Hill Cemetery — 11, 19, 28, 69
Forgionne, Joseph and Vernon — 30
Forrest Park — 65, 85
Frayser — 17
Friedel's Restaurant — 66
Frisco Bridge — 115
From Here To Eternity — 106-107
Front Street — 7, 50
Frulla Grocery Store — 19
Frulla, Claude, Eugene, and Pacifico — 19
Furlotte, Arthur — 97
Furlotte's Café — 97

— G —

Gaisman Park Swimming Pool — 21
Galloway, Mary — 65
Galloway, Robert — 61, 71, 84
Gamel's Drive-In — 47
Gammon, Ray — 91
Garner Lake — 102-103
Garner, Louis — 102-103
Garrison, Beatrice — 95
Gaston, John — 82-83
Gaston Hospital — 82-83, 88-89
Gaston Park — 83
Gaston Restaurant — 50, 83
Gayoso House/Hotel — 37
Germantown Performing Arts Centre — 75
Gilmore Seafood Restaurant — 31
Going To Market — 74-75
Goodwyn Institute — 42-43
Goodwyn, William Adolphus — 42
Great Memphis Pyramid — 40
Great Memphis Bridge — 115
Green Acres Motel — 49
Greene, N.T. "Brother" — 45
Gridiron Restaurants — 39
Grisanti Café — 91
Groupe, The (band) — 77
Guinozzo, John — 53

— H —

Halbert, Henry — 70
Haley Sundries — 7
Hall and Waller Associates — 41
Hall, Robert L. — 8
Halliburton, Nelle Nance — 28
Halliburton, Richard — 28
Halliburton, Wesley — 28
Halsey, Admiral William "Bull" — 81
Happy Hal Show, The — 65
Happy Hal's Toy Town — 65
Harbin, J.C. — 39
Harbin's Tourist Court — 39
Harkins, John — 82
Harms, Birch — 106-107

Harrison, E.L. Architects — 104-105
Hart Center — 77
Hartz, Brent — 40
Hayes, Isaac — 75, 107
Helen of Memphis / Helen Shop — 122-123
Henderson, Keith — 77
Hendrix, Ruth — 51
Herenton, Willie — 45
Hester Motel — 12
Hester, James R. — 12
Hicks Barber Shop — 7
Higbee School — 37
Higbee, Jenny — 37
Hinds, E. Clovis — 36
Hinton Funeral Home — 90
Hoadley Ice Cream Co. — 71
Hodges Field — 69
Holiday Inns — 39, 47
Hollingshead, R.M. — 89
Hollis, Harry N. — 13
Holman-Wade Florists — 122
Honeycutt Furniture — 25
Hopkins House — 112
Horse Shoe Diner — 12
Hot Tamale Road — 123
Hotel DeVoy — 113
Hotel King Cotton — 113
Hubbard, Edwin — 74-75
Huff-n-Puff Railroad — 102-103
Huntzicker, Mrs. William — 51
Hussong, Carissa — 103
Hutchison School — 28
Hutchison, Mary Grimes — 28
Hyde, J.R. "Pitt" — 95

— I —

Ida B. Wells Academy — 93
Idlewild Greenhouses — 59
"In-Curiosity" House — 116-117
Ingram, Helen R. — 122
International Harvester — 15
Iris Motel — 24

— J —

Jack Ruby Ambulance Co. — 90-91
Jackson, Andrew — 97
James Sanitarium — 53
Japanese Garden — 61
Jefferson Theater — 26
Jemison, W.D. and Sons — 17
John Gaston Hospital — 82-83, 88-89
John Gaston Restaurant — 50
Johnson, A.W.B. — 32
Johnson, Thomas G. — 23
Jones, James and Lowney — 106-107
Jones, Ronnie — 21
Jones, Walk C. — 87

— K —

Kansas City, Fort Scott, and Memphis Railroad — 115
Kaye Ice & Coal Company — 59
Kennedy General Hospital — 106

King Cotton Franks — 81
Kourdouvelis, Kris — 71
Kourvelas, Bonnie (Perkins) — 9, 66

— L —

Lakeland — 102-103
Lakeland Speed Bowl — 102
Lane, Richard C. and Alvira — 9
Langtry, Lillie — 121
Laskin Players — 121
Last Chance Records — 7
Laster Hardware — 12
Lauderdale Mausoleum — 28
Lauderdale School — 92-93
Lausanne School — 95
Lawrence Furniture — 29
Lawson, Eugene — 123
Leahy's Tourist Court — 106-107
Lee, Gypsy Rose — 107
Lemmon & Gale Dry Goods — 28-29
Lerner Shop — 13
Levine, Zachary — 123
Levy, J.C. — 60-61
Liberty Bell — 62
Liberty Cash Grocers — 19
Liberty Savings Bank — 13
Libertyland — 103
Linche, Frank and Maude — 123
Lion's Gate — 43
Litton Photographic Services — 27
Loew's Palace Theater — 32, 120-121
Loew's State Theater — 120-121
Longview Community Holiness Church — 93
Lovett, M.J. Grocery — 7
Lowry, Joe — 27
Lowry, Mary Frances — 21, 27
Lowry Private School — 21, 27
Luau Restaurant — 14-15, 67
Lyceum Theater — 120-121
Lyric Theater — 18, 26-27, 121

— M —

Maddox Seminary for Young Ladies — 53
Madison Theater — 26
Main Street — 29, 49, 53, 114
Mall of Memphis — 109
Marble Block — 22
Margolies, John — 24
Marjorie Duckett Dancing School — 44
Mary Catherine's Beauty Salon — 122
Mary Galloway Home for Women — 65
Maury School — 63
Maywood Lake & Beach — 81
McCalla, Wilford T. — 55
McIntire, John — 76-77
McKnight, Robert — 97
Meara, Patt — 107
Memorial Park Cemetery — 36-37, 45
Memphis Academy of Arts — 76, 96-97

Memphis-Arkansas Bridge — 73
Memphis Athletic Association — 121
Memphis Baseball Encyclopedia — 53
Memphis Belle B-17 — 8, 14, 35
Memphis Blues B-17 — 6
Memphis Botanic Garden — 61
Memphis Chicks — 53
Memphis Club — 18
Memphis College of Art — 65, 76
Memphis Flying Service — 117
Memphis Heritage — 97
Memphis Memoirs — 66
Memphis Park Commission — 21, 61, 71, 84
Memphis Pink Palace Museum — 22-23
Memphis Steam Laundry — 105
Memphis Theological Seminary — 119
Memphis Trades and Labor Council — 37, 38
Memphis University School — 95
Memphis Zoo — 60, 71
Mid-South Fairgrounds — 54, 60-61
Mid-South Service Station — 70-71
Miller, "Happy" Hal — 64
Miller, Claudette and Constance — 88-89
Miller, Elizabeth — 88
Mississippi River — 115
Mizell Plumbing — 25
Monk — 46-47
Montgomery, J.A. — 105
Morgan Keegan Tower — 65, 103, 113
Morgan, Allen — 95
Morgan, Jack — 81
Morgan, Robert — 8, 14, 35
Morris, John George — 66-67
Morris, Willie — 107
Morton, Lamar T. — 55
Mounce, Jimmy — 50-51
Mt. Arlington School — 6
Mulford Jewelers — 22
Mulford, John N. — 22
Municipal Swimming Pool — 61
Myar, Sam — 57

— N —

91st Bomb Group (H) Restaurant — 34-35
Napoleon, Phil — 56
Napoleon's Retreat — 56
National Cemetery — 13, 38
National Cibo House Corp. — 119
National Garage — 65
National Ornamental Metal Museum — 103
National Shelter Program — 101
New Chicago Civic Club — 45
Nineteenth Century Club — 120
North Parkway — 47
North Pole Sandwich Shop — 123
Northern, Andrew — 89
Novak, Frances — 88-89

— O —

Ogden, John — 86-87
Okey-Doke Lunchroom — 123
Ollie's Trolley — 114-115
Olswanger, Anna — 81
Olswanger, Berl — 80-81
One Memphis Place — 67
Orgill Bros. Hardware — 40
Original Memphis Five — 56
Orpheum Theater — 120-121
Oso Club — 77
Ossorio, Michael — 63
Our Market Grocery — 7
Overton Hotel — 16
Overton Park — 37, 48, 61, 71
Overton Square — 51
Overton, John — 97

— P —

Palomino Motel — 12
Panama-Pacific International Exposition — 62
Pancho's — 123
Pappy and Jimmy's — 50-51
Pappy's Lobster Shack — 50-51
Parking Can Be Fun — 33
Parkway Village — 94, 105
Pass, Herman and Mollie — 13
Peabody School — 6
Pearson, Dr. William — 57
Penetro — 10
Pentecost, Althea — 95
Pentecost-Garrison School — 95
Pepper Jingle Company — 75
Phil A. Halle Store — 122
Piggly Wiggly — 15, 23, 25
Pit Restaurant, The — 91
Plantation Inn — 107
Plough Pharmaceuticals — 11
Polk, Dr. Charles — 57
Polk, Margaret — 8
Pool of Hebron — 36
Poplar Plaza — 33
Poplar Street Depot — 62
Prana — 75
Presbyterian Day School — 95
Presley, Elvis — 75
Prewitt, Tom — 15
Pure Oil Company — 70
Pyramid, The — 40-41

— Q —

Quaker Oats Company — 78-79
Quale, Capt. Ralph — 68-69
Quinn, Helen and Arthur — 122-123

— R —

Railroad Salvage Company — 25
Raleigh Inn & Springs — 52-53
Raleigh Road — 13
Ramsey, Dr. Gordon — 57
Rawleigh, W.T. Company — 7
Ray Gammon's Restaurant — 91
Reeves, Carla — 11
Rendezvous, The — 51
Reuther, Walter — 15
Rex Club — 18-19
Rhodes College — 41, 91
Rhyne, J. William — 16
Rice, Carese — 10
Ridgeway Country Club — 18
Ringling Bros. Circus — 71
Riverside Drive — 9, 73
Riverview Urban Renewal Project — 72-73
Riviera Grill — 66-67
Robertson, Allen and Mary — 47
Robinson Apothecary — 83
Robinson, James and Mary — 83
Rodriguez, Dionicio — 36-37
Rogers and Hale, Architects — 16
Rogers, James Gamble — 16
Ronnie Jones Memorial — 21
Roosevelt, Eleanor — 96-97
Rosewood Barber Shop — 93
Rosewood Pharmacy — 93
Rosewood Theater — 93
Rothschild Sisters Dance Studio — 122
Roy Rogers Roast Beef — 15
Ruby, Jack — 90-91
Ruck, Leonard — 7

— S —

Safety Town — 94-95
Sammons, Lehman C. "Pappy" — 50-51
Saunders, Clarence — 23
Saymore Candy Co. — 57
Schering Plough — 11
Schmeisser, Harry Jr. — 63
Schwill, Otto — 59
Sea Isle School — 105
Sears Crosstown — 49
Second Hand Rose — 25
Second Presbyterian Church — 95
Sennett, Sue — 87
Seraphim Rose Books — 6
Sheffield High School — 8
Shelby County Cemetery — 89
Shelby County Courthouse — 16
Shelby County International Raceway — 102-103
Shelby Street — 9
Shellenberger's Art Studio — 122
Sherron Shoe Company — 32
Sherron, Thomas and Frank — 32
Shoney's — 109
Shuba, George — 53
Siesta Motel — 49
Signorelli, Frank — 56
Silver Bell Liquor Store — 12
Silver Dollar Inn — 12
Silver Horse Shoe Motel — 12
Silver Saver Super Markets — 12
Simmons, John — 7
Sivad — 48-49
Sky Rocket Bubble Gum — 57
Smith, Fred Jr. — 95, 114
Smith, Fred Sr. — 110
Snicker Flickers tv show — 65
Sombrero Restaurant — 123
Sounds Unreel — 27
Southern Association of Dance Masters — 45
Southern Bowling Lanes — 68-69
Southern Club — 18
Southern College of Optometry — 95
Southern Funeral Home — 6
Southgate Shopping Center — 69
Southland Mall — 94
Southwestern at Memphis (see Rhodes College)
Spandow, Florence Gage — 111
Spandow, William Eastman — 111
Spanish-American War — 38-39
Speedway Drugs — 47
Speedway Terrace Historic District — 47
Speedway, The — 47
Spencer and Barnwell Funeral Home — 45
St. Luke's Church — 122
St. Mary's School — 37
Stalnecker, Bette and Ed — 43
Starlight Supper Club — 113
Steak & Egg Kitchens — 111
Stepherson, Jack, Wesley, and Kenneth — 98
Stepherson's Big Star — 98-99
Sterick Building — 111
Stevens Sandwich Service — 111
Stewart, William and Natalie — 20
Stewarts, Inc. — 20
Story-Book Homes — 16
Summer Avenue — 12, 47, 91, 106-107
Swaffer, Lt. Calvin and Dorothy — 6
Sykes, Stephen — 116-117

— T —

Talent Party — 87
Tech High School — 66, 68-69
Tennessee Block Building — 29
Tennessee Brewery — 40
Tennessee Centennial Exposition — 40
Tennessee Trust Building — 119
Thomas Funeral Home — 6
Thompson Brothers Mortuary — 90
Three Sisters Building — 105
Tigrett, Pat and John — 40
Tipton, P.O. — 63
Toad Hall Antiques — 25
Toddle House — 105, 110-111
Tommy Bronson Sporting Goods — 101
Topp, Robertson — 37
Trickel, Glenn — 68-69
Tri-State Fairgrounds — 54
Tropical Freeze — 14-15, 109
Troutt Brothers Barber Shop — 35
Tubbs, Les — 10-11
Tucker, Sophie — 50
Tupelo Tornado of 1936 — 90
Turley, Susan — 46-47
Turner, Judge Kenneth — 77

— U —

Union Avenue — 32-33, 59
Union Station — 50
Unique Beauty Shop — 13
United Auto Workers — 15
United Confederate Veterans — 84
University of Tennessee — 18

— V —

Van Horn, John — 13
Van Powell, Noland — 105, 123
Vansickle, Betty — 87
Vesey, John — 21

— W —

Walker Elementary School — 92-93
Walker Street Trading Company — 7
Walker Temple AME Church — 6
Walker, George — 32
Walsh, LaVelle — 117
Warner Theater — 120
Weaver, Guy — 97
Welcher, Lynn — 55
Weona Food Stores — 15, 79
West Memphis, AR — 43, 107, 123
WHBQ TV/Radio — 48, 65
Whirlaway Club — 86-87
White House Motel — 47
White Station High School — 14-15
Whiz Auto Products — 89
Wiener, Donald and Russell — 57
Wilburn, Emma C. — 6
Wilde, Oscar — 83
Williams, Tennessee — 106
Williamsburg Colony — 105
Willingham, J.T. — 71
Willingham, William and Reginald — 70-71
Wilmoth, Charlie — 69
Wilmoth's Restaurant — 69
Wilson, Judge Julian — 118
Wilson, Kemmons — 38, 47, 114
Winchester, Marcus — 97
Withers, Beatrice — 68
WKNO-TV — 66
WMC Radio — 43
WMPS Radio — 81
Wolf River — 21
Wonder Bread — 20
Woods, Frank G. — 55
Woods, J. Douglas — 119
Woolworth's — 49
Wooten, Hoyt — 43
World's Fair (1904) — 62
Wright Diner — 91

Entertainment was a lot cheaper in my day. In fact, I often had to pay people to attend my accordion recitals.

But now, we'll make you a special money-saving offer!

Just call **1-877-467-1734** and mention "Vance" — or visit our website (www.memphismagazine.com) and enter "Vance" as the code — and you'll get **12 issues of *Memphis* magazine for just $10.**

That means you'll be able to keep up with me every month, while getting the very best that *Memphis* magazine has to offer. Each subscription also includes the annual Restaurant Guide and City Guide, so call now and tell them Vance sent you!

12 issues for $10.
Call 1-877-467-1734 today!

www.memphismagazine.com